Ideology and Educational Reform

Ideology and Educational Reform

Themes and Theories in Public Education

David C. Paris

Westview Press

BOULDER • SAN FRANCISCO • OXFORD

Copyright © 1995 by Westview Press, Inc.

Published in 1995 in the United States of America by Westview Press, Inc., 5500 Central Avenue, Boulder, Colorado 80301-2877, and in the United Kingdom by Westview Press, 12 Hid's Copse Road, Cumnor Hill, Oxford OX2 9JJ

A CIP catalog record for this book is available from the Library of Congress.
ISBN 0-8133-2341-X (hardcover) — ISBN 0-8133-2340-1 (paperback)

Printed and bound in the United States of America

The paper used in this publication meets the requirements of the American National Standard for Permanence of Paper for Printed Library Materials Z39.48-1984.

10   9   8   7   6   5   4   3   2   1

To the women in my life

Candace, Celia, Natalie, Stephanie

Contents

Figures

Acknowledgments

There are many people to thank who helped me in one way or another with this book. Several of my colleagues, Pat Neal, Pete Suttmeier, and Carol Drogus read earlier versions of some of the chapters and provided helpful advice. Their advice was reinforced by two anonymous readers of the complete manuscript who made other useful suggestions. Many other colleagues at Hamilton stimulated my thinking about education through their experiments in the classroom and in many informal conversations. I have received generous support for my research from Hamilton College's deans and presidents. Sally Carman and Basem Aly helped me prepare the manuscript. Six years on the local school board afforded me the luxury of listening to thoughtful discussions of immediate, practical problems in education. It also presented me with the task of balancing the competing demands on schools. Finally, my spouse and children have constantly wished me well with what one of my daughters calls "your story," even as they wished I would hurry up and finish. Any problems or errors are, of course, my own; I have not wanted for help and support.

David C. Paris

1

The First Triangle:
The Problems of
Educational Reform

It must be considered that there is nothing more difficult to carry out, nor more doubtful of success, nor more dangerous to handle, than to initiate a new order of things. For the reformer has enemies in all those who profit by the old order, and only lukewarm defenders in all those who would profit by the new order, this lukewarmness arising partly from fear of their adversaries who have the law in their favor; and partly from the incredulity of mankind, who do not believe in anything new until they have had the actual experience of it.

--Machiavelli

Nor would I hold up the sequence--from principles to problems to proffered solutions--as a perfect pattern laid up in some Platonic heaven, irreversible, like time's arrow. Though you would find it less tidy, it would not be absurd for you to start with your own proposed solutions and work backward. You might very well surprise yourself with the principles you found at the end, or would it actually be the beginning? In thought and rational discussion we must move back and forth along this path, which is not straight but triangular, with sides marked Principles, Problems, Solutions, except that at any point you may and almost certainly will generate a new triangle.

--Robert Dahl

Crisis, Consensus, and Optimism

In 1983 the National Commission on Excellence in Education declared that the United States was "a nation at risk" because of the poor performance of its schools. The report spoke in apocalyptic terms about a "rising tide of mediocrity" engulfing American education and compromising our economic and military position in the world: "If an unfriendly foreign power had attempted to impose on America the mediocre educational performance that exists today, we might well have viewed it as an act of war."[1] Because our national well-being was at stake, the commission argued, reform of the schools must be a primary national concern. Unlike reports of many other commissions regarding policy matters, this report's bleak portrayal of the schools and dire warnings made the front page of most major newspapers. *A Nation at Risk* succeeded in bringing national attention to the question of educational reform.

Once America's schools had been examined and found wanting, there was an outpouring of reports about schools and proposals for reform. At least a half-dozen other task forces and commissions reported in 1983; the results of several field studies were also published that year. Each year since has seen several reports on the state of education in general or on some particular topic for reform. In 1986 two task forces, the Holmes Group and the Carnegie Forum, offered proposals for changes in requirements, training, and working conditions for teachers. There has been considerable ongoing discussion of, and experimentation in, the organization and management of schools under the broad (and vague) rubrics of "restructuring" and "choice." More recently, there have been several reports on the preparation of students for entering the work world and the requirements for an internationally competitive workforce. As the reform movement has proceeded, almost every aspect of educational policy and process has been the subject of some kind of report or study.[2]

What typically emerges from this stream of reports and proposals is a multi-count indictment of the schools and other institutions, a list of policy and institutional failures. Too many students start school without a real chance of obtaining a decent education due to poverty, cultural deprivation, family problems, or simple abuse. Once in school, too few students acquire the most basic skills in reading, writing, and mathematics, let alone achieve high levels of skill in any subjects, especially math, science, and foreign languages. Achievement test scores may have stopped declining but previous declines have yet to be reversed, and in international comparisons of achievement, American students continue to fare poorly. These dismal academic indicators sometimes do not even take into account the significant proportion of students, perhaps a fourth or more, who drop out of the system altogether. Academic shortcomings aside, schools have also failed to maintain an orderly environment. Respondents to the annual Gallup poll on education routinely list discipline and drugs as the two most important problems facing schools. It is difficult to expect academic achievement when schools often cannot provide an environment conducive to learning. Finally, as if this weren't enough, institutions that might be expected to aid the schools in the process of reform--the family, church, and even the larger culture, including that usual suspect, television--are at best less supportive of the schools' mission than they were in the past; at worst, they are actually undercutting that mission.

Although the problems cited in *A Nation at Risk* and other reports were (and are) formidable, the reformers have typically been confident about the prospects for genuine change and improvement. Their confidence and determination has stemmed, at least in part, from the belief that there is a broad consensus on both the need for reform and on a general direction involving heavier academic demands and greater school accountability. For example, early in the reform movement one public official described what he saw as,

> fresh ideas, renewed commitment to educational standards, rising expecta-
> tions for teacher competence and student performance, impatience with
> trendy innovations and flabby practices, and a hot, bright faith in the impor-
> tance of high quality education for the individual and the nation alike. . . . At
> the risk of overstatement, I suggest that our society and culture are in the
> throes of an educational reform movement of epochal proportions. But for
> the first time in recent memory, this is an educational movement that draws
> its force neither from the federal government nor from the profession. It is
> very nearly a populist movement, led primarily by self-interested parents
> and employers and by the tax paying public.[3]

It is interesting to note the varied appeals contained in this passage. Not only had we reached some ideological turning point in the history of public education, we also potentially had the political wherewithal to carry out the required reforms. We *knew* what we wanted from the schools, what we wanted was widely agreed upon as being justified, and, neatly, it served our collective and separate interests. It makes a good script: American public, outraged by educational failure and animated by a "new consensus," demands the schools shape up. All that was needed for the "epochal transformation" to begin was the political will to achieve the widely agreed-upon goals of the reformers.

The states and the education "establishment" have responded to the calls for reform. Almost every state has made some changes to strengthen academic requirements and increase compensation for teachers. Some of the reforms for teacher training and certification proposed by the Holmes and Carnegie groups are being implemented. There have been some significant changes at the grass-roots level as well, including some promising experiments in restructuring, choice, and new forms of accountability. Businesses and other community groups have taken a more active interest, including forging formal partnerships with schools. There has been renewed interest in the problems of school finance, especially as the economic boom that accompanied early reform efforts has slowed. Some proposed reforms, such as merit pay, have been more or less given up as unwise or politically unworkable. Still others, such as plans for allowing parental choice or community-based management, seem to be gaining respectability even if they remain largely untested. Whatever else one might say about the reform movement, there has been no lack of activity.[4]

Whatever the long-term prospects of the reform movement, there is something rather cheering about all this rhetoric and activity. The ferment of the last decade indicates a willingness to acknowledge the depth and breadth of the problems of public education. The reform movement has raised serious questions of how to make the public schools work and generated a wide range of new inquiries and experiments in the schools. At its best the desire to see real educational improvement transcends political differences and approximates the proverbial "moral equivalent of war." The apparent commitment to this widely shared cause is a reason to be optimistic about the ultimate success of reform efforts.

At the same time, it is not surprising that despite all the rhetoric and activity, many have expressed doubts about the reform movement and few see tremendous changes. The neat script of a mobilized public spurring political and educational leaders to transform the schools simply has yet to be acted out. Those who sing as they march off to wars or their moral equivalents often stop singing and start grumbling once the battle is truly joined. The "enemy" is not so easily overcome, and the complexity and scale of the tasks of reform have become more apparent. Many of those charged with the task of reform have bemoaned a lack of progress or even a clear direction to the movement. For example, on the fifth anniversary of the 1983 "at risk" report, then Secretary of Education William Bennett delivered a rather pessimistic assessment of the movement's progress. "We are certainly not doing well enough, and we are not doing well enough fast enough. . . . An ethos of success is missing from too many American schools." The recent tenth anniversary of the "at risk" report was marked less by celebration of progress than by negative commentary about how little had changed. As the reform movement has continued, even its most ardent supporters have wondered about its prospects.

Perhaps such doubts were inevitable. The rhetoric that generates attention to educational problems (a "nation at risk") virtually guarantees that a "solution" is likely to be beyond our reach. The wide variety of studies, reports, proposals, and experiments in the last decade is testimony to the comprehensive nature of the original indictment of the schools and the scope of the proposed reforms. If the entire educational system is in need of reform, then there is no aspect of educational policy and practice that is beyond the purview of the movement. But this makes efforts at reform diffuse and even chaotic. There is little sense of how well we are doing when we are trying to do everything and do it all at once. Talk of "epochal" reforms runs more than the "risk of overstatement"; it risks making reform efforts inevitably fall short of expectations. Moreover, if the crisis is as severe and wide-ranging as the initial calls for reform suggested, then clear and dramatic reform is going to be a difficult, long-term proposition. If it took decades to create these problems, a quick fix is unlikely.

This apparent lack of progress may also indicate problems that go beyond inflated rhetoric, unrealistic expectations, and the formidable practical obstacles that confront reform efforts. It may indicate that, despite proclamations about a "new consensus" about education, we are not really sure how to approach and evaluate efforts at reform. The varied and occasionally contradictory proposals suggest that there may be no underlying vision guiding reform. For example, choice and voucher proposals vie for public approval with programs for increasing public school responsibilities for social services; there are simultaneous calls for national standards and greater grants of local discretion, and so on. Indeed, it may be that we have never known what we wanted from the schools or perhaps we have wanted too many and often conflicting things. Historically, there seems to be perennial dissatisfaction with the schools--almost every period in American history sees some educational crisis and efforts at reform. Many have observed that there are cycles of reform in which public or professional thinking moves from one pole to the other on some continuum. Perhaps we never seem to achieve our aims because they are never clearly in view or clearly in harmony.

The purpose of this book is to suggest that many of the difficulties of educational reform arise because of deep ideological problems concerning education. These problems more generally have their roots in liberal democratic theory. Specifically, this book will explore the varied and conflicting themes in public education--different ways of thinking about the aims of public education and how to realize them. These themes overlap and conflict with one another. Any effort at reform will inevitably address, consciously or unconsciously, these theoretical conflicts. Moreover, even taken separately, any approach to public education will face a dilemma of excess and deficit, a general ambivalence concerning state action in a liberal democratic society. Public schools will inevitably be open to the charge of doing too much or too little to achieve the appropriate aims of public education. And, not surprisingly, these are not the only theoretical or ideological problems confronting the schools. As an institutional expression of some of our most basic values such as liberty and equal opportunity, the schools often reflect different and conflicting interpretations of these values as well as some of the genuine difficulties of realizing them in practice.

Although this book will explore the theoretical and ideological problems confronting public education and efforts to reform the schools, these problems will not, indeed should not, be seen in purely abstract terms. Much of the argument here is that the meaning and significance of these problems depend on how they are dealt with in practice, how school practices and proposed reforms interpret or reflect varying themes and values. It is therefore necessary and desirable to discuss not only the key themes implicit in education policy but their practical manifestations as well, to look at the specific ways in which themes are played out institutionally. The following chapters therefore explore abstract considerations about liberal democratic political theory and the proper goals of public education as well as more concrete but no less important topics such as moral education, the relationship of education to jobs, and the school-based delivery of social services. Although practical responses to the ideological problems of education can never wholly resolve them--given that they are inevitable in a liberal democracy--they can provide more or less satisfactory ways of dealing with them. If this does not provide relief from our perennial dissatisfaction with the schools, it can provide a more theoretically informed way to evaluate current and future reform efforts.

The remainder of this chapter will discuss in a general way the kinds of problems, both theoretical and practical, confronting reform. Chapter 2 considers the prospects for discovering a "foundation" for educational policy in liberal democratic theory, specifically through the idea of neutrality. Liberal democratic theory permits a plurality of perspectives (themes), both in general and with regard to specific policy areas such as education. We therefore have a plurality of often conflicting ideals or themes that guide educational policy. Moreover, each individual theme faces conceptual, normative, and empirical difficulties. These conflicts and problems have their roots in the inevitable conflicts within liberal democratic theory concerning the legitimate role and scope of state power and the relationship of the individual to the community.

Chapters 3, 4, and 5 offer a thematic analysis of education policy by examining three major viewpoints regarding public education. Two of these, one emphasizing common moral or cultural education and the other emphasizing achievement and "human capital," have commonly been noted. A third theme, "clientelism," has also played a significant role in public education and promises to be increasingly important. Each chapter considers one of these themes by exploring some of its conceptual and institutional problems--including conflicts between and among themes--with specific reference to current reform proposals. The final chapter draws together some of the conclusions of this analysis and suggests some areas for future reform.

Current Reforms, Perennial Obstacles

What perhaps saved the reform movement from a premature death due to its own rhetoric was executive intervention, specifically the summit of governors convened by President Bush in fall 1989. That and a meeting the following year established six national goals for education to be achieved by the year 2000:

1. All children will start school ready to learn.
2. The high school graduation rate will increase to at least 90 percent.
3. American students will leave grades four, eight, and twelve having demonstrated competency in challenging subject matter including English, mathematics, science, history, and geography; and every school in America will ensure that all students learn to use their minds well, so that they may be prepared for responsible citizenship, further learning, and productive employment in our modern economy.
4. U.S. students will be first in the world in science and mathematics achievement.
5. Every adult American will be literate and will possess the knowledge and skills necessary to compete in a global economy and exercise the rights and responsibilities of citizenship.
6. Every school will be free of drugs and violence and will offer a disciplined environment conducive to learning.[5]

If the reform movement had not set forth, let alone accomplished, a clear agenda during the 1980s, executive leadership was now offering a new impetus and specific direction for the movement. Since these meetings, there have been numerous efforts at refining, especially through goals panels, the precise meanings of the aims and ways to measure them. For example, many expect there will be a voluntary program of national testing in the not too distant future.

It is somewhat surprising that the initial response to the setting of national goals was not to resist federal interference in what has traditionally been the responsibility of the states. The more common complaint was the apparent division of labor implied by this process, namely, that the federal government would declare the ends but leave it largely to the states to find the means. The setting of national goals at the instigation of the president was not accompanied by specific strategies for their implementation, let alone any promises of significant financial assistance from Washington. Rather, the focus was on outcomes and the difficult questions of implementation were left to the states and localities. It is fairly easy to criticize this division of labor, almost as easy as it is to specify national goals while leaving the hard work of implementation to others. Answering questions of implementation would be difficult enough, but it was also clear from the executive summits that little by way of additional resources would be available to help reform efforts. That money was neither the problem nor the solution was and is an article of faith in the reform movement.

A response, if not a remedy, to the gap between goals and implementation was offered in *America 2000*, unveiled by the Bush administration and its new secretary of education, Lamar Alexander, in spring 1991. *America 2000* is a hodgepodge of items, including rhetorical exhortations concerning reform, a progress report on the interpretation of the six goals, support for certain kinds of initiatives such as "choice" plans, and some new proposals for federal involvement in education. Specifically, among other proposals, it suggested national standards and voluntary tests, encouragement of parental choice, the creation of experimental "New American Schools" (now under way) that would serve as models for reform, and the establishment of job skill standards and Skill Clinics to ensure that students develop job-related skills. What is claimed to unify these various proposals, beyond their service to the six goals, is an emphasis on clearly stated standards and accountability, as well as the encouragement of community-based efforts and experimentation. Again, it is suggested that clear aims and political effort, rather than money, are the main ingredients for genuine reform.[6]

Certainly, there is something positive in the setting of national goals and the encouragement of educational experimentation. Besides the obvious benefit of focusing attention and effort, the goals reflect an appropriate mix of ambition and modesty. If we were to reach these goals in the specified time, all would probably agree that we had accomplished a great deal. Similarly, few could question the notion that our schools, and society generally, would be better off with fewer dropouts, better scores in math and science, and so on. The goals do reflect specific points of consensus about what would represent educational reform. Perhaps the clearest testimony to the general legitimacy of the goals is that the Clinton administration has made little or no effort to modify them. Indeed, it has further pursued the development of national standards. By and large the goals seem to reflect a nonpartisan statement of outcomes the schools should seek. The setting of these national goals thus seems to avoid (or at least attempts to avoid) knottier political and ideological questions. It does not seek to settle all differences about education or articulate some overarching vision about schools and society. If these goals, and the proposed means for implementing them, are not a solution to our educational problems, they represent a genuine effort that would, if successful, constitute real improvement.

The consensus represented by these goals, and their primary attraction, is thus pragmatic rather than ideological. If we can agree, preferably in as specific a way as possible, what our aims are, then we can work on ways to reach them. Whatever political differences might separate various groups, they can agree on some specific goals. If that consensus is not visionary, it is useful in concentrating attention and effort in a common cause--and making a common cause of school reform increases our chances of success. Indeed, this is typically the way of educational reform (or perhaps any policy advance) in a pluralistic society. While tolerating and even celebrating differences, we seek to establish working agreements where different views intersect or where compromises between and among differing views can be worked out. Once such consensus is established we can be optimistic about the prospects for reform or at least be comforted by the knowledge that fundamental political disagreement will not undermine them.

Despite the pragmatic attractions of this approach, it is also easy to be skeptical or even cynical about the prospects for real reform. Reform, in education or any other policy area, is going to confer advantages and disadvantages on various interests. Proclamations of consensus will not make these conflicts go away, and political opposition can limit or undercut the degree to which real changes are achieved. Even assuming goodwill and public-spiritedness all around, the sheer magnitude of the task of educational reform is daunting. Although we spend a great deal on education, and "more money is not the solution" has become a tiresome (and misleading) cliche, one could easily imagine a larger portion of our resources being profitably devoted to public education and being spent more effectively.[7] Thus, despite the apparent determination to change the schools and the setting forth of specific goals, it is not clear that we have the political and practical wherewithal to accomplish dramatic reform.

We may lack certain intellectual resources as well. Educational philosophy and psychology have hardly progressed to the point where we know what education should accomplish, let alone how to produce it. Again, every episode of crisis and attempt at educational reform in American history has been followed fairly quickly by another episode; there is a kind of "deja vu all over again" quality to the reform movement. We are somehow never satisfied with our schools, even after we have "reformed" them, and the current movement may seem to be yet another turn of the cycle of crisis and reform. Many of the substantive issues or themes cited in one era are often repeated or rejected in another. For example, many observers noted the similarity between the rhetoric of the most recent "crisis" and that which followed the launching of Sputnik--the schools are again urged to mobilize students to meet the rigors of international competition, although now the threat is more economic than political or military. Between these two "crises" there was a period in which reform efforts emphasized more personal, student-centered concerns. These cycles indicate that we do not always make clear and consistent, let alone attainable, demands of the schools. Indeed, we have often saddled them with multiple, conflicting tasks ranging from cultural integration to economic competitiveness, as well as asking that they take on new tasks as new problems arise.

To put the matter more systematically, there are three categories of doubts or questions about educational reform, or for that matter reform in any policy area: questions about the ideas or ideals guiding reform, doubts about the interests promoting or affected by reform, and finally questions about the institutional implementation of reform. The three i's--ideas, interests, institutions--suggest the kinds of things that must mesh for reform to be successful. They are the policy analog to Dahl's theoretical ("rational thought and discussion") triangle of principles, problems, and solutions. Like Dahl's triangle, these considerations are never wholly independent of one another, and we can seldom simply proceed from ideas to reforms in a straightforward fashion. Bringing together the three i's is difficult not only because of conflicts between and among them but also because each by itself poses problems for reform.

Ideas/Ideologies

The persistent dissatisfaction with public education and the accomplishments of previous reform movements reflect the extraordinary demands we place upon the schools. We have made them responsible for embodying and promoting our highest ideals. They also represent deep philosophical commitments--a faith in reason and in our ability to discover truth and control the future. Abstractions aside, we also have a long list of more or less specific tasks we demand of the schools that includes, among other things, the development of knowledge and skills, the promotion of common culture and citizenship, and preparation for productive work. In short, "We want it all."[8] Given the magnitude of these tasks, it should not be surprising that the schools are a persistent source of frustration. Whether through intellectual and moral failures, or because of the inevitable gap between ideals and reality, or simply because we are asking for too much, the schools never quite seem to live up to the very high hopes we have for them. Our constant crises may simply indicate that we have high and perhaps unrealistic expectations about what schools can and should do.

One way of trying to avoid making excessive or contradictory demands upon the schools might be to state more clearly and concretely what we expect the schools to do. The strategy of the recent reform movement, as noted previously, seems to be to avoid any elaborate, abstract statement of educational ideals as a rationale for recommended changes. To be sure, there are the usual rhetorical claims about the role of schools in enhancing competitiveness, opportunity, citizenship, and almost anything else we value. But the focus is on more specific policy goals that are offered as something upon which there can be wide agreement. It is implicitly assumed that whatever ideals we might have for the schools are best served by focusing our attention on these specific and measurable goals. Instead of being drawn into potentially divisive ideological wrangles about the purposes of public education, we will find a common, specific set of aims that can provide the focus for reform.

Again, the appeal of this strategy is primarily practical and political. It claims to provide a clear, consensual basis for reform. The goals are reasonably clear, and presumably there will be ways of measuring whether we have reached these aims. Moreover, they do provide the prospect of widespread agreement: who can oppose the idea that all children should be ready for school? Whether one values equity or excellence, citizenship or achievement, the proposed goals are arguably necessary for realizing any "higher" educational values we might have. Politically, the strategy of finding a common ground among otherwise disparate groups and demands has many precedents in American educational history. It also appeals to the pragmatic impulse of policymakers. Politicians and other policymakers typically do not have the luxury to take a long historical view of change and reform or to be very philosophical about public problems. The identification of education as a problem and its elevation on the public agenda demands a response. The tone of the reform reports, and even more in the discussion of national goals, is prospective and rhetorical rather than analytical and philosophical.

There are a number of reasons to doubt that the question of educational ideals can be so easily avoided through a consensus on specific goals. At least some observers and critics of the reform movement have suggested that this strategy avoids answering basic questions about the purposes of public education or, worse, offers dubious answers. For example, after summarizing all the forces that tend to make the schools resistant to change, one analysis suggests, "most of the foundation work of decent secondary education remains to be done, seven or eight decades after the system began to take shape." Similarly, Amy Gutmann argues that the use of rhetorical exhortations about excellence or getting back to basics does not give us any means for evaluating policy. "The problem is not that the reforms . . . are necessarily wrong, it is that we cannot judge them without a more principled understanding of our educational purposes." Any policy recommendations in the reform movement, she suggests, will presuppose a theory "about the legitimate role of government in education. Unless the theory is articulated, citizens cannot assess its principled merits or policy implications."[9] Still other, more critical comments note the tilt of the new consensus away from educational equity and characterize the discussion of educational reform as an "impoverished one . . . almost entirely lacking in a vision of schooling committed to equality and democratic citizenship." The clear implication is that the wrong ideas are being bandied about, and the path to reform must begin with the right ones (equality, democratic citizenship).[10] This kind of criticism suggests that we lack clearer or better principles to guide and evaluate reform, a failing that cannot be overcome by simply stating specific goals.

At the same time, the plea for foundation work, principled understanding, or a theory, however appealing, also involves certain difficulties. As will be discussed Chapter 2, there are significant limits on the degree to which any ideology or theory can provide satisfactory guidance for practice. Political theories or ideologies, especially in a liberal democratic society, will inevitably involve some significant ambiguities and, more important, some degree of incoherence that makes the simple translation of ideas into policy problematic. Consider the simplest possible case in which we set forth one value, say equal opportunity, that the schools are charged with promoting. What would it mean for the schools to maximize the goal of equal opportunity? It is easy to imagine several conflicting interpretations of this value. On the one hand it might mean that all students are given exactly the same curricular, personal, and financial resources as part of their education. But this conflicts with the notion that resources might need to be distributed unequally in order to adjust for individual capacities and needs; for example, extra expenditures for students with disabilities are seen as necessary for providing equal opportunity. It may also conflict with the notion of equal opportunity as outcome-related, for example, that educational outcomes, regardless of inputs, not be predictably disparate on the basis of sex or race. It is important to note here that these conflicts are not merely practical problems in implementing a guiding value, but are measures of incoherence surrounding that (and perhaps any) value itself. Moreover, a similar situation obtains when we consider more than one value, as any sensible theory or ideology must. For example, the value of equal opportunity almost inevitably conflicts with the right of families to provide advantages for their children, and these two values are not the only ones that might bear on educational or other policies.[11]

What separates the reform movement from some of its critics here is not whether the schools need improving, but how to think about educational goals and reform. Their different responses to this issue not only conflict but pose something of a dilemma. The reformers see the issue of goals as relatively transparent. It is easy to obtain agreement on things we want the schools to do (for example, the six educational goals), and the task, though still formidable, is primarily practical and political. We need to figure out how to get what we agree we want from the schools. The critics regard this strategy as at best superficial and at worst disingenuous. Agreement on goals, however worthy, is not a substitute for principled understanding. Without some broader theoretical view of what we want institutions to accomplish, the pursuit of concrete goals is unlikely to be satisfactory. It may even be self-defeating as we discover the pursuit of some goals may impede us from realizing other important values. In the worst case, the establishment of superficial goals avoids difficult but important ideological questions (for example, about equality and democratic citizenship) in favor of an implicit and even morally dubious view of schools' role in a democratic society. At the same time, however, the plea for a foundation or an emphasis on different (better) values ignores the inevitable ambiguity and conflict involved in the appeal to more abstract principles. It understates the problems in establishing foundational principles and, worse, risks holding reform hostage to inevitable, and perhaps irresolvable, ideological conflict inherent in pursuing such principles.

It is hard to believe that a country that produced Horace Mann and John Dewey could feel itself lacking a foundation for educational policy or, alternatively, would seek to skirt or avoid larger ideological questions. However, the problem is not a lack of principles but a false dilemma about making use of the principled help that is available. Namely, the reform movement and some of its critics seem to have offered a choice between setting specific goals that avoid the issue of fundamental educational aims, on the one hand, or producing a foundation--a clear, coherent, and just set of educational ideals--on the other. Much of the argument of this book is that neither solution is satisfactory or practical, or for that matter, reflective of our educational ideals and practices. Instead of attempting to avoid the plurality and conflicts of goals, the suggestion here is to expect them, clearly display them, and examine the ways in which institutions deal with them.

The thematic analysis offered here, as much by example as argument, suggests a compromise between the search for some foundational principles and the pragmatic pursuit of specific goals. This kind of analysis cannot sweep away the frustrations and anxieties associated with public education. Rather, it will suggest some of the reasons why we lack a foundation or deep consensus on public education and what that implies for the evaluation of policy. Since plurality is characteristic of liberal democratic thought, the analysis of policy cannot be theoretically determined. Instead it must take into account, in terms of specific institutions and contexts, different and often competing themes and the problems and conflicts they generate. Suggesting such difficulties, both in general and in educational policy in particular, does not mean that we are helpless or that the prospects for reform are hopeless. Rather it requires us to find a middle ground between the pragmatic but atheoretical approach of establishing specific goals and the theoretical but futile search for comprehensive principles. It requires us to somehow mix the more abstract concerns of ideology and the practical concerns of policy. We need to look at how institutions ultimately (and necessarily) deal with problems implied by various themes, taken separately or together.

Interests

Whether we seek a consensus on a foundation of basic principles or a more specific consensus on certain policy goals, the point of reaching agreement is to allow us to make better policy. Agreement of one kind or another helps avoid conflicts that make reform difficult or impossible. Unfortunately, we seldom find ourselves in a circumstance, in education or elsewhere, where there is widespread agreement about policy matters. Groups can sincerely disagree about the ideal parameters of policy, and interests adversely affected are hardly likely to agree with any proposed vision for reform. Whether by rationale or rationalization, policy disagreement is a permanent feature of our political life. Therefore the road from ideas about policy to genuine changes in institutions and practices must pass through the terrain of various interest groups in society. To be even remotely practical, any comprehensive view of policy generally, a theory or ideology, or even any specific policy proposal must anticipate its effects on existing political interests--on the relative power, status, and wealth of various groups in society.

If ideas and theories can change rapidly and dramatically, the groups who must anticipate the costs and benefits of change cannot. If reform is to be more than merely an analytical or speculative process, it must enlist the assistance of those interests affected by it. Of course, it is very difficult, if not impossible, to ask interests to be disinterested. Changes in policy, even modest ones, are likely to have some impact on interest groups. At least some of these changes will be, or will be perceived to be, negative. As Machiavelli pointed out, the prospect of reform will certainly generate opposition from those who benefit from current arrangements, the "old order," and probably arouse the suspicions ("incredulity") of others. Our hopes for reform, whether driven by general principles or specific goals, must be tempered by a sober understanding of the ways in which different interests might react to proposed changes.

Concern about the role of interests in the political process has always been a part of American politics generally and education policy in particular. The American constitutional design is built upon the expectation not only that interest groups will defend their positions but that they will seek to use political institutions to defend or advance them. Similarly, much contemporary political analysis of American politics has focused on the ways in which interest groups can block needed political actions. For example, it is commonly argued that the delegation of authority to public bureaucracies has often enlisted government in the essentially conservative task of protecting or advancing established interests. More generally there has been concern that advanced industrial societies become incapable of reform because interest groups so "clog" or "overload" the public sector that change for larger public purposes is rendered impossible.[12] Reformers past and present have often bemoaned the presence of special or entrenched interests blocking reforms.

The relationship of ideology and interests has also been at the center of debates about the American public education. Among historians, on the one hand, the orthodox account of public education in the United States portrays progressive changes in the public schools as a means of realizing and interpreting the nation's fundamental ideals of freedom and equal opportunity. Revisionist histories, on the other hand, point out the role of education in serving group or class interests and claim that rhetorical ideals are often the rationalization of those interests.[13] Not surprisingly, the reform movement and its critics reflect this tension. Much of the rhetoric of the reform movement in the 1980s stresses that public education is essential to our national well-being and is necessary for providing opportunities for individuals. Again, critics are more skeptical, suggesting that the reform movement is more concerned with developing human capital for corporate interests rather than providing educational equity. And it is a short step from skepticism to cynicism. Education reform is good politics, and educational interest groups have gained a great deal from the reform movement. Politicians and the education "industry" arguably have been the major beneficiaries of this education crisis and efforts at reform.

There is little point in trying to adjudicate between these two positions, in trying to assert the dominance of ideology or interest. Criticism of one position or theory often produces an equal and opposite error. If the orthodox account of American education understates the gap between principle and practice, the revisionist critique overstates the dominance of interest over ideology. If there is not a strict congruence between principle and practice in the history of American education or in the current reform movement, it should not be taken to mean that ideology is always and everywhere twisted to suit interests, class or otherwise. Ideology is not merely a snare and a delusion foisted upon the downtrodden by the dominant. But neither is it an impartial arbiter of interests, a purely neutral court of principled appeal that adjudicates conflict. If it were the former, segregated schools would still be with us; if it were the latter, arguments for educational equality and opportunity would have ended long ago. Ideology may serve to rationalize dominant interests, but not any rationalization will do. If it is a weapon for the powerful, it can also be for the weak.

It is important therefore not to place ideology or reform on one side and interest on the other, although it is common rhetorical strategy to do so. Those defending existing policies and institutions are not without ideological resources of their own. Their defense is not couched merely in terms of their interests, but in terms of ideological justifications legitimizing those interests. That is, few groups will say that some reform is unjustified because it gives them a diminished position in terms of wealth, power, or status. Rather, the diminished position is unjustified for some ideologically relevant reason. It is not always easy therefore to distinguish between rationale and rationalization. Occasionally, a case of the latter will be clear--to all but those offering it. Rhetorically attractive though it may be, it is often difficult to definitively dismiss a group's claims as merely a self-interested rationalization.

There will not be much discussion in this book of the myriad groups whose interests are affected by different themes and proposed reforms in public education. We can be confident that many of these interests can speak for themselves, and their stake in any orientation should be relatively clear. What can be said is why different groups might interpret a theme or policy in one way rather than another and what interpretations (and resulting institutional practices) are likely to generate political conflict and opposition. Although differing interests often agree on certain themes, they interpret them differently. For example, there might be widespread agreement on the desirability of moral education, but such a symbolic consensus is not the same as a deeper consensus. Discussions of specific policies in this area, as will be seen in Chapter 3, often involve considerable disagreement, for example, about the content of the curriculum, the proper role of the state in such matters, and so on. These conflicts will be viewed through the lens of perceived gains and losses, symbolic or material. The issue then is not how ideology serves the interests of society generally or some specific interest in society, but how different interests interpret, use, and even change basic ideological notions. These varying and often conflicting interpretations are worked out and ultimately embodied in specific policies and institutional arrangements.

Institutions

It is perhaps too easy to overestimate the role of interests in promoting or preventing reform. Interests do not float freely about the political realm. They are embedded in networks of laws, policies, practices, and organizations that define what can and cannot be done. These institutions, broadly understood, typically reflect the previous working out of the political play of interests and ideas. They reflect working agreements of how ideas are to be understood, policies are to be pursued, and costs and benefits are to be distributed. If consensus at an ideological level is often difficult to achieve and if conflicts among interest groups are always part of a free society, institutions reflect the perhaps inevitable need to come to some resolution of ideological and political conflict. If not solutions to policy problems, they represent working agreements about how policy in an area is to be conducted and to what ends, even if these ends remain the subject of ongoing interpretation and conflict.

At the same time, it has often been observed that many policies are altered, if not simply subverted, in moving from conception or legislation to execution or implementation. There have been numerous explanations for this phenomenon, many of them featuring bureaucrats--everyone's favorite scapegoats. Those charged with implementing policy are popularly portrayed as being too accommodating to special interests or too concerned with their own preservation and aggrandizement. Even when not self-seeking, bureaucrats are often seen as merely incompetent or intransigent, unable to implement policy properly and mired in pointless rules and routines. Institutions may reflect working agreements about policies, but that doesn't mean that institutions work.[14]

Certainly there is some validity in the common perceptions of bureaucracy, but they need to be complemented by two observations about institutions and implementation. First, implementation is a messy and difficult business. The neat connection between policy and results anticipated by those who make policy is a far cry from the reality of having to establish programs, deal with clients, and adjust to the inevitable variations in circumstances that arise in the course of administering a policy. In establishing a policy or program, most policymakers have in mind an image of how the policy normally should function, the nature of the typical transaction between the administering agency and the public, and the (beneficient) results of that interaction. Unrealistic expectations, unusual circumstances, and unintended consequences are the everyday world of implementation. This would be the case even if every policy and program were established anew. These problems are compounded by the fact that policies are often grafted on to a preexisting bureaucratic apparatus that has already more or less specified its task, established routines, and clarified its relationship(s) to various clientele. These must all be adjusted to the new demands of policy, and implementing even the apparently simplest changes can be a difficult task.[15]

Second, even as we recognize the practical difficulties of mobilizing institutions and actors to policy purposes, we may still underestimate the role of autonomous institutional practices in impeding reform. That is, we believe problems of implementation, though formidable, are not insurmountable; we retain an optimistic, quasi-engineering view of institutions as means to public ends. Although perhaps we neither can nor should think of institutions in any other way, it may also be that this view is somewhat inaccurate and therefore self-frustrating. Specifically, such a view might not take into account the relative autonomy of institutions, a notion expressed theoretically as the "new institutionalism." To oversimplify a bit, the new institutionalism suggests that far from being mere instruments, however (in)efficient, of policymaking, formal organizations independently "provide order and influence change in politics" and "define the framework within which politics takes place."[16] Within organizations, the centrality of rules and routines, the division of labor and expertise, and the elaboration of meaning all are integral parts of what policy will actually accomplish (or fail to accomplish). As we see organizations in this way, some of our traditional views of organizational behavior are altered, if not reversed. For example, instead of seeing organizations as solving problems posed elsewhere, we see them as solutions in search of a problem. Similarly, rather than viewing a sequence of decisions as rational or causal, we may see it as temporal, where timing is more important than some kind of logic. Though somewhat ill-defined, the new institutionalism suggests that ideas alone, however widely agreed upon, will not determine the prospects for reform. It is crucial to anticipate the ways in which those ideas are likely to be dealt with by the relevant administrative organizations.

Echoes of both views of the problems of implementation can be heard in discussions of the education reform movement. It is not surprising that teachers and administrators, as bureaucrats delivering a service, have been subjected to considerable scrutiny and criticism as the reform movement has proceeded. Initially teachers were cast as an interest group blocking reform, especially because of the role of unions; the discussion has now shifted to their acquiring better, more "professional" training and working conditions. More recently, discussions of restructuring, site-based management, and the like have suggested that schools as organizations can be reconfigured to make them both more efficient and effective. Similarly, part of the increasingly popular argument for choice plans is that schools confronting market forces tend not to have either large or intrusive administrations. It is often noted that private and parochial school bureaucracies are smaller and more effective than their public counterparts. In short, many reformers are suggesting that bureaucratic reorganization or elimination is a key element in reform.[17]

By whatever name--restructuring, site-based management, reorganization, choice--any significant organizational change in the schools is a massive chore. Educational organizations generally, and the delivery of educational services in particular, are relatively insulated from external influence. This may seem a remarkable claim, given the recurring concern about public education, and the many things--from broad cultural changes to state policies to the work of more specific groups such as textbook publishers or educational lobbies--that might influence schools. However, educational policy is characterized by features that tend to make it resistant to change by groups other than educators themselves.

To begin with, educational policy is both massive and diffuse. Simply because public education is a service that has to be delivered everywhere to everyone who requests it, there will be considerable discretion afforded educators and teachers--despite teachers' worries about professional status. Similarly, although educators complain about meddling parents and politicians, the schools have seldom been reconfigured to any particular purpose regardless of dramatic rhetoric about educational reform. On the contrary, the norm has been to keep schools out of politics, and many institutional arrangements and regulations are designed to do just that. Even when schools have been "reformed" the actual practices and policies of schools have often been only marginally changed, if at all.[18] Changing bureaucratic organizations may be difficult in any case. It is all the more so with regard to schools.

The institutional insulation and autonomy of the schools are consistent with the new institutionalism as well. Schools are a projected solution seeking a problem, whether it is economic competitiveness or equal opportunity or cultural integration. But the solution seldom involves dramatic organizational change; reform has typically involved the application of standard routines in response to problems. For example, Thomas Timar and David Kirp note that reform initiatives have generally been modified to fit more easily into the standard operating routines of schools while ignoring the need for a "fundamental redefinition of organizational roles."[19] Although it is tempting to dismiss these responses as mere self-interest on the part of educators, it might also be that this response is a logical or understandable way for schools as organizations to cope with demands for reform. The fitting of reforms into existing rules and routines is a way to provide order without massive and disruptive change. The proof of this kind of institutional autonomy lies not only in the ways in which particular reforms are molded to fit the organization; it also can be seen in our constant bewilderment about the basic structure of schools. It is commonly noted that schools, physically and organizationally, reflect outmoded assumptions (for example, that they are modeled on nineteenth century factories rather than twenty-first-century workplaces). But for all the talk about breaking the mold or restructuring, we somehow find it difficult to imagine, let alone move to, the appropriate school of the future. The current program of reform generally works within organizational forms that are often recognized as dubious, for example, concerning the use of time, age grading, and tracking. The net result is that schools may try to work better, though not necessarily differently.

The point here is not to suggest that institutions cannot be reformed. Rather it is to suggest that institutions simply are not as plastic as we might desire and they may even be an independent factor in determining what reform of various kinds ultimately means. Institutions will inevitably reflect how themes past and present are understood and interpreted. It is therefore important to not think of genuine reform as impossible, but to realize that ideas or themes must be given institutional expression and that this expression might be some distance from the idealized views of reformers and others. Both bureaucratic inertia and the relative autonomy of institutions are significant factors in the meaning and success (or failure) of reform. In any case, institutions must finally reflect, for better or worse, what themes will mean in practice. The ultimate meaning of reform will be determined by how institutions respond to new demands and policies.

Themes and Reforms

Reform, in education or in any other policy area, depends upon the smooth integration of the three i's. Ideally, there should be some agreed-upon ideas guiding reforms, various interests should see themselves as gaining, or at least not losing, by assisting the process of reform; and institutions should be mobilized or modified to make reform a reality. As noted above, each of these areas presents obstacles to the creation of a new order of things. Moreover, there is no formulaic way of overcoming these obstacles, since each side of this triangle is intertwined with and affects the others. Like Dahl's "triangular path," there is no sequence in going from educational ideals to practices. Rather, there is only a variety of themes and conflicts about their meaning and implementation.

Obviously shelves of books have, can, and could be devoted to exploring each of these categories, in general or with reference to a specific policy area such as education. Again, this book is primarily concerned with the first category, the ways in which ideals might guide educational reform. Specifically, it suggests that ideals should be considered as themes rather than theories providing principled guidance for specific policies. We must wrestle with the problems generated by different themes, taken separately or in conflict with one another. Addressing themes in this way neither provides systematic theoretical guidance nor avoids theoretical questions. Equally important, although we may not be able to answer many of the theoretical puzzles about the purpose(s) of public education, we necessarily provide better or worse answers in policy through institutions and practices. Examining the interpretation and ambiguities of various themes, their conflicts, and their practical implications can give us a clearer picture of some of the inherent problems confronting efforts to reform public education. If this picture does not provide a cure for our frustrations with public education, it might provide us with a clearer way of carrying on the policy discussion about educational reform, now and in the future. Such a discussion may not fully integrate the three i's, but it can suggest some of the ideological, political, and practical tasks at hand.

Notes

1. National Commission on Excellence in Education, *A Nation at Risk*. Washington, D.C.: U.S. Department of Education, 1983, p. 5.
2. Some of the major commission reports included R. Anderson and David Saxon, *America's Competitive Challenge*. Washington, D.C.: Business-Higher Education Forum, 1983; James Hunt, *Action for Excellence*. Denver: Education Commission for the States, 1983; Robert Wood, *Making the Grade*. Washington, D.C.: Twentieth Century Fund, 1983. Several major field studies were also published at about the same time, including Ernest Boyer, *High School: A Report on Secondary Education in America*. New York: Harper and Row, 1983; John Goodlad, *A Place Called School*. New York: McGraw Hill, 1983; Arthur Powell, Eleanor Farrar, and David Cohen, *The Shopping Mall High School*. Boston: Houghton Mifflin, 1985; Theodore Sizer, *Horace's Compromise: The Dilemma of the American High School*. Boston: Houghton Mifflin, 1983.

   The two major reports on the teaching profession were *Tomorrow's Teachers: A Report of the Holmes Group*. East Lansing, Michigan: The Holmes Group, 1986 and *A Nation Prepared: Teachers for the 21st Century*. Washington, D.C.: Carnegie Forum on Education and the Economy, 1986. For a succinct review of some of the issues concerning restructuring and choice, see Louann Bierlein, *Controversial Issues in Educational Policy*.. Newbury Park, Cal.: Sage, 1993, Chs. 3, 5. The major reports on economic productivity and education include *Workforce 2000: Work and Workers for the Twenty-first Century*. Indianapolis, Indiana: Hudson Institute, 1987; *Making America Work: Productive People, Productive Policies*. Washington, D.C.: National Governor's Association, 1988; *Investing in People: A Strategy to Address America's Workforce Crisis*. Washington, D.C.: U.S. Department of Labor, 1989; Ira Magaziner, *America's Choice: High Skills or Low Wages*. Rochester, N.Y.: National Center on Education and the Economy, 1990; The Secretary's Commission on Achieving Necessary Skills (SCANS), *What Work Requires of Schools*. Washington, D.C.: U.S. Department of Labor, 1991. The *Investing in People* report is certainly the most comprehensive of these, including two volumes of over 2,400 pages of background papers.
3. Chester Finn, "The Drive for Excellence: Moving Towards a Public Consensus," in Beatrice and Ronald Gross, eds., *The Great School Debate*. New York: Simon and Schuster, 1985, p. 75. See also Mark Yudof, "Educational Policy Research and the New Consensus of the 1980s," *Phi Delta Kappan*. 65 (1984): "Consensus is shaped around the basic mission of the schools. Children are in public schools to learn skills: to master reading, writing, and arithmetic; to establish a foothold in science;

to gain familiarity with modern computer technology; and, ultimately, to achieve a secure and productive job. Achievement counts. So does hard evidence of academic success or failure. But the softer variables relating to self and social interaction do not count. No more talk of open classrooms, identity crises, the culture of youth, and the diversities of ethnicity and race. The emphasis is on turning out engineers, scientists, computer programmers, health specialists, and other occupational groups that serve collective interests," p. 456.

4. For some of the initial state responses to the "at risk" report, see Milton Goldberg, *A Nation Responds*. Washington, D.C.: U.S. Department of Education, 1985. For a more recent summary and perspective on reform efforts, see Thomas Toch, *In the Name of Excellence*. New York: Oxford University Press, 1991; Bierlein, *Controversial Issues in Educational Policy*. For some political reactions, see Stanley Aronowitz and Henry Giroux, eds., *Education Under Siege: The Conservative, Liberal, and Radical Debate over Schooling*. South Hadley, N.J.: Bergin and Garvey, 1985.

5. U.S. Department of Education, *America 2000: An Education Strategy*. Washington, D.C.: U.S. Department of Education, 1991, p. 19. This is the final form for the wording of the goals first discussed in 1989. Not surprisingly, the wording, as well as the goals themselves, were subject to considerable discussion and negotiation.

6. *America 2000*, see sections I, II, III.

7. For all the talk about how much we spend on education, there is some evidence that our expenditures on primary and secondary education are *less* than those of many of our international competitors. See M. Edith Rassell and Lawrence Mishel, *Shortchanging Education: How U.S. Spending on Grades K-12 Lags Behind Other Industrial Nations*. Washington, D.C.: Economic Policy Institute, 1990; see also Albert Shanker, "The Myth of the Big Spender Debunked: U.S. Expenditures on Education," *New York Times*. Sunday, May 5, 1991, p. C6.

8. On the excessive expectations for education, see Henry Perkinson, *The Imperfect Panacea*. New York: Random House, 1977; Diane Ravitch, *The Schools We Deserve*. New York: Basic Books, pp. 32ff.; John Goodlad, *A Place Called School*. Ch. 1.

9. On "foundation work," Powell, Farrar, and Cohen, *The Shopping Mall High School*, pp. 27, 306ff. Amy Gutmann, *Democratic Education*. Princeton: Princeton University Press, 1988, p. 4.

10. On "equality and democratic citizenship," see Ira Katznelson and Margaret Weir, *Schooling for All: Race, Class, and the Decline of the Democratic Ideal*. New York: Basic Books, 1985, Ch. 1. More broadly, some have suggested that the reform movement was inspired by corporate needs for reproducing "human capital" and a reaction against more egalitarian views of education. See Christine Shea, Ernest Kahane, and Peters Sola, eds., *The New Servants of Power*. New York: Greenwood Press, 1990. Steven Tozer, Paul Violas, and Guy Senese, *School and Society: Educational Practice as Social Expression*, New York: McGraw Hill, 1993, Chs. 12, 13.

11. An especially compelling statement of this kind of conflict is offered by James Fishkin in *Justice, Equal Opportunity, and the Family*. New Haven: Yale University Press, 1983. For some of the complexities of equal treatment, see Deborah Stone, *Policy Paradox and Political Reason*. Glenview: Scott Foresman, 1988, Chapter 2. For a range of views, see also Norman Bowie, ed., *Equal Opportunity*. Boulder: Westview, 1988.

12. Respectively, Theodore Lowi, *The End of Liberalism: The Second Republic of the United States*. 2nd ed. New York: Norton, 1979; Mancur Olson, *The Rise and Decline of Nations*. New Haven: Yale University Press, 1982. For a more recent discussion, see Robert Salisbury, "The Paradox of Interest Groups-More Groups, Less Clout," in Anthony King, ed., *The New American Political System*. 2nd ed., Washington, D.C.: AEI Press, 1990.

13. For a review of the competing histories of American education, see Joel Spring, *The American School, 1642-1985*. New York: Longman, 1987.

14. For a discussion and partial critique of this view, see James Q. Wilson, *Bureaucracy: What Government Agencies Do and Why They Do It*. New York: Basic Books, 1989.

15. On issues of implementation, see Dennis Palumbo, *Public Policy in America*. New York: Harcourt Brace, 1988, Chs. 1, 4.

16. See James March and Johan Olsen, *Rediscovering Institutions: The Organizational Basis of Political Life*. New York: Free Press, 1989, pp. 16ff.

17. On restructuring, see Edward Fiske, *Smart Schools, Smart Kids*. New York: Simon and Schuster, 1991; on choice, see John Chubb and Terry Moe, *Politics, Markets, and America's Schools*. Washington, D.C.: Brookings Institution, 1990.

18. Larry Cuban, *How Teachers Taught: Constancy and Change in American Classrooms, 1890-1980*. New York: Longman, 1984.

19. Thomas Timar and David Kirp, "Educational Reform and Institutional Competence," *Harvard Educational Review*. 57 (August 1987), pp. 308-330.

2

The "Theoretical Mystique" and Thematic Analysis

In studying this subject we must be content if we attain as high a degree of certainty as the matter of it admits. . . . The question of the morally fine and the just--for this is what political science attempts to answer--admits of so much divergence and variation of opinion that it is widely believed that morality is convention and not part of the nature of things. We find a similar fluctuation of opinion about the character of the good. . . . Such being the nature of our subject and such our way of arguing in our discussions of it, we must be satisfied with a rough outline of the truth, and for the same reason we must be content with broad conclusions. Indeed, we must preserve this attitude when it comes to a more detailed statement of the views that are held. It is the mark of an educated man and a proof of his culture that in every subject he looks for only so much precision as its nature permits.

--Aristotle

These collisions of values are of the essence of what they are and what we are. If we are told that these contradictions will be solved in some perfect world in which all good things can be harmonized in principle, then we must answer, to those that say this, that the meanings they attach to the names which for us denote the conflicting values are not ours. We must say that the world in which what we see as incompatible values are not in conflict is a world altogether beyond our ken; that principles which are harmonized in this other world are not the principles with which, in our daily lives, we are acquainted; if they are transformed, it is into conceptions not known to us on earth. But it is on earth that we live, and it is here that we must believe and act.

--Isaiah Berlin

In the previous chapter, I discussed the movement for educational reform and some of the obstacles it faces. Competing and ambiguous ideas, conflicting interests, and problems of institutional implementation confront any proposed policy changes in a liberal democratic society. Education policy is no exception.

One implicit debate about the current reform movement concerns the kind of intellectual resources that we need to bring to bear in guiding policy. Some supporters of the reform movement declare that there is a consensus about the direction of educational reform. This consensus is often expressed in general rhetoric about excellence or competitiveness. Such rhetoric suggests that ideological or policy differences, if they exist at all, are minor. After all, who is against excellence? The task then is to translate this general consensus into specific educational goals, such as the six goals for the year 2000, and establish policies that will achieve them. Reaching agreement on specific goals may help us avoid immediate ideological or political conflict. Whatever else people might agree or disagree about, they can agree to these goals and move quickly to implement reforms.

Those skeptical or critical of the reform movement doubt the validity or utility of this rhetorical consensus. At best, it is argued, the current consensus fails to provide intellectual clarity--a deeper consensus--about educational aims and purposes. Beyond rhetoric about competitiveness and similar notions, there is little or no explanation why these goals have been set or what the relationships are between and among them. For example, little has been said about the potential conflict(s) between excellence and equity, although the former has been given more rhetorical attention than the latter. Some more specific aims seem to be given short shrift. For example, civic education seems to have a low priority relative to achievement in math and science.[1] In the absence of some more general statement of the ultimate rationale and priorities of the movement, it is difficult to evaluate the current goals. At worst, the absence of such foundation work may ignore or downgrade certain educational priorities and set an educational agenda that is inappropriate or inequitable.

The demand for a foundation rejects the pragmatic strategy of setting specific goals in favor of finding some broader theoretical or ideological guidance. This guidance might come from a broad theory of liberal democracy from which we could derive a persuasive account of the role of public education in our society. Alternatively, we might look to a specifically educational theory that sets forth principles concerning the proper aims of schools. Either would offer the possibility of achieving a more principled understanding of policy than a rhetorical, and perhaps inadequate, consensus that focuses on specific goals.

This chapter considers some possible ways of pursuing this theoretical strategy. Attempts to locate and justify basic principles of liberal democracy or public education often seek a certain kind of theoretical or ideological guidance (the theoretical mystique). This search is unlikely to be successful because it tries to go beyond a "rough outline of the truth" and seeks a "degree of certainty" beyond what liberal democratic society and policymaking within it "admits." Liberal democratic theory and policymaking in our society inevitably involve a plurality of values that overlap and conflict with one another. These "collisions of value" suggest that "the principles with which, in our daily lives, we are acquainted" resist being organized into some structured theoretical package. Instead of a theoretical approach to policy, a more thematic approach would take this plurality as a given for any policy area such as education. Examining several themes in a policy area can reveal the ideological problems and contradictions they generate ("incompatible values . . . in our daily lives") and, equally important, the ways in which institutions deal, or fail to deal, with them.

At first glance this detour into the theoretical mystique might seem a distraction, an abstract exercise far removed from issues of educational reform. However, there are two reasons for pursuing this strategy. First, many of the discussions in liberal democratic theory are analogous to debates about educational policy. For example, in both areas there are questions concerning the nature and role of consensus and about whether the state or the schools can or should be neutral in some sense. Second, in displaying some of the limits of the search for theoretical or ideological guidance we can also see some of the problems with a strategy that tries to reduce the problem of policy to the process of establishing specific, consensual goals. Neither theory nor politics alone provides an appropriate vehicle for analyzing educational policy and reform. A more thematic approach brings considerations of theory and policy closer together.

Liberal Democracy and "Neutral" Theories

The demand for foundation work or a more principled analysis of reform seeks some theoretical basis or explicit principles that can justify and guide educational policy. Such a theory would provide a basis for deriving conclusions about policies and institutions. If we could reach consensus on such principles, then we could use them in evaluating proposed reforms. Theory would guide practice; practice would be grounded in theory. The hope for such guidance and the temptation to seek it might be called the "theoretical mystique."

The hoped-for theory would presumably meet certain criteria. Like any good theory, it would be parsimonious, coherent, and comprehensive.[2] In formal terms, it would involve a relatively small number of general principles that fit together in a logical way. There would either be clear priorities among principles or they would be defined in a way that would avoid conflicts between or among them. Substantively, these principles would be well-established and relevant to the issues at hand. They might range from the broadest ideals of a liberal democratic society to more specific principles for public education within it. These principles could then be used to guide and evaluate educational institutions and policies--as well as efforts at reforming them. Even if there were some continuing disagreement about their application in particular cases, there would be consensus on a basic set of principles for discussing policy.

To just state these criteria is to see how difficult it might be to obtain such theoretical help and how tempting it might be to seek instead consensus on specific policy goals. It would seem to be very difficult to obtain any systematic guidance from liberal democratic theory or some more specific theory concerning education. There are many varieties of, and disagreements within, liberal democratic theory.[3] Likewise, there are any number of overlapping and competing theories about the appropriate goals of public education and the role of schools in our society.[4] Certainly we can describe in general some of the things to which liberal democratic ideology is committed, including limited government, individual rights and freedoms, popular sovereignty, and so on. Similarly, we can list many of the things we want public schools to do, including imparting basic skills, encouraging citizenship, and preparing students for the world of work. But these bundles of commitments are understood and arranged in a wide variety of ways, ways that do not obviously lend themselves to theoretical encapsulation. These kinds of disagreements cast doubt on the prospect of achieving a deeper theoretical consensus as a foundation for evaluating policy.

Any such doubts are compounded by the fact that liberal democratic societies are inherently suspicious of foundations or any orthodoxy that might inhibit debate and dissent. Part of the appeal of our society is the variety of political and philosophical commitments it allows. Our orthodoxy seems to be not to have an orthodoxy. Conflicts concerning liberal democracy or education may seem even more pervasive and intractable because we invite disagreement and dissent. This not only lessens the prospect for achieving a deeper theoretical consensus, it casts doubt on its desirability.

Still, it is tempting to try to find those principles, for liberal democracy or education policy, that might be recognized as fundamental. The question then is where to look for such principles. One strategy, though certainly not the only one, involves an implicit or explicit appeal to a concept or principle of neutrality. As will be seen below, this appeal may take a variety of forms. Following Aristotle, we might broadly distinguish between what might be termed "external" and "internal" appeals. The former involves neutral principles that are alleged to reflect the "nature of things." They reflect some external reality or philosophical principles that are not dependent upon historical or cultural understandings. The latter, internal principles, are those that reflect some shared (neutral) understanding within a society or practice; they arise from human agreement or "convention." In drawing a distinction between external and internal principles, it is important to remember that the terminology is not sacrosanct. The former could easily be termed general, objective, broad, or philosophical, and the latter might be termed local, conventional, narrow, bounded, or political.[5]

Ultimately, in whatever form, these appeals typically fail because the expectations that underlie them, the theoretical mystique, are too demanding. To oversimplify a bit, the formal requirements of a good theory are contrary to the substance of liberal democracy and the inevitable "collisions of value" in policymaking. We are unlikely to obtain the theoretical guidance sought through appeals to neutrality. Rather, we need to explore other, more thematic ways of dealing with the inevitable plurality of values in theory and policy, and this is well illustrated by debates about educational policy.

External Neutrality

Neutral Because Objective

Liberal democratic theorists have repeatedly attempted to provide an objective foundation for their political beliefs. As one observer puts it, "It has been the objective of many liberal writers to demonstrate that their political conclusions logically follow from either incontestable metaphysical claims or indisputable factual evidence."[6] Such principles would be neutral in the sense of being objective. That is, *all* rational individuals with the same access to evidence and argument would recognize these principles as being true. Proposals for foundational principles have included theological, moral, and philosophical arguments, for example, about God-given human rights, as well as appeals to allegedly scientific principles in sociology or psychology (utilitarianism). The appeal of finding such an external point of certainty is obvious. It potentially provides the foundation for justifying liberal democracy and adjudicating policy issues within it.

This foundational project has always faced severe obstacles. As noted previously, there is a tension and ambivalence in the liberal tradition concerning foundational claims. Liberal democratic philosophers and politicians have simultaneously sought incontestable principles while proclaiming tolerance of diverse and conflicting foundational beliefs. Therefore claims to have discovered some externally neutral principles, an objective foundation for policymaking, are likely to be open to skeptical challenge. The enforcement of such claims as a kind of orthodoxy is unacceptable. Moreover, there is a similar tension between establishing noncontentious or readily demonstrable first principles and ensuring that those principles can speak to political issues. Metaphysical claims and factual evidence that are politically relevant are likely to be disputed.[7]

Recent intellectual developments have further undercut the idea that liberal democracy can be understood and justified through some externally neutral or objective principles. In many intellectual disciplines and endeavors, particularly those generically called "postmodern," the very possibility of objectivity, or neutrality, has been called into question. The "incredulity toward metanarratives" has invited challenges to any and all political claims and beliefs. The postmodern viewpoint emphasizes the role of cultural perspectives in determining what is rational, objective, and so on. For example, the movement for multiculturalism often suggests that Western understandings have no special, objective standing but are only one of a variety of cultural forms and choices confronting us. As one title puckishly puts it, "Reality isn't what it used to be."[8]

A similar, but more specific, critique of liberal democratic theory's philosophical foundations is offered by communitarian theorists.[9] Despite many differences among these theorists, they share some general arguments. Liberal democratic political theory, it is claimed, is confused or wrong in its philosophical assumptions. Specifically, its theoretical arguments are not historically self-conscious enough. For example, individual rights are treated as transcendent principles rather than the historical and contingent choices of our community. Too little notice or credit is given to the ways in which cultural, historical, and institutional factors influence moral judgments and personal identities. Similarly, these assumptions lead to political views that are too individualistic. Because individuals in liberal society see themselves as separate from any community, our society is dangerously atomistic. The excessive emphasis on individual autonomy and rights, it is argued, has corrupted public discourse and created or exaggerated many social problems. Once these values are seen as socially constructed or historically situated, then better (less individualistic, more communitarian) alternatives can be more readily considered. Like the postmodern viewpoint, the communitarian critique suggests there is no externally neutral point outside of our cultural perspectives and historical traditions.

Neutrality as a Principle

If these criticisms suggest that we cannot locate some "incontestable metaphysical claims" perhaps what is needed is a principle that recognizes their contested nature. Instead of seeking neutral principles (the neutrality *of* principles), we might instead explore neutrality *as* a principle. To say, for example, that the state should be neutral with respect to matters of

religious belief seemingly provides a way of addressing church-state relations without undercutting the commitment to religious autonomy and
diversity. Or, more generally, it might be argued that because individuals
deserve equal respect the state should somehow be neutral with respect to
individual conceptions of the good.[10] For example, this might be taken to
imply that the state should not use educational institutions to impose certain values. Discovering or suggesting principles that are neutral in this
way is attractive because it simultaneously provides some basic philosophical principle(s) that are consistent with pluralism and diversity.

Although the idea of neutrality *as* a principle governing liberal democratic societies is appealing, it is important to note, as communitarians suggest, that this concept must be viewed in both a historical and a cultural
context. The idea that the state should be neutral vis-a-vis religious beliefs
is not a neutral notion but a product of the specific evolution of our society.
More important, what it means to be neutral here depends heavily on historical interpretation and institutional practice, rather than obvious inferences from a given principle. For example, as recently as thirty-five years
ago mandatory prayer in the schools was not viewed as violating the state's
neutrality toward religion. Now prayer in the schools is impermissible,
and there are numerous other cases in which the definition of neutrality
has shifted. In short, neutrality as a principle is less some external point of
guidance than a notion that must be situated in terms of specific historical
understandings and institutional practices.

A good illustration of the problems with neutrality as a principle is the
notion of "neutral dialogue" suggested by Bruce Ackerman. "Neutrality,"
he claims, is a philosophical principle that governs all claims about moral
and political issues: "Neutrality: No reason is a good reason if it requires
the power holder to assert: (a) that his conception of the good is better than
that asserted by any of his fellow citizens, or (b) that, regardless of his conception of the good, he is intrinsically superior to one or more of his fellow
citizens." This principle of neutral dialogue, Ackerman claims, recognizes
that "nobody has the right to vindicate political authority by asserting a
privileged insight into the moral universe which is denied the rest of us."[11]
At the same time, this principle supposedly can be used to derive policy
results. For example, it is claimed to support egalitarian distributions because it does permit individuals to say, "I'm at least as good as you are,
therefore I should get at least as much." The appeal of Ackerman's neutrality principle lies in its claim to be a rational (external) philosophical
principle that is neutral between or among individuals and their various
claims ("nobody has . . . a privileged insight") yet powerful enough to
produce inferences concerning policy.

There are a number of problems with Ackerman's proposal. For example, it offers a neutrality principle that is not really neutral. The inference from the principle to "I'm at least as good" is meaningless without some measure of value ("shares" of some good such as money or power) against which to measure "at least as much."[12] Once such a measure is brought into the dialogue, the principle is no longer neutral because it presupposes the good(s) to be equally distributed. Moreover, the principle itself presupposes a liberal democratic view of the world. The idea that no "conception of the good" can be offered as superior is more a part of our cultural view than an established philosophical principle. But this is circular, as one critic puts it, "because you cannot prove that there is no good common to all persons by preventing anyone from raising the question in the first place."[13]

These criticisms illustrate some of the difficulties and tensions inherent in the search for external principles generally--whether they are more positive philosophical (metaphysical) or scientific ("indisputable factual") principles or neutrality as a principle of the sort offered by Ackerman. Certainly one would not want to deny outright the possibility of finding such principles. However, any proposed external principles will likely face the trade-off between neutrality and adjudicative power--the more neutral a principle, the less likely it is to speak to important issues. Ackerman's view of neutrality as a principle reinforces this point. If it is truly neutral it does not say anything by way of justifying liberalism, or anything else, being a kind of radical skepticism. When it is interpreted in ways that give it adjudicative power ("I'm at least as good"), it becomes considerably more contentious. The more it meets some theoretical criterion (external neutrality) the less likely it is to be able to speak to substantive issues. Thus Ackerman's argument is a kind of *reductio ad absurdum* for arguments developed from externally neutral principles.

As will be seen below, contemporary liberal theorists have generally accepted the notion of limits on external defenses of liberalism. They have concentrated their efforts on defining liberal democratic political culture and responding to communitarian critiques of it. Before we examine this turn to internal neutrality, it should be noted that the quest for an externally neutral foundation, the impulse to seek more certain and more coherent justifications, is not illegitimate. The attempt to solve the puzzles and contradictions of social life in a rational way is an enduring and appealing feature of liberal democratic culture. To suggest limits on such theoretical aspirations is not to endorse the postmodern critique of objectivity and rational debate. That these arguments are, as communitarians suggest, in some sense contingent, historically and culturally situated, and therefore not absolutely certain, does not make them irrational or arbitrary. The lack of some "incontestable metaphysical principles," or even a useful principle denying the existence of such principles, does not prevent us from appealing to relevant philosophical, scientific, or metaphysical theories.

Rational policy argument inevitably involves, implicitly or explicitly, such broad appeals. They cannot be avoided by agreements on specific policy goals. As noted in Chapter 1, any consensus on policy will imply some broader views on the proper role of government, goals of education, and so on. In short, it will implicitly appeal to ideological principles. Although these appeals cannot provide a foundation for policy, they can provide a basis for rational consideration of the inevitable plurality of perspectives and "collisions of value" in a liberal democracy.[14] Indeed, the expectation that there can be reasonable disagreements in evaluating policy is one of the distinctive features of the liberal democratic community.

Internal Neutrality

"Overlapping Consensus"

The demand for "incontestable metaphysical claims," is probably too severe and not attainable in any case. Instead of trying to find some external principles as a foundation for policy, perhaps all that can and should be sought are consensual principles shared *within* liberal democracy. Instead of attempting to stand outside our culture and traditions, we should ask what principles underlie the liberal democratic community. Meeting a test of internal neutrality of this sort is less demanding than finding objective principles. It allows us to propose or discover some principle(s) that underlie our tradition even if they cannot be objectively grounded. These principles would be internally neutral in the sense of reflecting common commitments of otherwise diverse individuals and groups. They would provide a consensual basis for discussing institutions and issues and for clarifying our commitments and their implications for policy.

Again, it is obvious that our society shares many broad principles. We believe, among other things, in individual rights and liberty, the rule of law, and equality. The question then is whether--in general or for some specific policy area--these beliefs can (or even should) be expressed in a theoretical form that can be applied to policy. Here, as in the case of external neutrality, finding a theory "in which all good things can be harmonized in principle," as Berlin notes, "is a world altogether beyond our ken." It is inconsistent with the varied principles and commitments within our society, "and it is here that we must believe and act."

Perhaps the most fully developed case for shared (internally neutral) principles of this sort has been offered by John Rawls. In what seems to be a departure from his earlier accounts, Rawls claims that his two principles of justice (of equal liberty, for just distribution) are "political, not meta-physical."[15] By this he means that they do not reflect any agreed-upon philosophical (metaphysical) argument. Rather he claims that his two prin-ciples represent "the kernel of an overlapping consensus" in the liberal democratic tradition. They are or could be agreed to by "each of the oppos-ing comprehensive moral doctrines influential in a reasonably just demo-cratic society." Even if partisans of various metaphysical positions inter-pret these principles in their own ways, he claims, they can still agree to his principles as a "political charter" for liberal democratic society. Consciously or not, Rawls' shift from a metaphysical to a political interpretation of his theory implies concessions to the communitarian critique. Instead of ask-ing basic philosophical questions, Rawls is attempting to articulate what the liberal democratic community is by suggesting what principles might be internally neutral among groups within it.[16]

Rawls seeks this overlapping consensus because, first, he doubts the utility of attempting to develop a deeper philosophical rationale for his (or other) principles. He claims that his conception "deliberately stays on the surface, philosophically speaking," meaning it is independent of "disputed philosophical, as well as disputed moral and religious questions." He seeks to avoid these questions because the "diversity of doctrines--the fact of pluralism--is . . . a permanent feature of the public culture of modern de-mocracies." Second, confining our attention to shared political principles, as opposed to seeking "truth about an independent . . . order" (external neutrality), will better serve what Rawls sees as the "task of political theory" in a liberal democratic society. Namely, political theory should provide principles that form the basis for a "shared, workable order" among groups that hold different and even incommensurable positions on philosophy, morality, and politics. It aims at discovering, articulating, and obtaining consensus on those principles that, regardless of other differences, are shared by all segments of our society.[17]

If we assume this task of political theory, the question then becomes whether Rawls' two principles--or any small number of logically ordered principles--are widely shared and powerful enough to perform this task. There are several ambiguities and problems that suggest a negative an-swer to this question. These problems would confront any attempt to en-capsulate our shared commitments in some logically structured theoreti-cal form.

First, there is an important ambiguity about whether the claim that cer-tain primary principles are consensual or internally neutral is an empiri-cal, anthropological claim or a normative, rhetorical one. For example, Rawls' claim that his principles represent the "kernel of an overlapping consensus" might be initially taken in an empirical or anthropological way, as reporting what our "tribe" believes to be its basic, shared principles.

Alternatively Rawls' claim might be seen as normative or rhetorical. That is, the two principles are offered as persuasive definitions of the charter of liberal democracies. All groups in a liberal democratic society will, upon reflection, agree to them. It is critical to note here that this rhetorical conception is not wholly separate from the empirical one. It would make little sense to offer a persuasive account of charter principles, understood as political, if they bore no discernible relationship to common understandings.[18] Nonetheless there remains some, perhaps inevitable, ambiguity about this mix of elements.

On either account it is not clear that Rawls' two principles or any other contenders can represent the kernel of an overlapping consensus. For example, as an empirical matter, it is doubtful that Rawls' egalitarianism is widely shared. The public mind, past or present, might in fact be better represented or codified by some libertarian principles or some form of rule utilitarianism. But these, and other philosophical principles, also conflict with one another, as well as with Rawls' views. These conflicts indicate that, as an empirical matter, there is probably no underlying consensus.[19]

If Rawls were primarily offering an empirical claim for his principles one might expect some detailed historical or anthropological argument. Instead one finds more standard philosophical arguments--for example, arguments about moral persons, the priority of liberty, and so on. This suggests that Rawls is engaged in the more rhetorical task of providing a persuasive definition of charter principles. However, as with the empirical approach, it is not clear that Rawls' principles would be able to win widespread or meaningful allegiance or that some other proposed "core" principles might not claim an equal or greater ability to do so. This is particularly true if we allow, as Rawls does, different groups to interpret proposed charter principles in their own way (that is, retain many or all of their preexisting allegiances). It is not clear then why groups would prefer Rawls' principles to other contenders or vice versa. In short, there are good reasons to doubt that Rawls' principles represent, either empirically or rhetorically, liberal democratic society's underlying consensus.

Another problem concerns the practical role such principles might play. They may be understood as either guides or boundaries to political debate. On a strong interpretation these principles serve as guides. They provide good reasons for political proposals and criteria for judging political institutions, "a publicly recognized point of view [of] . . . what are recognized among them as valid and sufficient reasons singled out by the conception itself." Alternatively, these principles or others might be understood as weaker constraints or boundary conditions on political discussion and institutions. Liberal societies are predicated on allowing the existence of a plurality of conceptions of the good. Some shared principles, as a political charter, set the parameters within which the pursuit of potentially incommensurable goods is possible. On either understanding, whatever disagreements remain are dampened because they are discussed on the basis of consensual principles, "as theorems, as it were, at which their several views coincide."[20]

Both notions of consensual principles face problems and there is some tension between them. If various parties are free to use principles as strong guides in their own ways, any consensus may be more symbolic rather than real. For example, Rawls notes that our tradition is of (at least) two minds about liberty and equality, with Locke and Rousseau representing contending camps. But if the modern partisans of these positions interpret shared principles in their own ways, their disagreement is not, at least not obviously, lessened. They merely have another language in which to express it. Similarly, the weak view is potentially too weak to accomplish the task of political theory. For example, one might agree with Rawls that principles of liberty and equality are in some sense basic, boundary principles for liberal democracy but then wonder about their practical significance. These boundaries are still open to differing interpretations, and the principles do not provide any guidance for other conflicting claims.

Indeed, these two conceptions suggest a dilemma in themselves. On the strong view, Rawls' principles or similar candidates as guides are unlikely to have consensual status. If they really do have some power to determine important political outcomes, they may not be seen as consensual by those whose views lose out. The strong conception may be too strong for consensus. Alternatively, if they are seen as weak, then the shared basis may be more readily agreed upon, but this provides a largely symbolic sharing--liberal democrats are committed to liberty and equality, somehow understood, and little else. Again, as Rawls notes, each group will interpret basic principles in its own way. Thus a strong, guiding interpretation is likely to fail to be consensual, and the weaker, boundary view may not play a significant role in lessening disagreement.[21]

The above criticisms at least allow the possibility that there is some coherence to our tradition and, more important, that its coherence can be expressed in one or a few principles. Actual traditions may be a poor approximation of these theoretical ideals. For example, there may be some deep consensus about the importance of rights, but not their absolute priority over considerations of consequences. Neither of these reflects procedural values that might have a similar status. Perhaps more important, the shared understandings in our society may include virtues that are not deducible from principles such as those offered by Rawls. These may reflect traits of character or attitudes, for example, toward work or marriage.[22] It may be that charter principles, if they exist at all, are more numerous and complex than Rawls' argument allows, extending beyond political values or principles to ideals of character and conduct. It is doubtful that liberal democratic political culture can be encapsulated in Rawls' two principles or any similarly spare form.

The point here, then, is not that liberal democratic societies lack consensus about values and principles. Rather, the problems with Rawls' political account suggest that such consensus is unlikely to take the theoretical form of a few logically ordered principles that are widely shared and commonly understood. Although there may be internally neutral principles, they may overlap and be interpreted in conflicting ways that defy the kind of theoretical expression offered by Rawls. Indeed, similar problems are likely to arise with attempts to find such principles in specific policy areas, for example, education.

"Democratic Education"

It might be wondered whether the search for overlapping consensus in liberal democratic society is simply too abstract, too removed from the concerns of educational policy to be very promising. Perhaps the theoretical guidance that is needed should be sought in a theory that is more directly concerned with education in a liberal democratic society. If there is no well-structured consensus about liberal democratic principles there may be some consensual (internally neutral) principles concerning education policy. Again, we certainly agree on at least some educational values and principles. The question is whether these can be articulated and organized in a way that helps guide our policy debates.

A recent formulation offered by Amy Gutmann is particularly interesting, because of both its theoretical self-consciousness and its emphasis on the political goals of public education. As noted previously, Gutmann is critical of the lack of principled analysis in the reform movement. Rhetorical exhortations about excellence and agreements on specific goals, she rightly points out, do not give us sufficient means for evaluating policy. Like Rawls, however, she is wary of any foundational account that recommends a "moral ideal of education." Philosophical theories may set forth some moral ideal of education--for example, rooted in conservative or liberal ideology, understandings of human nature, functionalist views of society--from which we may infer possible answers to educational questions. But these theories leave us with no way to deal with inevitable disagreements among them about educational aims. Neither do they tell us who has authority to make decisions about education or what kinds of limits there are, and must be, on that authority in a liberal democratic society.

Therefore, Gutmann argues, what is needed is a *political* ideal, a theory that sets forth how authority over education is to be exercised in a democratic society. That is, even as individuals differ in their moral ideals, they share a political commitment to democracy. Specifically, there is a common "commitment to share the rights and obligations of citizenship with people who do not share our complete conception of the good life."[23] A theory of democratic education, then, can provide such a political ideal because it reflects "our deepest convictions" and the "deepest shared commitments of a society." Although there will be conflicts between and among moral ideals of education, a democratic theory of education, if properly framed, can say a great deal about what the primary purposes of schooling are as well as speak to many specific controversies in education.

Gutmann derives the principles for her democratic theory by surveying the major alternative political views--the family state, the state of families, and the state of individuals--on authority over education. She rejects each of these as ceding either too much authority to the state to determine the good life or too little by turning over education to families or "neutral" professionals. A democratic theory of education, she claims, can avoid these problems and preserve the strengths of the alternatives. It can do so in a positive way by recognizing the importance of empowering citizens to make educational policy in ways that enhance democracy. At the same time, it must also limit public power "[in ways] that preserve the intellectual and social foundations of democratic deliberations."[24]

The positive side of this task is what Gutmann calls "conscious social reproduction." Democratic authority over education should be exercised by local communities for the civic purpose of giving students the knowledge and skills necessary to play their role as democratic citizens. Our many disagreements concerning educational aims, Gutmann claims, "presupposes a common commitment to recreating the society that we share." This common commitment implies, procedurally, that education should be democratically controlled. Substantively, it implies that the schools should not only transmit certain kinds of knowledge and skills but should also actively engage in "cultivating character," teaching virtues of toleration and critical deliberation appropriate for a democratic society. "Conscious social reproduction" therefore is not neutral, for example, between the claims of tolerance and bigotry. Rather it suggests that teaching tolerance is an important positive aim in preparing students to be citizens in our society.

These positive aims must be accompanied by limits on democratic authority over education. It is obvious that democratic control can produce undemocratic outcomes. Gutmann suggests two principles, nondiscrimination and nonrepression, that constrain democratic authority over schools. The first forbids exclusion of any educable child from an education "adequate to participating in the political processes that structure choice among good lives." The second suggests that education may not be used to restrict rational consideration of "competing conceptions of the good life and

good society." These constraints serve the cause of conscious social reproduction by ensuring that democratic authority will not foreclose the future
effective participation of democratic citizens. It will neither exclude students from educational opportunities nor impose a vision of the good life
upon them.[25] On the basis of these principles Gutmann proceeds to address a wide range of specific educational issues.

There are several similarities between Gutmann's discussion and Rawls'.
Her distinction between moral and political ideals of education roughly
parallels Rawls' distinction between metaphysical and political principles.
Her appeal to "shared commitments" that underlie different political ideals is quite similar to Rawls' version of an "overlapping consensus." Like
Rawls, Gutmann derives her principles by surveying and rejecting the major alternatives and trying to capture features they have in common with
her principles. Finally, like Rawls, she views the task of theory to be judging and guiding practice in light of our deepest convictions.

Not surprisingly, many of the things that can be said about Rawls' political principles of justice can be said about Gutmann's theory of democratic education. First, there is the question of whether the appeal to shared
convictions is primarily empirical or rhetorical. Gutmann is perhaps clearer
than Rawls that her appeal is to the latter, to desirable principles rather
than the actual beliefs or practices of the regime. Still, her rhetorical appeal
may not, rightly or wrongly, square very well with other widely held sentiments that might reflect our deepest convictions. For example, many
might place greater emphasis on the personal, academic, or economic importance of education, as distinct from its political aims.[26] Moreover,
Gutmann's account also faces a dilemma concerning the strength of her
principles. She does not regard them as weak or merely symbolic. Her
numerous specific applications suggest quite the opposite. But reading
them in a strong way invites criticism, both as to whether the application
of her principles is appropriate and whether such application suggests that
we ought not (or do not) accept these principles. For example, Gutmann's
argument that her principles forbid teaching creationism in the public
schools (even when taught in a way that does not promote religious beliefs) seems to infringe upon a potentially legitimate sphere of democratic
authority. At the same time her suggestion that school authorities could--
unwisely, but not illegitimately--ban certain books may not reflect widely
shared beliefs about free inquiry; it may also be inconsistent with her principle of nonrepression. More generally, Gutmann's theory can and has
been criticized for giving priority to the political aims of education over
other aims, for emphasizing the importance of democratic control over in

dividual freedom, and for producing some dubious results, both in its own terms and in terms of other legitimate concerns.[27]

Many of these specific criticisms stem from different and competing ways to understand the proper role of the schools, particularly their relationships to individuals and families. Gutmann's separation of "moral" ideals from her "political" ideals assumes that conflicts among the former can be made coherent by subordinating them to the latter. Competing moral perspectives on the schools, however, may not be so readily reduced or subordinated to internally neutral principles of the sort offered by Gutmann. Insofar as alternative (moral) ideals suggest different policies--for example, a more libertarian view on the power of families and individuals versus school authorities--it can be argued that these moral claims ought not be subordinated to some political ideal. Indeed, it is not clear that the distinction between moral and political ideals can be maintained.[28] Finally, "our deepest convictions" may not have the kind of coherence represented in either the form or substance of this, or any, theory. Rather we are, as Gutmann's critique of other theories and analysis of policies suggests, persistently pulled in different directions by different (moral) perspectives on the schools, including her own.

Overall, these specific criticisms are less important than their indication of some of the problems implicit in the search for theoretical guidance of a certain sort. Although Gutmann claims that her theory is merely a "guide to moral reasoning rather than a set of rigid rules," it nonetheless attempts to articulate a few ordered principles that will guide policy in this area. Gutmann's recognition of the problems of foundationalist claims does not lead her to abandon the associated search for some small set of primary principles. Like Rawls' political principles, her theory claims to reflect our deepest convictions (internal neutrality). As with Rawls, the attempt to find a few principles to guide policy confronts competing principles that are prima facie legitimate, trade-offs between theoretical acceptability and practical applicability, and inevitable ambiguities in application.[29]

This is not to say that the political aims of education might not be very important, even primary, in public education. Some support for this view will be offered in Chapters 3 and 6. Moreover, as will be discussed below, Gutmann has rightly pointed to one of the most fundamental tensions concerning education, namely, the relationship of the state to individuals and families. However, the conflict(s) between the state and individuals and families, as well as between and among aims for public education, cannot be so readily "harmonized in principle" through the kind of theory offered by Gutmann.

Theories and Themes

Although it apparently cannot be realized, the theoretical mystique is both understandable and laudable. It attempts to subordinate policy to principle and provide principles that can guide and serve as a basis for evaluating policy. The aspiration to objectivity or claims for externally neutral principles seeks some objective foundation for liberal democracy. The search for principles that constitute an overlapping consensus is limited to our particular tradition but seeks the same end, neutral theoretical guidance for institutions and policies. More specific theories such as Gutmann's also seek to put policy on a principled basis, albeit for a particular policy area.

The theoretical mystique implies certain expectations and demands concerning the relationships among principles, the nature of consensus and justification, and the relationship of theory to practice. The goal of theoretical inquiry, in general or in a policy area, is to obtain a consensus on a small number of consistent, broad principles from which inferences can be drawn about justice, education and so on. Again, such principles would meet the formal requirements of a good theory—coherence, scope, and parsimony. Substantively, they would provide a reference point for rational justification of particular commitments or policies, practices, or institutions. Justification would be a matter of citing these principles and using them to constrain or derive consequences. Current or proposed institutions and policies could then be judged on a rational, principled basis. Power would be subordinated to, and guided by, reason.

The search for theoretical guidance of this sort is understandable but flawed. It is flawed because it generates excessive and contradictory demands, particularly in a liberal democratic society. Externally neutral, metaphysical, principles are difficult to come by in any case, but especially so in a society given to skepticism about such claims and tolerant of differences in fundamental beliefs. A more political approach that seeks internal neutrality expressed in an overlapping consensus or small number of principles conflicts with the variety of beliefs and plurality of ways of interpreting fundamental values in a liberal democratic society. As it is with liberal democratic theory generally, so it is in broad policy discussions within our society. There are, for example, competing educational aims and values that cannot be transcended by appeal to our deepest convictions, allegedly expressed in a small set of principles. The demands of theory (in Berlin's words, "this other world") seem to be in tension, if not outright conflict, with our moral intuitions and the nature of liberal democratic society.

Suppose, however, we begin to relax some of these theoretical demands and expectations. For example, in moving to a "political, not metaphysical" approach Rawls explicitly avoids the demands for external philosophical justification. The task of theory, as he defines it, is less closely aligned with philosophical inquiry--the disinterested search for truth through reason and analysis--than with cultural interpretation for a practical purpose. Rawls seeks to describe and articulate our culture's underlying commitments, its overlapping consensus, as a practical response to its basic problem, the "fact of pluralism." This political approach focuses more directly on the description and interpretation of our society's underlying principles. Locating these internal points of consensus within our society would provide theoretical guidance for policies and institutions. The problem, as noted above, is that Rawls retains certain theoretical expectations about the form and nature of these principles (parsimony, coherence, comprehensiveness) as he attempts to engage in cultural interpretation. Metaphysical expectations about theory conflict with the political culture the theory purports to reflect.

The demands of the theoretical mystique might be relaxed even more. Going further in this political direction might lead to a less structured interpretation of the principles underlying liberal democratic society. In response to the communitarian critique, some theorists have tried to define and defend liberal democratic societies in terms of a bundle of principles that are broadly and generally shared. These overlapping commitments may not have the clear structure of a theory. They do, however, reflect the broad framework of shared principles within which diverse pursuits are possible. For example, Stephen Macedo argues that liberal democratic societies have "a basic political commitment to public reasonableness," to "open justifications openly arrived at." This commitment is expressed in distinctive concepts of "citizenship, virtue, and community . . . located in an ideal of liberal constitutionalism."[30] The major political institutions in liberal democracies reflect this commitment and make such societies more hospitable to certain ideals and ways of life and less to others. Similarly, William Galston suggests that our society does have a view of the human good that involves a number of dimensions. These include respect for life, normal development of basic capacities, fulfillment of interests and purposes, freedom, rationality, social relations of various kinds, and subjective satisfaction. Our institutional arrangements promote these values and are in turn supported by virtues found in the social, political, and economic spheres of liberal society that are vital for the continuing health of these institutions.[31]

Arguably this approach reflects our shared views more accurately than a more spare, axiomatic account. Commitments to public reasonableness and other virtues as well as specific institutional commitments to the rule of law and constitutional and market arrangements are all part of what defines and distinguishes a liberal democratic community. Although these commitments are not reducible to some theoretical formula, they nevertheless provide principles to which we can appeal in evaluating policies. These appeals do not lead to unique solutions because of differences in the interpretation of principles and the need to weigh and balance them against one another.[32] Nevertheless, this kind of account seems to better describe liberal democratic society in terms of a number of interrelated commitments. It offers a more robust, pluralistic account of our society, its view of the human good, and virtues appropriate to it.

Without gainsaying the value of this approach, it does suggest the possibility of going still further to close the gap between theory and policy. If the logic of theorizing shifts toward cultural interpretation for a practical purpose, then one way to fulfill the task of theory would be to look at some specific policy area in our society. Namely, we might start with a policy area, describe the competing themes or perspectives concerning it, see what theoretical problems and puzzles are embedded in it, and evaluate how these are (or are not) dealt with in liberal democratic society. Instead of moving from theory to policy, a thematic approach would start with policy problems in liberal society and explore their theoretical implications and conflicts. Such an approach would not reject philosophical or theoretical criticism but attempt to situate it more directly in issues and institutions.

A thematic approach then does not, at least not initially, seek much "distance" from ordinary policy debates in the liberal democratic community. It begins by displaying the plurality of themes in a policy area, in this case education, and looking at the values these themes reflect, their internal puzzles and contradictions, and their conflicts with one another. The expectation is that there are several perspectives or themes concerning policy and that these themes variously overlap and conflict with one another. Institutional settlements and practices reflect the ways in which these themes have, for better or (and?) worse, been given practical expression through the interplay of ideas, interests, and institutions. To speak of "settlements" is not to say that issues and problems have been appropriately resolved but merely to highlight the ways in which our society has interpreted its aims and values. This must also include some description of the ways in which institutions and policies embody a theme, or several themes, simultaneously. Finally, such an analysis is not, nor should it be, merely descriptive. It must also, as part of the task of political theory, critically evaluate these themes and their institutional manifestations, separately and together.

Thematic analysis suggests a somewhat different understanding of the task of political theory and how to bring theory to bear in analyzing policy. Its theoretical expectations are drawn mainly from the ways in which liberal democratic society discusses and deals with policy issues. Specifically, it involves at least three departures from the requirements of the theoretical mystique discussed previously. It assumes that we must deal with an irreducible plurality of primary values, takes a different view of the nature of consensus and justification in a liberal democratic society, and places a greater emphasis on political or institutional resolutions of conflicts between and among principles. In general these elements suggest that theorizing need not be radically different from ordinary political discussion but can be part of the fabric of ongoing policy debate.[33] Such an approach further shortens the distance between theoretical and political discourse by trying to reflect (and reflect upon) problems in our society. More important, such an approach suggests how we might examine debates over policy, in this case educational reform, in a way that avoids both atheoretical goals or aspirations to theoretical unity.

Plurality

A thematic approach assumes, both in general in liberal democratic society and in any specific policy area, that there is a plurality of principles and values that does not form any neat theoretical structure. These principles have been interpreted differently at various times and, perhaps more important, weighed and balanced against one another in different ways. Again, the liberal democratic community is not neutral regarding all political claims, but does allow and even invite differences in ordering and interpreting a variety of basic values. These varied interpretations give rise to several different political perspectives (egalitarians, libertarians, and so on) as well as different metaphysical, (scientific, religious, or philosophical) beliefs underlying them. We cannot expect these principles to be neatly encapsulated in some theoretical package. The plurality characteristic of liberal society is likely to go "all the way down," even as we share a number of values.

As it is with liberal democratic theory generally, so too it is in most policy debates in our society. There will typically be a plurality of values and aims within or across policy areas that may or may not always be consistent with one another. A thematic approach would highlight the different and competing perspectives in a policy area. These themes, taken separately or together, can be described in terms of the ways in which their key concepts are understood and how they are (more or less) realized and implemented in institutions. The three different themes or perspectives in education policy described below and in the following chapters provide different views of the appropriate aims of public education. Not only do these suggest different, if overlapping, directions for the schools, they are each open to different and conflicting interpretations. Even within a policy theme plurality is the rule rather than the exception.

This plurality of general perspectives and policy themes implies the possibility of several justifiable positions on many political issues. That these collisions of value do not lend themselves to theoretical resolution does not lead to a philosophical or political free-for-all. The absence of a small set of shared, structured first principles does not mean that political discussion and debate are necessarily either irrational or inconclusive. Reasons must be offered for invoking a certain value or principle in a given situation. For example, an individual may provide an argument for a certain educational policy because it advances equality as he or she understands it. To do so does not mean that he or she is likewise committed to always placing equality over other values in educational matters or to deny that other individuals might see the situation as falling under a different value such as liberty. Similarly, an individual may find that his or her own principles compete and need to be weighed and balanced against one another, or, perhaps tragically (or typically), some values cannot be satisfied at all. Reasonable disagreement on political issues does not necessarily constitute a threat to the stability of society, but rather a healthy--and typically liberal democratic--adjustment of principles and practices to new ways of thinking and historical and social developments.[34]

Consensus and Justification

Consensus in a liberal democratic society is not built upon a few theoretically ordered principles. Rather, it is a "thick" consensus in which multiple, overlapping values are widely shared, though interpreted in various ways.[35] To adopt Rawls' terminology there is an "overlapping consensus" but it has many "kernels" that correspond to the multiple perspectives within the liberal democratic community. To be sure, some principles, such as individual rights, may generally have a more secure status, but their presumptive priority is not immutably fixed nor is their interpretation always agreed upon. Similarly, in any policy area such as education there will be consensus about numerous, overlapping aims but these will also be subject to conflicts of both principle and interpretation.

Viewed in this way, there is more consensus in our society than liberal democratic theorists (or, for that matter, communitarians) seem to fear but it has less structure than they might wish or hope. Consensus about values is often not expressed theoretically or philosophically but in general or assumed agreements about specific institutions, laws, and policies. A great deal is, and perhaps even must be, taken for granted about how people may or may not, should or should not act in some specific context. Even when there are conflicts in interpretation or between and among values, these are not typically resolved by appeal to first principles. The legitimacy of certain values and procedures for resolving conflict is generally taken for granted, and questions that are raised are usually contextual rather than fundamental. The issue at stake is usually what the relevant value or principle is and how it is to be interpreted in the particular case, not what is required by some clearly ordered theoretical system. Consensus on a number of more or less general values, including procedures for resolving conflict, is less a foundation upon which other commitments are built, or a kernel that is at the center of things, than a patchwork quilt of elements knit together in a variety of ways.[36]

Just as there are differences between our everyday and more theoretical notions of consensus, so too there are differences between ordinary and theoretical justifications. Ordinary justifications often, perhaps typically, do not involve much theoretical elaboration. Unlike more theoretical justifications, ordinary (political) justification begins, and often ends, with a form of contextual justification. We justify our values and commitments in the first instance by appeals to some widely held value or the rules within some institutional setting or practice. For example, we justify a change in employment practices to better conform to norms of equal opportunity. Similarly, the rules of a school may be invoked to require or prohibit something. Often, that is all the justification that is needed or sought, and at most what is at stake is the invoking or interpretation of the relevant value or rule. Of course, disagreements about these may lead to the broader consideration of consensual values or institutional purposes. The discussion (or, perhaps, political conflict) may then turn to still broader (higher) principles, which presumably cut across specific institutions and practices. Conflict at this level may eventually involve the clash of more comprehensive perspectives and the use of political procedures to adjudicate the conflict--for example, court cases that challenge the authority of school officials vis-a-vis students. This kind of conflict is one of the factors that creates an impulse to seek some theoretical clarity, to find some philosophical or metaphysical principles to adjudicate conflict.

Given these various levels of argument, consensus on what counts as an adequate justification may often be reached at a relatively low level. A call for further justification may or may not be appropriate. Again, in a setting such as the schools, or in liberal democratic society in general, certain principles are simply shared and taken for granted. More important, these justifications, made locally or contextually, against the background of an institution or practice apparently meet the test of being "political, not metaphysical." At any step up the justificatory ladder consensus may be achieved among individuals or groups that a policy or practice is justified. Each may agree for different (metaphysical or political) reasons. These are only inadequate as justifications if we add formal or theoretical requirements that they must be subsumed under broader principles of a certain sort. As a practical matter, the search for broader, more theoretical justifications may not lessen disagreement or enhance the consensual pull of the argument. In fact, we sometimes decide our values or principles have to be modified to better conform to our intuitions about practices or particular cases. Also, the result is often that consensual political processes settle or adjudicate what cannot be resolved by rational appeals to higher values or principles. Once we abandon the theoretical expectation of justification as involving primary principles, there may be several styles of justification, including those that are more contextual and local,[37] and some types of justification that are simply the result of political processes.

Institutions and Policies

The shift away from a primarily theoretical view of consensus and justification requires us to look at specific institutions and policies as part of evaluating our theoretical ideals. Institutions and policies represent the ways in which various principles and values have been understood and implemented. For example, equal opportunity has generally been interpreted in the school setting as meaning that individuals will be given an equal chance to develop their skills and talents. Of course, the schools have been challenged as not providing this equal chance, and often this challenge involves a different interpretation of what equal opportunity means in both theory and practice. In any case, the school as an institution will reflect conflicting interpretations of values like equal opportunity and their relationships to other values.

Examining institutions and policies in this way is also important because we routinely expect them to try to achieve several values simultaneously. In the absence of some theoretical ordering for the plurality of values, institutions and policies will necessarily represent better and worse responses to the various values and the tensions between and among them. It may be that institutions and policies can satisfactorily realize several values that would otherwise seem to be competing or even conflicting. For example, the schools are supposed to provide equal education, interpreted as a common base of knowledge and skills for each student. At the same time, equal education has also meant that the schools should respond to differing students' needs and talents through different curricula, for example, remedial or accelerated programs. The general response to the tension between these two notions is an institutional division of labor, a tendency toward commonality in the primary school that gives way to differentiated curricula in secondary school (although neither does one to the exclusion of the other). Regardless of the merits of these tendencies, they do reflect the idea that different values might predominate in certain circumstances but not in others.[38] A mixed program involving several values that might not be wholly consistent in theory may be acceptable or even sensible in practice. Looking at specific institutions and policies may suggest how and under what circumstances various values may be achieved.[39]

It might be objected that contextual justifications or institutional resolutions of this sort are not really justifications at all, or are parasitic on a more complete or theoretical notion of justification. This may seem especially true when political processes are invoked to justify settling issues when there is persistent disagreement. That some resolution might be obtained by political procedures does not mean that such settlements are rationally justified. Political agreement or resolution is not rational argument.

Certainly, no one would wish to say that a political consensus reflected in some institution or policy is always rationally justified. But, again, once we make principles political, not metaphysical, it becomes less clear that we can establish some external philosophical or theoretical authority to contradict such political settlements. When political consensus within a community--for pragmatic purposes and based on differing reasons--replaces some other (metaphysical) means for determining justificatory adequacy, theoretical appeals are no longer clearly independently authoritative. A consensus on some institutional practice or policy, for example regarding the schools, is not obviously less justified if some higher consensual principle(s) cannot be readily introduced to support it. Relevant, broader philosophical arguments may be less likely to obtain or maintain consensus. Similarly, if resort to agreed-upon political procedures leads to an accepted settlement of a disagreement about a policy or practice, for example, a court decision about student rights, further philosophical appeals may not create consensus since philosophical disagreement may have been at the root of the conflict in the first place. If this makes theoretical inquiry dependently authoritative, perhaps that is all it ever can (or even should) be in a liberal democratic society.[40]

In sum, if we move away from the expectations generated by theoretical inquiry, a different view of theorizing about the liberal democratic community emerges. Plurality is a more typical and even desirable state of affairs than theoretical agreement on some small number of neutral principles. A thick consensus of overlapping principles and practices can be maintained without a deeper consensus on some foundational principles. Philosophical arguments may not typically resolve disagreement or override democratic political processes. Contextual justifications emphasizing the preponderance of good reasons in the face of competing principles is more typical, and perhaps more likely to obtain consensus, than foundational arguments. A mixed program that tries to accommodate several, perhaps competing, values is the most likely result, and its justification may be more or less elaborate and sometimes merely political. Finally, institutions must ultimately deal with the several values or themes in ways that will be more or less satisfactory. Thus, instead of viewing policy from a theoretical perspective, there is an alternative thematic perspective involving a plurality of moral principles, contextual considerations and political processes, and actual practices and institutions.

Thematic Analysis and Public Education

In terms of education policy, then, a thematic approach would begin by describing the major perspectives on the purpose(s) of public schools, anticipating a plurality of aims and values. It is fairly easy to establish that there are numerous and diverse expectations for the schools. Indeed, it is often suggested that part of the problem is that we want it all. We demand that the schools do more things than they are capable of doing well. Diane Ravitch provides a short, formidable list of some the goals of public education:

- Reduce inequality among individuals and groups by eliminating illiteracy and cultural deprivation.
- Improve the economy and economic opportunity by raising the nation's supply of intelligence and skill.
- Spread capacity for personal fulfillment by developing creative energies.
- Prove to be an uplifting influence for the nation's cultural life by broadly diffusing the fruits of liberal education.
- Reduce alienation and mistrust while building a new sense of community among people of similar education and similar values.
- Reduce prejudice and misunderstanding by fostering contact among diverse groups.
- Improve the quality of civic and political life.[41]

Although a common complaint has been that the schools have been asked to do too many things, it is hard to see anything on this list that we would gladly remove. It represents an overlapping consensus about public education that involves a plurality of aims and values. We could easily add more specific or general goals to this list even though at least some of these aims may simply be beyond the ability of the schools to achieve. It is hard to imagine the schools achieving everything on the list, and the situation is only complicated by differing interpretations of the aims and the potential for conflict between and among them.

Any list like the one above suggests that there is more than one aim we expect the schools to pursue. One way of organizing these aims would be to describe and analyze a smaller number of major themes that make sense of these purposes. A theme might be thought of as a perspective, a way of viewing and thinking about the schools. It provides a more or less coherent way of organizing or knitting together the various values and goals relevant to a policy area. Like political parties within a polity, different themes suggest different ways of understanding, and acting in, the policy realm. Just as different parties might emphasize common values but interpret them differently, so too different themes will variously overlap and be in conflict with one another. Just as a political party might be made up of several groups or coalitions, there are also variations on any theme that also may overlap and conflict. Thus conflicts arise not only between and among themes but within individual perspectives as well.

Chapters 3, 4, and 5 examine three major themes or orientations toward the public schools. Each side of this "second triangle" represents a general account of the primary purposes of public education, the rationale and key values implicit in them, and the institutional arrangements and practices they imply (see Figure 2.1). Each theme provides a distinctive perspective on the primary aims and values of public schools in a liberal democratic society. For any theme there are policies and practices that typify its orientation toward the role of the schools. Finally, each theme also sets forth the primary problems confronting the schools, suggesting the areas in which reform efforts should be concentrated.

As noted in Figure 2.1, each theme taken separately faces certain problems--conceptual, empirical, practical, and normative--independent of its relationship to other themes. Moreover, as will be seen in the succeeding chapters, within each theme there are variations that are in tension, if not outright conflict, with one another. As might be expected, ideological plurality, both within and among themes, cannot be easily or fully overcome. The problems and conflicts in this "second triangle" continually exist and confront educational policy and efforts at reform. We therefore need to examine critically the various interpretations of each theme, the problems they confront, and how those problems are addressed in educational policies and practices. The institutional responses to the problems of an orientation will reflect whether and how its values can be realized in practice, especially in relationships to other themes.

The three orientations toward the public schools that will be examined are, first, the common school perspective that emphasizes the political and cultural functions of the schools. The schools aim to provide the same education to all and, more important, to transmit common moral or cultural understandings. The second orientation, the human capital view, aims at promoting and recognizing individual achievement as a means of serving the larger society. Specifically, it is primarily concerned with the schools' preparing students for their economic roles. Often discussions of American educational history and philosophy note the differences and tensions between these two orientations, and critics of the current reform movement have suggested that there is too much emphasis on the economic role of schools. In any case, there is a third orientation that has gradually become more important for public schools, particularly as they have been forced to deal with the effects of urbanization, immigration, and other social dislocations. "Clientelism" reflects an orientation of the schools toward meeting a range of individual needs that may or may not be traditionally seen as academic. The wide variations on this theme, including choice plans and the provision of social services through the schools, are becoming an increasingly prominent aspect of public education.

The image of a triangle is intended to convey the notion that different orientations toward the public schools are analytically separate yet practically connected. Though we can analytically separate these orientations and examine them as different themes, they are inextricably linked to one another. Rhetorically, we can and typically do gloss over any potential differences among these orientations by claiming that quality education for all will serve the various demands placed upon the schools. The result, called "merged rhetoric" in Figure 2.1, claims that schools can simultaneously meet these various demands. For example, it is claimed that quality education is the best preparation for both work and citizenship as well as a response to many of our problems beyond school. Higher academic standards can both provide a common cultural background and better prepare students to take their place in a highly competitive world. Caring teachers and support services can meet individual students' distinctive needs, academic or otherwise. Schools can more effectively reach out to the community and deal with problems in ways that support their academic tasks.

This overlap is more than rhetorical. As a practical matter, our institutional arrangements seem to reflect the attempt to combine these various aims. For example, as noted previously, there is a mixed program with the primary schools reflecting more common concerns and the secondary schools being more closely linked to the economic issues of productivity and competitiveness. The variety of support services throughout the schools anticipates the needs of their "clients," even beyond the classroom. There will be at least some (and perhaps considerable) overlap because practices associated with any theme can be reinterpreted in terms of others. For example, a common school orientation implies a certain view of the schools' clients as well as their relationship to the economy. An emphasis on economic productivity and human capital will suggest what is common among students, namely their relationship to the market. Not surprisingly, then,

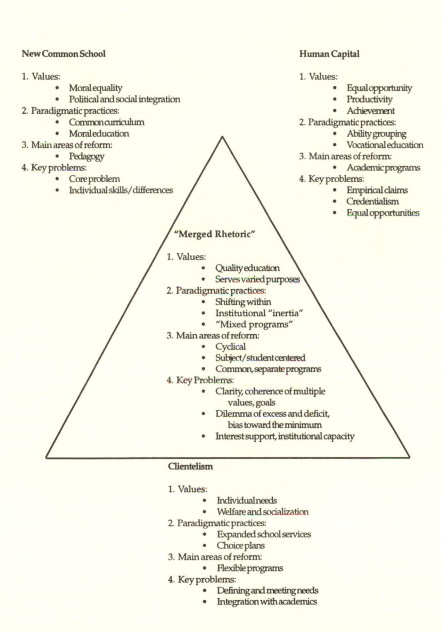

New Common School

1. Values:
    - Moral equality
    - Political and social integration
2. Paradigmatic practices:
    - Common curriculum
    - Moral education
3. Main areas of reform:
    - Pedagogy
4. Key problems:
    - Core problem
    - Individual skills/differences

Human Capital

1. Values:
    - Equal opportunity
    - Productivity
    - Achievement
2. Paradigmatic practices:
    - Ability grouping
    - Vocational education
3. Main areas of reform:
    - Academic programs
4. Key problems:
    - Empirical claims
    - Credentialism
    - Equal opportunities

"Merged Rhetoric"

1. Values:
    - Quality education
    - Serves varied purposes
2. Paradigmatic practices:
    - Shifting within
    - Institutional "inertia"
    - "Mixed programs"
3. Main areas of reform:
    - Cyclical
    - Subject/student centered
    - Common, separate programs
4. Key Problems:
    - Clarity, coherence of multiple values, goals
    - Dilemma of excess and deficit, bias toward the minimum
    - Interest support, institutional capacity

Clientelism

1. Values:
    - Individual needs
    - Welfare and socialization
2. Paradigmatic practices:
    - Expanded school services
    - Choice plans
3. Main areas of reform:
    - Flexible programs
4. Key problems:
    - Defining and meeting needs
    - Integration with academics

FIGURE 2.1 The "Second Triangle": Themes in Public Education

efforts at educational reform will seek, in both rhetoric and practice, to combine or blend all three orientations in acceptable ways.

Although they are bound together conceptually, rhetorically, and institutionally, it is important to analytically separate these themes. As can be seen in Figure 2.1, each "side" represents a distinct way of describing the schools' mission, ordering its priorities, and setting forth key principles and practices. Each offers a picture of what the schools might look like if its agenda were the only one pursued. Looking at each theme separately points up their strengths and weaknesses and clarifies some of the conflicts and tensions between and among them. It allows us to explore how well justified any theme is in both theory and practice. Equally important, it goes beyond any agreement on specific goals and suggests how we should evaluate such goals by putting them in a broader theoretical context. Saying that "we want it all" does not tell us clearly what "it" is and whether we can have all of it. By looking carefully at each of the primary thrusts or themes of public education and its specific institutional manifestations, we can understand what is at stake in the rhetoric and proposals for reform that somehow combine them.

Although there is no logical bar to achieving a variety of aims or even having "it all," there is always the potential for conflicts in aims and values, even if only in differences in emphasis and priorities. Because each vision provides a different kind of idealization of what the schools should do, each theme stands as a potential or actual critique of the others. More important, this potential for conflict among themes is often more than theoretical. For example, it has been commonly noted that there are tensions, if not outright conflicts, between the common school and human capital themes.[42] This is often expressed as a conflict between "equality" and "quality," or "equity" and "excellence" manifested in a variety of policy issues from ability grouping to school finance. There are numerous other differences in policy that might be derived from these themes as well. More generally, the overall picture of the public school is quite different among them, suggesting different institutional configurations. At any given time a pattern of policies and practices represents how we weigh, balance, and combine these different demands.

These orientations are not theories in the sense that we could test them to see if they correspond to "what's out there." They are not merely versions of the way the world functions, although they do--indeed, must--involve some empirical claims, for example, about the relationship of schools to the economy. But they also involve a counterfactual element. They depict the way the world ought to work and might work if social institutions were changed and a certain vision pursued in a certain way. When the ideals expressed by a theme and current realities clash, it might lead us to temper our ideals, to be more realistic. It might also lead us to speculate about what might be done to make reality better conform to our ideals. Therefore when critically examining a theme, we must look at what kinds of empirical claims are involved in it as well as looking at programs or policies as ways of better realizing (or perhaps failing to achieve) its values. Inevitably then any discussion of a theme will be incomplete, since the possibilities for interpreting and realizing some vision can never be fully exhausted.[43]

That some holistic, comparative test of themes is very unlikely does not mean that we must forego rational criticism or comparative evaluation of them. We can assess how well-justified the various claims associated with a theme are. First, any theme will involve some empirical claims about both existing relationships and possibilities for programs and institutions. Assessing these empirical claims can give us some sense of their validity and possible ranges of application. Besides making empirical claims, each theme has its own conceptual and normative framework. Certain concepts will be central to understanding a theme, and there will inevitably be normative claims about what is desirable, permissible, and so on. These key concepts and claims can be examined for ambiguities and incoherence that have consequences for policy. There will inevitably be conceptual problems and differences in interpretation that will render a vision open to various criticisms, both by those who share an orientation and those who emphasize an alternative. This process of criticism should take seriously the theme as it is "situated"--understood and interpreted through specific policies and practices.

Such criticism will often raise larger philosophical and theoretical questions, including basic questions about the proper role of the state, notions of individual autonomy, equal opportunity, merit, and many others. One such philosophical issue that arises in all three themes might be called the "dilemma of excess and deficit." It derives from a traditional philosophical problem of liberal democracies, namely the legitimate scope of state authority versus the individual. There is a persistent antagonism against government on behalf of individual liberty, even as it is expected that government will take on a variety of tasks. As Gutmann notes, the various political ideals of education also reflect the tension between the state, on the one hand, and individuals and families, on the other. Although mandating and providing education has generally been regarded as a legitimate state function, it has also been limited by the rights of individuals and families--these being open to wide interpretation, of course. The dilemma, then, is that as the state takes on any educational task(s), it may be be criticized as doing too much, overstepping the bounds of state authority, but if it fails fully to pursue a task it may be charged with doing too little. Indeed, it might be open to these charges simultaneously.

Thus not only do we have differences concerning *what* the aims of public education should be, reflected in the three themes and variations within them, we also have the problem of *how far* the state should pursue any vision. Each theme suggests a different orientation and aims for the schools, and within each theme there will be variations in how the theme is understood. Moreover, for each theme there will be both a minimum and a maximum version of what an orientation requires, creating the dilemma described above. Thus each theme faces conflicts and problems, both considered separately and in comparison with others.

There is no permanent resolution to these issues, either theoretically or practically, since they reflect conflicts and dilemmas that are a natural part of liberal democratic ideology. What a thematic approach focuses on is not these deeper philosophical conflicts but rather on how they are addressed in specific institutions and policies.[44] These problems are dealt with politically on an ongoing basis by constantly negotiating a mixed program combining aims in specific institutions, seeking the "right" point between excess and deficit, and working out the details of programs and policies. For the most part, these practical, political resolutions tend to have what might be called a "bias toward the minimum." That is, for ideological reasons concerning the role of the state and political reasons concerning interests and institutional inertia, the schools will generally tend to pursue the minimal version of some theme or variation on it. This in part explains the tendency for reformers in any era to want the schools to do more and to be rather frustrated as reform efforts typically fail to meet these often inflated expectations.

Again, it is important to note that these political resolutions, minimal or otherwise, do not resolve the underlying theoretical issues since disagreements between and among a plurality of perspectives may go "all the way down" to basic philosophical disagreement. Rather they reflect the necessity of coming up with more or less satisfactory institutional responses to the demands of policymaking. A thematic analysis then must ask a series of questions that addresses both the theoretical and practical aspects of the prominent perspectives on public education. What does a theme suggest are the primary aims of public education? What kinds of hypotheses and empirical evidence are relevant to the theme in question? How well does such evidence support the vision put forth by a theme? Empirical issues aside, how coherent and defensible are the concepts, arguments, and ideals suggested by a theme? How defensible or desirable is its image of the role of public education? Finally, what kinds of practices or policies exemplify what a theme suggests? How successful have we been at realizing its vision and how likely are we to be able to realize it, especially as it relates to other themes? Addressing these questions can suggest the strengths and weaknesses of each theme--its justificatory adequacy in terms of coherence, empirical soundness, and normative defensibility. It can also suggest how or whether various themes can be combined. The exploration of these questions will not suggest "the answer" to the problems of educational reform, nor will it put our choices beyond criticism. Nevertheless, it can provide a broader, more theoretical basis for evaluating policy.

Notes

1. R. Freeman Butts, "Citizenship as a National Education Goal," *Education Week*. December 11, 1991, p. 36: "But something terribly important has been missing throughout the two years these discussions have continued. . . . Missing has been the preeminent recognition that the primary purpose and overarching goal of universal, free, public schooling in the United States is its civic mission."

2. Herbert Feigl, "The Orthodox View of Theory," in Stephen Radnor and S. Winokur, *Analyses of Theories and Methods in Physics and Psychology*. Minnesota Studies in the Philosophy of Science, Volume IV. Minneapolis: University of Minnesota Press, 1970.

3. See Norberto Bobbio, *Liberalism and Democracy*. London: Verso, 1990; David Held, *Models of Democracy*. Stanford: Stanford University Press, 1987.

4. For example, see Gerald Gutek, *Philosophical and Ideological Perspectives on Education*. Englewood Cliffs, N.J.: Prentice-Hall, 1988.

5. An example of external neutrality might be the idealized scientist who is supposedly neutral between or among theories or the philosopher who pursues objective (logical or moral) principles that all individuals with access to the same evidence and arguments will acknowledge as true. Similarly, a neutral party in a war stands outside the conflict. This sense of neutrality is associated with the idea of disinterest or noninvolvement. An example of internal neutrality might be a referee or judge who deals with situations within some local culture or practice. Neutrality here is applying the rules (of law, of a game) without reference to the persons involved but on the basis of recognized or settled principles within a practice. It is associated with the idea of impartiality. For a more detailed discussion of this distinction, see David C. Paris, "The 'Theoretical Mystique': Neutrality, Plurality, and the Defense of Liberalism," *American Journal of Political Science*. 31 (November 1987), pp. 905-940.

6. D. J. Manning, *Liberalism*. New York: St. Martin's, 1976, p. 119.

7. For example, the laws of physics may be externally neutral but have no clear (or any) implications for political institutions. Proposed laws of psychology and economics might be politically relevant, but current theories, and any future proposals we might imagine, are hardly likely to be considered neutral.

8. The phrase "incredulity toward metanarratives" comes from Jean-Francois Lyotard, *The Postmodern Condition: A Report on Knowledge*. Minneapolis: University of Minnesota Press, 1984, p. xxiv. For an accessible survey, see Stephen White, *Political Theory and Postmodernism*. Cambridge: Cambridge University Press, 1991.

Walter Anderson, *Reality Isn't What It Used to Be: Theatrical Politics, Ready-to-Wear Religion, Global Myths, Primitive Chic, and Other Wonders of the Postmodern World.* San Francisco: Harper, 1992.

9. The major communitarian works include Alasdair MacIntyre, *After Virtue.* Notre Dame: University of Notre Dame Press, 1981; Michael Sandel, *Liberalism and the Limits of Justice.* New York: Cambridge University Press, 1982; Charles Taylor, *Hegel and Modern Society.* New York: Cambridge University Press, 1979; Robert Bellah, et al., *Habits of the Heart: Individualism and Commitment in American Life.* New York: Harper and Row, 1986; Benjamin Barber, *Strong Democracy.* Berkeley: University of California Press, 1984. For a review and critique, see Patrick Neal and David C. Paris, "Liberalism and the Communitarian Critique: A Guide for the Perplexed," *Canadian Journal of Political Science.* XXIII (September 1990), pp. 419-439.

10. See Ronald Dworkin, "Liberalism," in Stuart Hampshire, ed., *Public and Private Morality.* New York: Cambridge University Press, 1978, pp. 113-143.

11. Bruce Ackerman, *Social Justice in the Liberal State.* New Haven: Yale University Press, 1981, p. 11.

12. On measures of value, see James Fishkin, "Can There Be a Neutral Theory of Justice?" *Ethics.* (January 1983), pp. 348-356. Indeed, Ackerman's initial inference here to "I should get at least as much" is puzzling. It implies that any claim to superiority will entail a claim to be at least as good, the latter being the only thing that anyone is permitted to claim, given the neutrality principle. This seems, at the very least, to distort the logic of claims to superiority or value that do (must) make comparisons. Whether this inference is valid or sound is not crucial to analyzing the relationship of liberalism and neutrality as discussed in Ackerman. See Benjamin Barber, "Unconstrained Conversations: A Play on Words, Neutral and Otherwise," *Ethics.* (January 1983), pp. 330-347.

13. Patrick Neal, "Liberalism and Neutrality," *Polity.* 17 (Summer 1985), p. 666.

14. For a persuasive view of rational practice that does not require a theoretical foundation, see Thomas Spragens, *Reason and Democracy.* Durham, N.C.: Duke University Press, 1990. For a discussion of the irreducible plurality of "rational ideologies," see David C. Paris and James Reynolds, *The Logic of Policy Inquiry.* New York: Longman, 1983, Chs. 7, 8.

15. The first expression of this new interpretation is John Rawls, "Justice as Fairness: Political, not Metaphysical,"*Philosophy and Public Affairs.* 14 (Summer 1985), pp. 225-251, on "the kernel," p. 229, on "comprehensive moral doctrines," p. 246. His two principles: "1. Each person is to have an equal right to a fully adequate scheme of basic rights and liberties, which scheme is compatible with a similar scheme for all. 2. Social and economic inequalities are to satisfy two conditions: first, they must be attached to offices and positions open to all under conditions of fair equality of opportunity; and second, they must be to the greatest benefit of the least advantaged members of society." John Rawls, *A Theory of Justice.* Cambridge: Harvard University Press, 1971, pp. 60, 302.

16. Further development of this new viewpoint may be found in Rawls, "The Idea of an Overlapping Consensus,"*Oxford Journal of Legal Studies.* 7 (1987), pp. 1-27; "The Priority of Right and the Ideas of the Good,"*Philosophy and Public Affairs.* 17 (1988), pp. 251-276; "The Domain of the Political and the Overlapping Consensus,"*New York University Law Review.* 64 (1989), pp. 233-255. On staying "on the surface," "Justice as Fairness," p. 230; on the "fact of pluralism" and "the task of

political theory," "The Idea of an Overlapping Consensus," pp. 3-4. Rawls has assembled these arguments in *Political Liberalism.* New York: Columbia University Press, 1993.

17. For a sampling of criticism of Rawls' political turn, see the symposium in the summer 1989 issue of *Ethics.* For a recent review see Stuart Hampshire, "Liberalism with a Twist," *New York Review of Books.* 40 (August 12, 1993), pp. 43-47.

18. This is a version of "reflective equilibrium" in which a fit is sought between principles and considered judgments. See Rawls, *A Theory of Justice.* Cambridge: Harvard University Press, 1971, pp. 46-53.

19. For an analysis and critique of the empirical claims about overlapping consensus, see George Klosko, "Rawls's 'Political' Philosophy and American Democracy," *American Political Science Review.* 87 (June 1993), pp. 348-359.

20. On "sufficient reasons," see Rawls, "Justice as Fairness ," p. 229; on "limits" and "theorems," see pp. 249, 247, respectively.

21. For a further discussion of this dilemma, see Paris, "The 'Theoretical Mystique'," pp. 917-921.

22. See Jeffrey Stout, "Liberal Society and the Languages of Morals,"*Soundings.* 69 (Spring 1986), pp. 32-59, especially pp. 34-38.

23. Amy Gutmann, *Democratic Education.* Princeton: Princeton University Press, 1988, p. 47.

24. Gutmann, *Democratic Education,* p. 14.

25. Gutmann, *Democratic Education,* pp. 43-47.

26. See George Sher, "Educating Citizens," *Philosophy and Public Affairs.* 18 (Winter 1989), pp. 68-80. "Clearly goods such as intellectual excellence and the matching of talents to social needs have a value that is independent of their contribution to democracy. But why then should democracy's demands be lexically prior to theirs?" pp. 76-77.

27. Respectively, see Nadine Strossen, "Review of *Democratic Education* by Amy Gutmann," *Journal of Law and Education.* 19 (Winter 1990), pp. 147-159; Sher, "Educating Citizens,"; Jonathan Marks, "Democratic Education," *Michigan Law Review.* 86 (May 1988), pp. 1140-1147.

28. See David Hansen, "Remembering What We Know: The Case for Democratic Education," *Journal of Curriculum Studies.* 23 (1991), pp. 459-465; David Post, "Liberalism and its Discontents: A Review of Berger, Tarcov, and Gutmann," *American Journal of Education.* 96 (August 1988), pp. 533-555.

29. Post puts it nicely, "That she can go far with this method indicates a consensus on many core democratic values in America. That she does not from this approach obtain a comprehensive theory only reminds us that, after all, America is not a single society, but one composed of many overlapping communities. And the probability that these are conflicting cultures is exactly what Gutmann would deny." "Liberalism and its Discontents," p. 553.

30. Stephen Macedo, *Liberal Virtues.* New York: Oxford University Press, 1990, on "open justifications," p. 38, on "liberal constitutionalism," p. 272.

31. William Galston, *Liberal Purposes.* New York: Cambridge University Press, 1991.

32. James Fishkin calls this situation "ideals without an ideal." See his *Justice, Equal Opportunity, and the Family.* New Haven: Yale University Press, 1983, pp. 169-193.

33. Michael Walzer puts it in this way: "The sophist, critic, publicist, or intellectual must address the concerns of his fellow citizens, try to answer their questions, weave his argument into the fabric of their history. He must, indeed, make himself a fellow citizen in the community of ideas, and then he will be unable to avoid entirely the moral and even the emotional entanglements of citizenship. He may hold fast to the philosophical truths of natural law, distributive justice, of human rights, but his political arguments are most likely to look like some makeshift version of those truths, adapted to the needs of a particular people: from the standpoint of the original position, provincial; from the standpoint of the ideal speech situation, ideological." "Philosophy and Democracy,"*Political Theory.* 9 (1981), p. 398.

34. On invoking different values in different "spheres," see Michael Walzer, *Spheres of Justice.* New York: Basic Books, 1983. In technical terms this view of plurality suggests "intuitionism" as the moral theory most compatible with liberal democracy. As J. O. Urmson describes intuitionism: "Maximization of the general welfare is not the only primary reason for action, since fidelity to contract is also one. . . . If it be recognized that there is a plurality of primary moral reasons for action, the complexity of many situations seems to make it implausible to suppose that we are guided (presumably unwittingly) by any decision-procedure when we weigh up pros and cons. I also doubt whether our moral beliefs have the internal harmony requisite for a decision procedure to be even theoretically possible; since this seems to be not an irrational anomaly but our ordinary predicament with regard to reasons in most fields, I find this conclusion neither surprising nor unduly distressing." We can just as easily substitute terms relevant to policy for the moral reasons cited by Urmson and see this as an appropriate characterization of "our ordinary predicament" in policy matters. J. O. Urmson, "A Defense of Intuitionism," *Proceedings of the Aristotelian Society.* LXXV (1974-75), pp. 111-119.

35. On "thick" descriptions, see Clifford Geertz, *The Interpretation of Cultures.* New York: Basic Books, 1973, Ch. 1.

36. Another image might be, in Ludwig Wittgenstein's terms, that our shared values are "family resemblances": "I can think of no better expression to characterize these similarities than 'family resemblances'; for the various resemblances between members of a family: build, features, color of eyes, gait, temperament, etc. etc. overlap and criss-cross in the same way. . . . And we extend our concept[s] . . . as if spinning a thread we twist fibre on fibre. And the strength of the thread does not reside in the fact that some one fibre runs through its whole length, but in the overlapping of many fibres. . . . But if someone wished to say: 'There is something common to all these constructions--namely the disjunction of their common properties'--I should reply: Now you are only playing with words. One might as well say: 'Something runs through the whole thread--namely the continuous overlapping of those fibres'." Ludwig Wittgenstein, *Philosophical Investigations.* trans. by G. E. M. Anscombe. New York: Macmillan, 1953, p. 32.

37. Don Herzog describes "contextual justification" in this way: "Nothing is certain, nothing is fixed, in such an argument. We have no incentive to find immutable premises, no reason to devote much energy to epistemology, theology, metaphysics, and the like. We cannot plausibly claim that our conclusions should be applied in all times and places. A contextual justification may then seem much weaker than a foundational one. But successful foundational justifications are phi-

losophers' pet unicorns; we have yet to see one. Contextual justifications provide a preponderance of good reasons, so they are good enough to qualify as justifications even if they do not deliver the certainty that foundational arguments might." *Without Foundations: Justification in Political Theory.* Ithaca: Cornell University Press, 1985, p. 225.

38. This notion of meaning is consistent with the perspective of the "new institutionalism" discussed in Chapter 1. The schools' routines and practices provide a more or less conscious way of institutionalizing the meaning of equality.

39. For further discussion of the idea of a "mixed program," see David C. Paris, "Fact, Theory, and Democratic Theory," *Western Political Quarterly.* 40 (June 1987), "The idea of a 'mixed program' suggests that what are generally conflicting ideologies may each have some applicability in democratic practice. . . . Research that is mindful of the possibility of mixed programs is more likely to clarify serious practical inconsistencies between or among problem-solving strategies . . . [and] clarify if and when different problem-solving strategies will prove useful as well as when mixed programs will lead to incoherence in policy." pp. 232-233.

40. On the distinction between "independent" and "dependent" authoritativeness in social inquiry, see Charles Lindblom and David Cohen, *Usable Knowledge,* New Haven: Yale University Press, 1980, Ch. 1. To say that theoretical inquiry may be only "dependently authoritative" is unsatisfactory only if the expectation is that theory will guide practice rather than reflect and interact with it or, in the current phraseology, that philosophy takes priority over democracy. The academic or theoretical impulse is to somehow go beyond ordinary discourse and practices to some greater degree of justification or theoretical unity. Otherwise it would seem that philosophy is being subordinated to democracy when the adequacy of political justification ought to be primarily determined by philosophical or theoretical criteria. It is important to note that the argument here is not to reverse these priorities, to suggest that democracy takes priority over philosophy, or that contextual justifications should supplant foundational ones, or that cultural interpretation supplants philosophical inquiry. Rather, the point is that the search for theoretical closure (through neutral principles) or philosophical distance resolves these tensions by favoring the latter over the former in each of the above pairs. When we note the other horns of these dilemmas--the thick consensus and contextual justifications rooted in institutions and practices--these tensions are not so readily resolved in this way. On the conflict between philosophy and democracy, see Richard Bernstein, "One Step Forward, Two Steps Backward: Richard Rorty on Liberal Democracy and Philosophy," *Political Theory.* 15 (1987), pp. 538-563; Richard Rorty, "Thugs and Theorists: A Reply to Bernstein," *Political Theory.* 15 (1987), pp. 564-580.

41. Diane Ravitch, *The Schools We Deserve.* New York: Basic Books, 1984, pp. 32-33.

42. Concerning this conflict, see Joel Spring, *American Education, 1642-1990.* New York: Longman, 1990, Chs. 7-9; Alan DeYoung, *Economics and American Education.* New York: Longman, 1989, Chs. 5-7, 10.

43. "Presumably scientific theory is not aimed at bringing anything into existence. . . . Ideology, on the other hand, suggests which of several possible worlds ought to be chosen, often suggesting the means for realizing the preferred order . . . ways of *acting* to bring about appropriate political change. Ideology *necessarily* serves a practical action-guiding function, providing guidance concerning those

things--institutions, practices--which we create and maintain. It is a 'theory' which inevitably contains a practical intent." Paris, "Fact, Theory, and Democratic Theory," p. 224.

44. Obviously this kind of thematic approach is not unique and it can take several forms. For example, in a broad historical study, James Morone points out that the continual conflict between an antagonism toward political authority and a "democratic wish" for community produced many of the (ironic and even contradictory) features of the American administrative state. The theoretical conflict has never been resolved, but "the Americans negotiated their dread of public power as they constructed their administrative institutions." *The Democratic Wish*. New York: Basic Books, 1990, p. 4. Another example is Jennifer Hochschild's detailed study of the success of desegregation efforts in various cities; it notes a persistent dilemma between democratic control and the rights of minorities. See *The New American Dilemma: Liberal Democracy and School Desegregation*. New Haven: Yale University Press, 1984. Although these two works differ in their approach, both point to fundamental conflicts that are dealt with, for better or worse, only through specific institutional arrangements that do not resolve the underlying theoretical issues. The approach taken here is similar, although it is somewhere between the broad historical sweep of Morone's work and the more detailed policy/case studies offered by Hochschild.

3

The Common School Theme:
Moral Education and
the "Tie That Binds"

Those articles in the creed of republicanism, which are accepted by all, and which form the common basis of our political faith, shall be taught to all. But when the teacher, in the course of his lessons or lectures on the fundamental law, arrives at a controverted text, he is either to read it without comment or remark; or at most, he is only to say that it is the subject of disputation, and that the schoolroom is neither the tribunal to adjudicate, nor the forum to discuss it . . . political proselytism is no function of the school; but that all indoctrination into matters of controversy between hostile political parties is to be elsewhere sought for, and elsewhere imparted.
--Horace Mann

Yet herein lies a paradox, for the very traits that traditionally have defined the "goodness" of women, their care for and sensitivity to the needs of others, are those that mark them as deficient in moral development. . . .When one begins with the study of women and derives developmental constructs from their lives, . . . [a different] outline . . . begins to emerge and informs a different description of development. In this conception the moral problem arises from conflicting responsibilities rather than competing rights and requires for its resolution a mode of thinking that is contextual and narrative rather than formal and abstract. This conception of morality as concerned with the activity of care centers moral development around the understanding of responsibility and relationships, just as the conception of morality as fairness ties moral development to the understanding of rights and rules.
--Carol Gilligan

Chapter 2 considered what kind(s) of theoretical help might be available for evaluating and justifying policy, including educational policy. Theoretical approaches based on the idea of neutrality are too demanding. They do not reflect the plurality at the heart of the liberal democratic tradition, the value conflicts that arise in a liberal democratic society, or the practical and institutional ways in which these problems are resolved. An alternative to a theoretical approach is a more thematic analysis that involves the examination of various themes as they have been developed and are currently embodied in institutional practices. It expects that in any policy area there will be a variety of more or less conflicting themes. These inform a mixed program of institutions and practices that seek to resolve or compromise the various conflicts within or among themes, as well as between values and practices. Displaying these themes provides the opportunity for criticizing them and their practical manifestations separately, as well as assessing their actual or potential conflicts. It is likely therefore to be truer to the policy world that we ordinarily confront. Understood as thematic analysis, this kind of theoretical criticism is thus rooted more firmly in ongoing policy debates and political practices.

Themes in a policy area are like the various strata in a geological formation that have been layered in and shifted through successive historical periods. The various themes in American public education have likewise been established and changed as the schools have developed. The first theme is that of the common school. The founding ideal of American public education was to provide a common, equal education to all. That education would, first, ensure the basic literacy essential for the political, economic, and social life of all citizens. But it would do more than simply develop basic skills. It would help forge a social bond by providing common moral and political understandings to otherwise different individuals and groups. What Horace Mann called "the great balance wheel of the social machinery" would make differences in status and background secondary to the fundamental equality of citizens. The provision of a common cultural and political background, the "creed of republicanism," would create a civic identity that superseded narrower identifications. In the absence of a common or state religion, the schools would be the "tie that binds" together an otherwise diverse society.[1]

One constant feature in the rhetoric of American education is that some minimum level of public education should be available equally to all. Ensuring basic education is seen as so important that the practices of having the state provide it and making it compulsory have hardly been questioned.[2] This is an implicit admission of the limits of the liberal democratic tradition's individualism. Liberal democratic *theory* portrays individuals as more or less rational creatures who confront each other and society naturally ready to engage in commerce and politics. In practice, we are far less confident that individuals can be fully prepared for life in a liberal democratic society by their diverse families or other separate, private communities. There must be something that binds together free, separate individuals--some common core of skills, knowledge, or value commitments--without which our commitment to freedom threatens to dissolve into anarchy. In liberal democratic theory, this is usually established by philosophical argument, for example, concerning the terms of a social contract. In practice, however, such a core must be actively created by groups and institutions, and the public schools have typically borne a major share of this burden.

Though practical in this sense, the idea of the common school is intimately connected to the moral vision expressed in liberal democratic theory. The ideal that all individuals should have an equal, common education seems a logical, practical extension of their basic moral equality. Without a basic education, political freedom and economic opportunity are meaningless. An individual without basic skills is cut off from full participation in civic and cultural life as well as the opportunity to advance economically. Ideally, the provision of a common education thus embodies respect for the moral equality of individuals and enhances their freedom. It also has collective political significance. If we are something more than a collection of separate individuals and groups, then there must be some identifications and beliefs that bind us together. There has always been the expectation that public education would provide some common skills or experiences that would bind together an otherwise diverse society. The public school offers the prospect of helping to create that common ground by giving individuals a shared experience, as well as basic knowledge and skills, that mute differences in background and belief.

In this chapter I discuss the evolution of, and variations on, this theme and some of the current problems and controversies surrounding it. A brief history of the notion of a common school describes a shift away from a moral toward an academic variation on this theme. The shift toward an academic variation reflects both the difficulties in finding some common ground in public education, what will be termed here the "core problem," as well as the influence of other themes and aims that arose as the public schools developed. In any case there is both overlap and tensions among these variations of the common school theme, as illustrated by recent proposals for new common curricula and programs for moral education. Similarly, each variation contains within it both minimum and maximum possibilities that are likewise in tension with one another, creating versions of the dilemma of excess and deficit. Although the schools' response to these problems has tended toward the minimal academic variation, the suggestion offered here is that more can and should be done to emphasize and enhance the unavoidable moral role of schools. Indeed, many of the ways in which moral education can be enhanced are already present in schools' curricula and practices.

"Whose Moral Values . . . What Religion?"

As it evolved in the nineteenth century the idea of the common school was to promote, in locally controlled and publicly supported schools, a basic standard of literacy and a common set of values. By the middle and latter parts of the century a system of tax-supported common schools had gained ascendancy and been recognized in constitutional law. The popular image of the common school is often connected with the "three Rs," an emphasis on basic literacy and skills, as well as a tightly controlled classroom. Actually, the goals of the common schools were considerably more ambitious than simply teaching the basics. The teaching of basic skills was seen as a vehicle for providing a general moral education. More specifically, the aim was to teach a kind of "Protestant-republican ideology" extolling religious faith, hard work, civic virtue, and patriotism. Combining political and religious imagery, Mann put the ideal of the common school very succinctly when he wrote that "the creed of Republicanism . . . the basis of our political faith, shall be taught to all." Lessons involving Bible reading and the McGuffey series went well beyond basic literacy or some common cultural references. They were strongly didactic and unashamedly Christian. The goal was to produce virtuous citizens whose political-moral outlook would be strongly supportive of American institutions and ideals.[3]

It is interesting to note the parallel between Mann's appeal to consensus in terms of a "creed . . . accepted by all" and Rawls' notion of an "overlapping consensus." In both cases there is an agreement on some basic principles that underlie otherwise diverse views. The recognition and endorsement of that consensus provides the practical service of responding to the "fact of pluralism." This view of the common school might be seen as a practical means to accomplish the task of theory, to promote a consensus that can limit political conflicts and preserve pluralism. Locating that consensus and expressing it in educational practices--the "core problem"-- has never been easy. What is appropriately part of a common education, its core, is always a subject for potential political dispute, reflecting the deeper tension of consensus and diversity in a liberal democratic society. Although it is important for the schools to promote a political consensus (creed), it is also crucial that they not be seen as engaged in imposing partisan views (indoctrination). Vigorously pursuing consensus might be seen as compromising diversity (excess); conscientious respect for diversity might be seen as not doing enough to build commonality (deficit).

These problems aside, it is easy--perhaps too easy--to argue that we have never fully pursued the ideal of a common, fully inclusive school. For example, it has often been suggested by revisionist historians that the supposed consensus or ideals of commonality reflected certain interests rather than notions "accepted by all." The drive for publicly supported schools, it is argued, was primarily aimed at subordinating religious minorities and the working class rather than extending equal citizenship to all.[4] Thus, the emergence of the common school may have been less a matter of consensus than the vision of some specific groups. The principles of "Protestant-Republican virtue" that supported the dominant political, economic, and moral order became the ideology of the common school. As successful as it ultimately was, the common school movement was resisted by groups such as Catholics who, with some justification, saw this allegedly nonsectarian moral education as threatening their beliefs. Similar kinds of opposition formed around differences in class, race, and language, for example, German immigrants who formed schools to have education conducted in their own language. Thus whatever romantic notions we might have about the original common school, its moral lessons and claims to reflect consensus were controversial from the very beginning.

Even assuming the best of intentions all around, there have always been conceptual problems deciding what is or should be the core of the common school. The original common school was, for a variety of reasons, simply not inclusive enough to define a ground truly common to all. Both in the past and now, conflicting interests and problems of interpretation and implementation have made this ideal difficult to achieve. The battles over religious readings in the nineteenth century have become battles over school prayer and the teaching of creationism. The racial and linguistic divisions of the nineteenth century currently manifest themselves in debates about Afrocentrism, multiculturalism, and bilingual education. These disputes raise questions about what, if anything, is common in the common school.

In a pluralistic society in which cultural, political, and intellectual differences are not only to be tolerated but respected, the search for a common core will inevitably lead to substantive disputes about what is implicitly or explicitly taught. The ideal of common education, particularly as it has had moral overtones, has repeatedly collided with the reality of a segmented, pluralistic society. R. Freeman Butts phrases the problem confronting the common schools quite well:

> When the Founders' dream of a unified, cohesive, whole republican society was confronted by segmental tests of religion, race, language, and behavior, the rule for public education became infinitely more complex and difficult than the Founders could have imagined. No longer would simple literacy, moral values, history, or the study of forms of government fill the public need. Segmentation raised all sorts of questions: Literacy in what language? Whose moral values based on what religion? Whose history? Study of what government? The common school movement constantly had to face such

questions pertaining to its role in building civic cohesion in a society marked by diversity and particularism.[5]

This is a particularly concise statement of the core problem. That is, what ought to be common in the common school? If the schools' role is to produce civic cohesion, political or moral integration, how can it do this without compromising some individuals' or groups' autonomy?

It is a short step from these questions to the dilemma of excess and deficit. As the schools try to address these questions they open themselves to criticism as doing too much or too little to promote commonality. Promoting certain cultural or historical understandings risks the charge that the state is imposing its values on individuals or groups, compromising their autonomy. To avoid these questions, for example by professing neutrality on matters of value, risks the charge of doing too little to build civic cohesion. (It may also be very difficult for the schools to be, or be perceived as being, neutral on many issues of morality and culture.) Often both types of criticism occur simultaneously. For example, with regard to bilingual education the schools have been criticized for promoting English as the primary language in ways that compromise cultural diversity and for doing too little to promote a common language by offering expansive bilingual programs.

In response to these problems the schools have steadily retreated (or been forced to retreat) from both morality and commonality in education. By 1872, required Bible readings were eliminated on constitutional grounds, but by that time Catholics had created their own school system to protect and promote their religious beliefs. The relationship of that system to the public schools has been a bone of contention and an issue of constitutional law ever since. Racial segregation was exempt from the demands of common education in the nineteenth century, and many would say it still is. Linguistic differences were folded into programs for "Americanization," but more recently the question of bilingualism has prompted disputes about a shared "official" language. The potential for segmentation on the basis of some dimension of group identity is ever expanding and it continues today. It can range from Christian fundamentalists creating their own schools to the creation of a high school for gay students in New York.

Similarly, the ideal of a genuinely common curriculum has been progressively diluted as the system of American public education has developed. First, the ideal of common education, past and present, has been most fully realized, if at all, at the elementary level. As the secondary schools have developed in the twentieth century, they have generally rejected a truly common curriculum in favor of differentiated academic programs allegedly more suitable to individual abilities, needs, and likely economic futures. Commonality in the secondary schools consists mainly in shared space, extracurricular activities, and school identity. Certainly there are core subjects, but these are often offered differently to various academic groups. There have been, and will continue to be, many arguments about the legitimacy of these differences--whether they are a sensible meshing of skills and subjects or an artificial means of sorting students into likely career paths. In any case, the educational program at the secondary level is typically less common than in the primary schools. We simply do not provide the same education to all students beyond a certain point.[6]

The ideal of the common school has also been diluted because of a shift from a moral to a more academic focus, again especially at the secondary level. For Mann, the development of academic skills was the occasion or instrument for moral instruction in, among other things, a creed. It was not academic in the contemporary sense of exposing students to the wide range of knowledge represented by different subjects. As the schools have become secularized and "comprehensive," the common ground has become academic. There is a focus on subjects, knowledge, and skills, and moral issues are handled indirectly, if at all. Moreover, the demands that schools develop "human capital," another major theme in public education, suggest differentiated curricula that ready students for broad occupational categories. Additionally, these divisions have, rightly or wrongly, been seen as the proper application of a more student-centered pedagogical approach. In any case these pragmatic and pedagogical concerns are somewhat removed from the moral and political ones of the common school.

In many ways this shift is not surprising. Moral education has always been a touchy subject. Even in Mann's statement at the beginning of this chapter, there is the recognition that "controverted" issues pose a problem for the public schools and that "indoctrination into matters of controversy" is something to be avoided. As noted previously, the common schools of the nineteenth century had difficulty finding common moral ground, most notably between Protestants and Catholics. Consensus about academic standards and areas for study has always been more readily obtainable than consensus on moral topics. Commonality is more likely to be found in the former area and more likely to implemented without conflict and controversy. Political conflict aside, it would seem that any program of moral education, especially a didactic one, would risk going beyond the legitimate authority of the state. The topic of moral education conjures up, at best, difficult questions of autonomy, indoctrination, and the preservation of minority rights and, at worst, images of brainwashing and fundamentalism.

As the public schools became increasingly secularized, moral education, as Mann might have understood it, took two forms. One was fairly visible and didactic, the other hidden. First, the teaching of civics and the promotion of good citizenship were seen as appropriate forms of didactic moral education in the schools. There has been widespread agreement that civic education is a legitimate concern of the schools, one that poses less of a clear challenge to the particularities of language, race, or culture. Whatever differences there are among Americans, there is supposedly, and perhaps necessarily, a common political order to which they all pledge allegiance. Second, and perhaps equally important, the schools have also continuously engaged in moral education simply by exercising their authority, typically in accord with the values of the community. The so-called "hidden curriculum" also reflected, at least until fairly recently, a consensus that schools could act in the place of parents and set rules and expectations governing behavior. The schools' exercise of authority in these matters was hidden only in that it was not formally academic or programmatic. It was simply assumed that schools would exercise this kind of control, both as part of the process of administering the schools and as an extension of parental authority. What Robert Hampel calls the "scripts of adult authority" were continuous between school and home.[7]

Even in these areas there have been controversies about commonality and diversity and the legitimate extent of state authority. For example, the zeal to promote patriotism has occasionally overstepped constitutional bounds. A 1924 Ku Klux Klan-inspired law in Oregon that would have abolished parochial schools was struck down. Similarly, in 1969 the Supreme Court defended students' rights to peaceful political protest (the wearing of armbands) in *Tinker v. Des Moines*. More recently, in *Wisconsin v. Yoder* the Court allowed Amish students to opt out of schooling before the usual age as an expression of religious freedom. These decisions suggested that promoting support for the political system or community mores may go too far, even though the more common complaint, then and now, has been that the schools do not do enough to promote good citizenship. And there have also been instances in which the schools are criticized for teaching the wrong civic lessons. For example, some groups have wanted the schools to provide a civic education that is more critical of the American system. In the 1930s social reconstructionists suggested that the schools might dare to build a new social order, as have more contemporary proponents of critical or liberation pedagogies.[8] Civic education has thus had its share of controversies about what will be taught and how far the schools should go in promoting certain ideals.

There have been similar controversies concerning the role schools might play in moral education through its rules and practices, the hidden curriculum. Historically, the schools' authority in these areas was largely unquestioned. Conflicts were often resolved by the exit of the disaffected rather than a change in the institution. It has become less clear, at least since the 1950s and certainly since *Tinker*, what the schools' range of authority is and how far it can seek to influence or prescribe behavior. These the courts have been more sympathetic recently to claims of authority by school officials, the net result has been that schools now act less like relatively unrestrained moral authorities *in loco parentis* and more like state agencies cooperating with (or perhaps attempting to control) clients. Issues of discipline and punishment, search and seizure, and the use of facilities are all potential matters of constitutional law but more typically are the subject of ongoing negotiation between and among parents, students, faculty, and administrators. The reconceptualization of the schools' legal powers and the larger cultural trends concerning the exercise of public authority have led to the relaxing of the "scripts of authority" and the renegotiation of "treaties" concerning the schools' moral authority and power.[9]

Whatever its problems and controversies, much of the history of public education in the United States has been variations on the theme of the common school. Each generation has sought to define its version of the essential elements of the common school. At various times institutional settlements concerning the core of common schooling have been negotiated, and then later challenged and renegotiated. Solutions to this problem have always faced the dilemma of excess and deficit. In the current reform movement there are a number of controversies and proposals concerning curricular reform and moral education. These are the most recent manifestations of the theme of the common school and its major problems. Before looking at these specific issues it is useful to restate the major variations on this theme and the dilemmas and problems the variations face.

Variations on a Theme: "What?" and "How Far?"

The general evolution of the theme of the common school seems to have produced questions and problems but few obvious solutions. Any version of the common school theme faces two questions, "What?" and "How far?" (Figure 3.1).[10] Answering those questions will almost inevitably generate some version of the core problem and the dilemma of excess and deficit. In each case the typical response to these problems has been a bias toward the minimum as a politically safe, potentially consensual, and institutionally easy position. Not surprisingly, reformers interested in creating some version of a new common school tend to demand more in some sense. The question then is to what extent these proposals might be expected to adequately deal with the problems that lead to the bias toward the minimum. Before addressing that question, it is important to clarify how the variations on the theme of the common school answer the questions "What?" and "How Far?"

	Moral/Civic	Academic
Maximum	Didactic moral education Prosocial/citizenship education	Common culture, curriculum Appropriate subjects, thinking skills
Minimum	Values clarification	Basic literacy, numeracy

FIGURE 3.1 **Variations on the Common School Theme**

The first "what?" issue that any contemporary version of a common school must confront is the distinction between moral/political education, broadly understood, and academic education. The latter category seems transparent enough. For example, whatever else the schools might offer to all students equally, we can reasonably expect them to promote basic skills, especially literacy and numeracy. Even as we move beyond this minimum, there is probably considerable consensus about some more advanced skills or knowledge all students should have upon completing school. Still, there are knotty and politically controversial questions about the content of such a curriculum. The academic version of the common school faces the issue of what, if anything, beyond basic literacy ought to be provided to all students. Leaving aside the question of whether there should be one curriculum for all, there are continuing controversies, such as the debate over multiculturalism, over what might be in the curriculum. Moreover, it is not clear that even the minimal notion of common education can be totally free of such conflicts. For example, the problem of bilingualism indicates that even the notion of "basic" literacy can be contested.

Academic matters aside, there is a difference, even if only in emphasis, between this academic version of the common school and a more explicitly moral vision. The latter would focus on the schools promoting certain moral ideals, including certain virtues and notions of good citizenship. That is, the schools would encourage individuals to endorse some moral principles and to view relationships to society, particularly the state, in a certain way. The schools have generally sought to promote certain ideals of citizenship by, among other things, teaching students their constitutional rights and responsibilities or encouraging them to vote. In recent years, however, the schools have often shied away from any program in moral education. They have often limited discussion of moral questions to "clarification," which keeps the school from taking a position on potentially touchy moral subjects. These minimal efforts are, of course, some distance from the more aggressive and didactic program of the original common school and, as will be seen, some proposals of current reformers as well. In any case, such an emphasis on moral education is different from a central concern with academic skills and subjects. Any program of common education will need to address the issue of what its focus is, whether it will try to emphasize academic, as opposed to moral, education and how it might do both in some combination.[11]

The questions of "what?" then, arises both between and within each variation of the common school theme. In either variation there are questions of what should be the common ground in public schools. These difficulties are exacerbated by the dilemma of excess and deficit. For either variation the schools can be accused of doing too much or not enough. Basic literacy may be seen as too modest an academic goal but more ambitious notions of literacy and culture may be seen as overstepping the bounds of state authority. Similarly, regarding moral education, there has been an ongoing controversy about whether the schools should take a didactic approach or strive for a posture of neutrality, for example through programs like values clarification--assuming they address the issue at all. A strong commitment to substantive values is likely to be opposed by groups who want a different set of values taught. Here again the schools are open to the charge of doing too little by trying to avoid moral education or too much as they try to promote some values. Setting priorities and finding the balance between extensive and minimal demands plague both variations on the common school theme.

These problems create a bias toward the minimum in two ways. First, in each area the safer, more consensual course is to avoid taking on a more ambitious program. It is easier to agree on basic skills, to engage in flat pedagogy that covers neutral content, to avoid controversial topics in order to find a common academic program that could be given to all students. Similarly, the schools' avoidance or profession of neutrality in moral matters is less likely to generate controversy or raise issues of imposition. For all its problems, values clarification at least seems nonthreatening to parental beliefs. Second, there is a bias toward the minimum in the tendency to seek an academic version of the common school and downplay or avoid the topic of moral education. It is easier and safer politically to define the academic goals of the school rather than to say in a more straightforward way what kind of person the school hopes to produce. Although this cannot totally rescue schools from the core problem and related dilemmas, it does avoid the potentially more contentious issues of what values and beliefs the schools should promote. To pursue these issues would involve developing a more robust version of the common school ideal, one similar to Mann's original vision. This risks opposition from those who disagree with the moral values the schools would seek to promote or those who would see such a project as a threat to parental prerogatives, or both.

These general statements of problems and dilemmas do not imply that there is no plausible or rationally defensible way to promote a common school. Indeed, as will be seen, there are different segments of the reform movement that are promoting more ambitious academic or moral versions of a new common school. Noting these variations on the theme and the problems they face--the core problem and the dilemma of excess and deficit--provides a means for discussing and evaluating the proposed reforms. Again, a recapitulation of these problems does not lead to some answer or specific solution but does suggest what should be considered as the problem is negotiated in practice. If this does not produce solutions, it can suggest what is at stake in the various alternatives, how resolutions of these problems are or might be negotiated through institutions and practices, and even why some alternatives and resolutions might be preferable to others.

The "Academic" Variation: Reform, Discipline, and Academics

As the reform movement got under way in the mid-1980s the focus was squarely on curriculum and requirements. Academic achievement had to be improved across the board if the schools were to play their role in maintaining America's position in the world, especially its economic position. More requirements and higher standards were proposed for both students and teachers. More time would have to be spent on academic tasks, and greater emphasis would need to be placed on measurable achievement, especially in standardized tests. Indeed, the "at risk" report did not hesitate to spell out what a curriculum in the new basics should look like, how long the school day and year should be, and how the teaching profession should be organized. In all these areas the thrust of the reform movement was on doing more in order to produce better academic results.

For all the "at risk" report's specificity about the new curriculum and standards, the early reform reports were rather vague about whether their requirements would apply to all students equally, let alone what would be done with those less-accomplished students having trouble coping with existing demands. The "at risk" report tried to finesse the equity question by claiming that excellence and equity would not be traded against one another even as it argued "the variety of student aspirations, abilities, and preparation requires that appropriate content be available to satisfy diverse needs."[12] Similarly, the report spoke of raising both "the floor and the ceiling" of educational achievement without making clear whether the "room" was open to all equally. This vagueness was in part a function of a lack of clarity about what the guiding ideals of reform should be. It was also an attempt to avoid any direct response to perennially debated issues of tracking and ability grouping. Can or should we have the same curriculum for all students? Should students taking the same subjects work in groups of mixed ability or only with those at their level? Obviously, these are more than pedagogical questions. They raise serious issues about what constitutes an equal education and the schools' obligations to students who differ in ability and achievement.

At the same time, one segment of the reform movement has consistently argued for a modernized version of the common school that extends through secondary education. It is a rather diverse group, ranging from cultural conservatives to more liberal educators, reporting on the results of field studies of schools. The proposals that have been offered are as diverse as the group that has offered them. They range from setting very minimal, but rigorously enforced standards for all students to more elaborate proposals concerning curricular revision. There are proposals for minimal goals of "literacy, numeracy, and knowledge for responsible citizenship," suggestions for a more expansive curriculum that emphasizes traditional subjects or a notion of "cultural literacy," as well as more recent arguments about thinking skills, "to use minds well." Despite their differences, these proposals suggest that all children receive essentially the same education.[13]

It should also be noted that this plea for a common academic focus has often been accompanied by a rejection of the economic emphasis in much of the rhetoric of reform (a theme to be discussed in the Chapter 4). Among those promoting this kind of curricular reform, there is considerable skepticism about the role of public schools in enhancing economic performance. Schools, it is argued, simply cannot be held responsible for America's economic decline or recovery, and it is unreasonable to expect schools to be able to adjust their curricula and practices as rapidly as technologies and economic needs change. Moreover, separation of different groups of students on the basis of likely future economic roles is rejected as academically unsound and morally dubious. As Ernest Boyer puts it, "Putting students into boxes can no longer be defended. To call some students academic and others nonacademic has a powerful and, in some instances, devastating impact on how teachers think about students and how students think about themselves."[14] What limited economic role the schools play is best served through an appropriate common curriculum.

Whatever the similarities or differences among these these proposals for common academic requirements, they indicate that the rhetoric of equal education continues to have a powerful impact on discussions of reform. The framing of education goals for the year 2000 often echoes the theme of an inclusive, common education: all students will start school ready to learn, all will learn to use their minds well, every adult will be literate and so on. The thrust is clearly egalitarian. Many of the reforms must touch everyone in essentially the same way. The goals also specify subject-matter competencies that should be tested at grades 4, 8, and 12 for international comparison. There is considerable discussion about the possibility of having a voluntary program of national testing that will provide a benchmark for achieving these aims.[15] These goals and the prospect of national examinations are moving us ever closer to a truly national curriculum and common standard of education.

The "Discipline" Problem

Most reformers, whether proponents of a new common school or otherwise, generally agree about the nature and origins of the recent decline of the schools. It is only a slight exaggeration to say that the reform movement sees the schools' problem as a lack of discipline. Specifically, it is explicitly or implicitly assumed that the decline of the schools began with the relaxation of both personal and academic standards in the late 1960s and early 1970s. As authority in the larger society was being challenged, and social and cultural controls relaxed, it is perhaps not surprising that the authority of schools would likewise be challenged and changed. The powers of school authorities in matters large and small shifted both legally and by dint of custom and culture during this period. There was, it is argued, a comparable loosening of academic requirements reflected in diluted general curricula and decreased requirements in favor of open schools, student-centered curricula, relevance, and so on. These resulted in the declining test scores and other measures of achievement at the heart of the "nation at risk" report.[16] The weakened authority and legitimacy of the schools made it more difficult for them to make demands, academically or otherwise, on students. What the schools could once command, it seemed, now had to be negotiated with the result that expectations, and therefore achievement, declined.

The "discipline" problem then really has two dimensions. Most obviously, the weakening of the authority of school officials over student conduct put many schools in such disarray, made them so disorderly, that academic matters were not and could not be addressed. The public at large has generally seemed less concerned with academic excellence and international competitiveness than with domestic tranquility. Gallup polls have consistently indicated that order and discipline, along with drugs, are seen as the most serious problems in the public schools. The academic and other aims of the reform movement could not be pursued without the creation of some basic order in the schools. If the schools were not orderly, new curriculuar requirements or other reforms would be meaningless. The national education goals have explicitly recognized this problem by setting the goal of "schools free of drugs and violence."

However, the problem of discipline goes beyond the more obvious instances of "drugs and violence." A number of field studies, many of which promoted the idea of a new common school, suggested that there were discipline problems of a sort even in schools that were apparently orderly. The atmosphere in otherwise orderly schools and classrooms was flat. It lacked a sense of purpose or urgency, let alone a drive for excellence. One study compares the high schools to shopping malls, "another consumption experience in an abundant society," in which there is variety, consumer choice, and neutrality about what is valuable.[17] Students drift through school more concerned with friends and extracurricular activities than with academics. Faculty, unsure of their professional status or mission, revert to the safest form of teaching by covering material on schedule. The classroom generates little by way of intellectual excitement or interest. A sense of mission is lacking, and in its place are mostly tacit "treaties" whereby students and faculty and administrators agree not to demand too much of one another. The decline of the general authority of the school in nonacademic matters reinforces the lack of direction in the academic program and makes these treaties all the more convenient and attractive. Thomas Toch puts it most bluntly and negatively, suggesting that the "apathy and alienation that pervade . . . the nation's public secondary schools" is the major obstacle to genuine reform.[18]

Beyond maintaining basic order, the remedies suggested for the discipline problem have been a mix of curricular and pedagogical proposals. A minimalist version of the new common school would certify that students had attained certain basic skills and leave further academic achievement or specialized training to other institutions. For example, early in the reform movement Theodore Sizer argued that the schools can and should only demand that each student achieve "literacy, numeracy, and sufficient knowledge for responsible citizenship." Because a liberal society must be wary of compulsion or indoctrination, these must be both the minimal and maximal compulsory goals of public education.[19] Similar, but distinct versions of setting a minimal standard for all students are proposals for certification tests in high schools. For example, Oregon has a proposal for a common test to be give to tenth-graders that leads to a "Certificate of Initial Mastery." The certificate would presumably guarantee that a student has passed some basic educational threshold. Oregon's proposal also provides for special assistance to students who do not meet standards as well as direction toward college or training and apprenticeships for those that do. In these proposals then there is the setting of some minimal standards, albeit for somewhat different reasons, with the promise of strict accountability for schools' achieving them.

Of course, there have also been proposals for more extensive common curricula suggesting that basic education of this sort simply is not enough for some legitimate contemporary purposes of a new common school. Even those who advocate a more minimal notion seem to believe or sense that something more must, if not be required, at least be available. Although focusing on minimal aims has the obvious attraction of avoiding potentially contentious arguments about what all students ought to know, other proponents of a new common school see the avoidance of this question as precisely the problem with the schools. They take a more explicit and expansive view of what constitutes a basic, general education. For example, E. D. Hirsch's argues that common cultural perspectives, embodied in "hazy background knowledge" of certain facts and concepts, is essential if all individuals are to have the opportunity to participate fully in society. Those who are cut off from this common culture will be unable to avail themselves of the opportunities society offers. Perhaps most important, Hirsch claims, what are seen to be academic deficiencies, such as lack of writing skill, are indicative of a lack of cultural exposure rather than a lack of ability. A truly equal education must offer this cultural exposure to all. Unfortunately, Hirsch's argument, partly through his book's emphasis on a highly specific "index of cultural literacy," has been regarded as a kind of mindless version of education via trivial pursuit. Its more serious and plausible argument is that schools must provide for cultural integration of all students equally by giving each student a thorough grounding in a range of subjects.[20]

The more conventional way of offering a more expansive, common education is by trying to describe the elements of an appropriate, nontracked curriculum. There has been no shortage of such curricular proposals in the reform movement. There have been calls for a "revival of the humanities," increased emphasis on math and science, more foreign languages, and so on. One typical proposal was offered in *James Madison High* by then Secretary of Education William Bennett. He suggested a detailed curriculum of common subjects with a very modest set of electives. Each student would be required to complete certain academic sequences. Equally important, there would be few or no exceptions made to these requirements and no differences in the way they would be presented to different students. There are other examples of proposals for common curricula that take a similar approach.[21] Finally, the more recent discussion in favor of national tests, many have noted, would have the effect of standardizing curricula. By encouraging (or, in effect, requiring) schools to teach to the test, a greater degree of commonality would be introduced into school curricula.

For all the talk about curriculum and testing, the primary focus of reform on behalf of common education is the culture of schooling and, more specifically, the issue of pedagogical style. That is, the treaties governing many schools do not lend themselves to academic achievement, regardless of curriculum, because they do not involve pedagogical approaches that promote intellectual interest. Many of the field studies of schools describe the typical classroom as a rather dull place in which teachers talk, students (sometimes) listen, and relatively little real thinking or learning occurs. In part this is a result of too much emphasis on curricular coverage. There is too much emphasis on transmitting numerous facts and covering many topics rather than explaining a few fundamental concepts and relationships. This produces a flat, neutral atmosphere rather than stimulating interest, curiosity, and engagement. It is simply contrary to what is increasingly recognized as good pedagogy--active student involvement with subject matter that involves more dialogue and increased emphasis on critical thinking, writing, and speaking. As many effective schools have already demonstrated, it is important to create a climate of expectations that all students can have academic success and that the school (and students) will make the necessary efforts to do so. The point is to do this for all students by providing a fixed standard of quality, general education for a single track of students.

Recently there have been several projects that have put less emphasis on the traditional subject matter of the curriculum and more on broadly pedagogical issues. They are concerned with how to motivate students and teachers to give their best effort in the academic enterprise. Indeed, these models for a new common school often explicitly reject any highly specific, subject-based curriculum precisely because it is perceived that it will become teacher-centered and test-bound. Often these efforts fall under the rubric of "restructuring" since they involve significant changes in ordinary school practices, such as the use of time and the means of assessment. They also involve giving greater discretion to the schools and teachers to figure out what will work best at the building or classroom level. For example, the Coalition of Essential Schools, a group headed by Theodore Sizer, suggests that the principles governing curricula should be "helping adolescents learn to use their minds well" by realizing that " 'less is more' . . . curricular decisions are to be directed toward the students' attempt to gain mastery rather than by the teachers' effort to cover content."[22] Expectations for mastery are for all students and involve "the students' demonstration that they can do important things." It is expected, of course, that these restructured schools can meet the major academic goals for the year

2000 and do it in a way that goes beyond test achievement to genuine understanding and critical thinking.[23]

The Core Problem

The various academic versions of a new common school have some obvious attractions. They each set forth a conception of the core elements of public education that is arguably appropriate, attainable, and consensual. There is a great deal of consensus about general subjects that students should understand and skills they should have. Still, it is also important to note that these versions vary considerably. To emphasize cultural literacy over basic skills or an expansive view of the curriculum over a narrower one ("less is more") creates very different policies. Certainly these are not exclusive options, and a mixed program is probably an inevitable and desirable result. Similarly, any one of these options or some mix thereof reflects some more or less provisional settlement of the core problem, simply because there is no permanent solution to be discovered. Rather, determining what are the appropriate common elements in public education is more or less continually open to contest and negotiation. For any proposed requirement (for anything beyond the most basic skills), whether in terms of subject or content, there is always the potential for objections that propose something different or something more or less ambitious. Equally important, these inevitable variations suggest that the question of developing an academic version of the common school is inseparable from the broader question of moral education.

First, any definition of common education will start with basic skills of literacy and numeracy in some sense. Few, however, would say that that is sufficient; the emphasis on skills cannot eliminate questions about what all students should know. On the one hand, these questions may seem transparent. Students should know the basics in a range of subject areas as measured by achievement tests or other appropriate measures of "mastery" that indicate that they have reached certain levels of knowledge, skill, and understanding. To be sure, these expectations will be periodically adjusted to accommodate new forms of knowledge and revised expectations (for example, "computer literacy"), but there is certainly some core of academic subject areas that are the basis for any curriculum.

On the other hand, once specific curricula are proposed, questions almost inevitably arise, and there have been several controversies about what should be in a common curriculum--and whether it should be common at all. For example, in offering a "curriculum of inclusion" a New York advisory group suggested that the biases in existing curricula are not only pedagogically unsound but actually detrimental to the self-esteem of minorities.[24] At the very least the place of minorities, women, and other cultures should be elevated in the curriculum. In some instances it has been proposed that a distinct "Afrocentric" curriculum be offered in schools with large African-American populations. This perspective has of course been controversial. Similarly, the New York proposal has been widely criticized for undercutting the idea of a common curriculum or suggesting one that is in its own way as much or more biased than the curriculum it is to replace.[25] Suffice it to say that such a curriculum is some distance from other "common" curricula that have been proposed such as Hirsch's notion of a common, essentially "Western" view of cultural literacy. Although an academic definition of commonality may pass muster in areas such as math and science (even though here too there have been some questions), the areas of social studies and literature are a curricular minefield for the issue of commonality. And, of course, traditional areas of study are not the only topics of debate. Conflicts with parents and other public officials about sex education, creationism, bilingualism, the treatment of religion in texts all indicate that there are conflicts about what ought to be the core of the curriculum in the public schools.

Again, in specifying any common curriculum the schools will face the dilemma of excess and deficit. On the one hand, the schools may be charged with imposing certain cultural or moral notions on students, for example, through curricular portrayals (or absence thereof) of certain groups. The claims for bilingual instruction or multicultural education both suggest that the schools are going too far in creating a common curriculum, compromising legitimate desires for linguistic and cultural identity. In the face of such potential for controversy, the schools have often taken shelter in the neutral coverage of material. They thereby open themselves to the charge of doing too little to promote a common culture or morality. Often the pursuit of neutrality and avoidance of controversy simply leads to inaccuracy. For example, some historians have pointed out that the treatment of religion in history textbooks has done too little to promote a proper understanding of the religious influences in American history and culture. Fearful of church-state controversies, textbook publishers and administrators have not done enough to promote a common, let alone accurate, understanding of the role of religion in American life.[26] Thus the multicultural critique suggests the state has gone too far in promoting a view of history and culture, and those complaining about treatment of religion in textbooks suggest that the state has done too little to promote a common, or even accurate, historical understanding.

It is also important to note that these problems cannot be avoided by placing a greater emphasis on skills rather than content coverage. For example, it might be tempting to believe that agreement on common skills and performances demonstrating basic mastery can avoid the core problem. There can be little disagreement that we want students to learn to use their minds well, to be excited about their work in school, and perhaps above all to get into the habit of putting forth their best effort all the time. However, the arguments about curricula indicate that in saying we want students to use their minds well, we envision something more than some disembodied intellectual skills. If the subject matter is biased, if it ignores certain groups, cultures, or topics, then students cannot use their minds well. Equally important, to raise questions about the effect of the curriculum on students' understandings about different races or cultures (or on some students' self-esteem) is to ask what kind of beliefs and attitudes the curriculum aims to foster. Whatever one thinks of issues like multiculturalism, they do raise questions about what results the school will or should aim to produce. These in turn are inevitably issues of moral education.

Academics and Morals

This unavoidable link between academics and moral education is well illustrated by the controversy about multicultural education. But that controversy is merely a very visible illustration of a more general issue. Even if there were no objections on the ground of fair treatment of different groups, past or present, it would still be legitimate to ask why certain subjects and skills were deemed essential for all students. The same point can be made in a more positive way. If we believe that there is some reason for compulsory schooling beyond achieving basic literacy, then it would seem that there is some moral purpose and urgency for requiring further education. The advocates of the common school such as Mann were clear that they wanted to produce a certain type of person with a certain outlook. Today we are considerably less confident, and somewhat vaguer, about both what we want the schools to produce and the legitimacy of such a goal. Such a larger purpose can be defined primarily in academic terms but it will inevitably lead to the addressing of moral issues through, among other things, definitions of common curriculum and skills. That is, implicit in these curricular controversies is the moral and political issue of what kind of person is envisioned emerging from the schools.

Perhaps most important, the emphasis on curricular coverage or academic skills to the exclusion of moral education may be self-defeating. Many of those promoting an academic focus have suggested that the tone of most classrooms is "flat," "emotionally neutral," and so on. At least part of the explanation for this should now be clear. Beyond simplifying the practical task of teaching by reducing pedagogy to subject matter coverage or emphasis on (vague) skills, this style avoids those issues that have the potential for producing controversy. By avoiding issues that might involve the school in moral education, teachers are inclined to act pedagogically in ways that are academically less than desirable. If we want to produce critical thinkers, the questions that give rise to critical thinking must matter. They will often involve controversial and unavoidably moral topics. To try to constrain academic topics to the safe coverage of subject matter is contrary to any program that values academic excellence. The question of moral education is thus not so easily avoided by an emphasis on academic subjects or skills.

These are less killing objections to proposals for a new common school program than a persistent conceptual problem of liberal democracy manifested in terms of public education. Public educational institutions should be open to examining and even redefining what constitutes core subjects, even as calling all facts and principles into question is impractical and undesirable. As noted above, this may lead to conflicts. But attempting to avoid conflict and criticism produces the bland pedagogical style that is commonly observed. In the face of the core problem teachers and administrators adopt a defensive posture. To go beyond the minimum to address controversial topics and to raise difficult questions is to risk raising someone's ire about indoctrination or contradiction of family and community norms. Seeking refuge in a neutral posture through emphasis on curricular coverage or emphasis on skills to avoid controversy is an understandable, if undesirable, response to the core problem.

This situation is both worse and better than it might seem. In the worst case, the curriculum and instruction within it becomes a kind of zero-sum game in which teaching a subject in any way guarantees some sort of objection. For example, some Christian groups have challenged the teaching of biology in the standard way as violating their religious freedom and imposing a state-sponsored religion ("secular humanism"). Legislative attempts to mandate coequal treatment for creationism and evolution have been successfully challenged on the same grounds. At the same time, this intractable theoretical conflict is made less destructive than it potentially is because of institutional practices and policies that reflect greater degrees of consensus or common ground than many of the more visible controversies would lead us to believe. There are simply many areas of the curriculum and specific topics that are widely agreed upon. The curricula in most public schools overlap in many ways. Similarly, there is also considerable consensus about some of the intellectual skills schools should foster. For example, few would question the notion that we want students to consider different viewpoints, understand different cultures, be at least moderately skeptical and inquisitive. Admittedly, this agreement is often honored more in the breach than the observance, given the typically flat style of the classroom. Nevertheless, these broad areas of consensus at least make possible a greater degree of commonality than we might otherwise suspect on the basis of theoretical speculation alone.

Certainly, noting such a consensus does not resolve instances of the core problem such as multiculturalism. But it does remind us that these very visible controversies are departures from a more general, broad consensus. Not surprisingly, such challenges have led to a reconsideration of what should be in the curriculum, for example, in history or social studies. These in turn have led to practical responses that try to broaden what is taken to be "common" consistent with the legitimate claims of diversity. For example, some responses to the challenge of multiculturalism suggest a broader, more critical "warts and all" history that is more accurate factually and also suggests a common, if diverse, heritage. As Diane Ravitch puts it, this kind of pluralistic account teaches that "cultural pluralism is one of the norms of a free society . . . the United States has a common culture that is multicultural."[27] Finally, it is important to realize that this kind of evolving consensus on academics inevitably raises, and involves the school in, the enterprise of moral education. Any notion of a new common school only makes sense in terms of some moral purposes. Academic commonality, or for that matter excellence, is not independent of of the moral aims of the school. The ways in which schools engage, directly and indirectly, in moral education set the framework within which academic pursuits and problems should be evaluated.

Moral Education and Consensus

To recast the issue of a new common school in terms of moral education might seem to be jumping from the frying pan into the fire. If there are controversies about academic versions of a new common school, it would seem even more difficult to address the notion of moral education in the schools. Agreement on algebra is more likely than agreement on abortion. Nonetheless, as the reform movement has proceeded, there have been calls for explicit moral education in the schools, and the idea has been given at least verbal support by a surprisingly broad group. For example, both Mario Cuomo and William Bennett, politically opposite in all other things, gave similar speeches supporting the idea of didactic values education. Similarly, leaders of teachers' unions have voiced their support for teaching "the political vision . . . that unites us as Americans" that "must be taught and learned," and California's superintendent of public instruction, Bill Honig, voiced similar support because, as he put it, "We've ended up with students who are ethically illiterate." Politics may create strange bedfellows, and on the issue of moral education, rhetorically at least, everyone seems to agree, as Bennett put it, that "we should 'teach values' the same way we teach other things."[28]

Although such endorsements of moral education are a safe and largely rhetorical exercise, they are also in part an understandable reaction to school disorder and other problems such as drug use and teenage pregnancy. If nothing else, the schools must take a stand, it is argued, against those things that make education impossible. Beyond responding to these problems, the calls for moral education are also a reaction to curricula, popular during the 1970s, that seemed to emphasize the process of making moral judgments rather than the substance of those judgments. For example, exercises in values clarification were popular. These and similar programs took the most minimal approach to moral education, implying that the teaching of any specific values was a potential violation of student autonomy. Students were encouraged to clarify how they felt about moral problems, even if these feelings ran counter to the prescriptions of adult authority or common moral sentiments. Such exercises fit neatly with school administrators' pronouncements that the school should be neutral on moral matters. As one district superintendent puts it, "Whose version of ethics would we use? It's outside the scope of our charge to teach morals." Just as the treaty on academic matters seemed to make few demands on teachers and students, so too this posture of neutrality generally ignored moral issues.[29]

The apparent relativism of this approach fairly begs for a strong reaction in the other direction. Instead of worrying about *how* students think about moral matters, it is argued that we should focus on *what* they think, making sure they think, and do, the proper things. Specifically, calls for moral education often take a form similar to Mann's precept in the nineteenth century. The place to find principles "to be taught to all" is in consensus. For example, Bennett dismisses "time-worn doubts about 'Whose values will be taught?' and 'How?'," by offering a list of consensual values that the schools should promote:

In defining good character we should include specific traits such as thoughtfulness, fidelity, kindness, diligence, honesty, fairness, self-discipline, respect for law, and taking one's guidance by accepted standards of right and wrong rather than by, for example, one's personal preferences . . . there is a good deal of consensus among the American people about these character traits. . . . Not only is there a consensus among the American people on the elements that constitute good character, most Americans want their schools to help form the character of their children.[30]

Again, this appeal is not confined to the right of the political spectrum. Cuomo also suggests that schools should promote allegiance to fundamental or core values: "at the core of every society is a set of moral values, a code of behavior, a credo . . . Even here in our uniquely free society where diversity of belief is protected . . . there is a rough--but clear--national understanding of what is right and wrong, what is allowed and forbidden, what we are entitled to and what we owe . . . real, tangible, specific values. And we can teach them to our young specifically."[31] These statements reflect a remarkable confidence that there are widely shared and easily known values worthy of promotion by public institutions. Consensus on basic or core values is both the rationale for, and substance of, educational policy.

Perhaps more than proposals for a common curriculum, the demand for moral education is the modern echo of the ideals of the common school. Again, common literacy and skills were not the only, or perhaps even the primary, goal of the original common school. Explicit moral training was part of the curriculum as well. Then, as now, there were explicit appeals to a core of common (consensual) beliefs that formed the foundation for good character and citizenship. Equally important, it was believed that this creed was consistent with liberty and pluralism. Far from being a violation of political or religious diversity, the common school supposedly reflected the intersecting beliefs of various groups. Current reformers also cite an equivalent credo, a set of shared beliefs about values such as those listed above. The schools should, it is argued, use these values to "reinvent the modern equivalent of the McGuffey reader."[32]

There are some interesting comparisons between this argument for a program of moral education and the argument for neutral principles offered by Rawls discussed in Chapter 2. Both appeal to widely held, fundamental values in order to pursue a practical purpose. Both avoid providing any fuller (metaphysical?) justification for these consensual values, but for different reasons. Rawls seeks to avoid potentially divisive philosophical issues in order to discover an overlapping consensus; however, the promoters of moral education believe such a justification is available, but unnecessary. Philosophical exploration of what we know to be right and wrong is less important than active promotion of basic values. It is striking that as political philosophers struggle with the question of what values or principles, if any, bind or should bind our society, some politicians and educators are quite confident about a broad consensus on basic values.

These comparisons raise the heretical (for political theorists, at least) possibility that the view of basic values offered by these reformers may be a better way of approaching the task of political theory than Rawls' approach. If, as Rawls and his communitarian critics seem to agree, it is important to understand how our community defines itself, then the open-ended set of values provided by the proponents of moral education seems to be a more accurate portrayal of an overlapping consensus than Rawls' principles. It may be empirically and rhetorically sounder because it cites many of the virtues that are either assumed or ignored in Rawls' account. It thus seems to offer a more comprehensive basis for agreement. At the same time, it does not seem to fall prey to being too weak because it suggests a range of virtues and implies a fairly strong, prescriptive understanding of them as guides to character and conduct. Finally, if the task of theory is primarily practical, to develop a working consensual agreement based on a tradition, then didactic education in a "credo" would seem to be an obvious way of fulfilling that task. If this is the case, then we might simply tell the theorists to get out of the way and let politicians and practitioners articulate and teach core values. Political theory might help clarify these conceptions, but these would be refinements of the more elemental task of simply asserting (and teaching) what we already all know.

It is, of course, not as simple as this. Just as theoretical consensus has proven elusive, if not dubious, neither has a practical consensus on moral education been obtained, at least not in the form suggested by those calling for it. The most important issue, of course, concerns what specific values the schools will promote. The proponents of moral education suggest that there are consensual values that can be readily agreed upon and taught, and a number of states have worked at developing lists similar to those offered by Bennett and Cuomo.[33] It should be noted, however, that when such a list becomes an issue, the potential for agreement may be diminished. Even where there have been agreements about such a list, it has not been clear that the values on the list could be taught in a way that is both nontrivial and noncontroversial. Like Rawls' principles, any list of values may be consensual, at the price of being merely symbolic, and if more than symbolic it may not be genuinely consensual. Certainly we can tell children that it is wrong to lie, steal, and so on, but many of our moral problems involve issues where the implications of these basic values are in dispute. For example, it is one thing to teach that murder is wrong and quite another to say whether abortion is murder. It is one thing to list core values; it is quite another to establish a specific curriculum in moral education that does not offend some groups. A listing of values may not constitute a specific consensus about what is to be taught under the banner of moral education.

The problem here is not a lack of consensus about many moral values. Few would contest the lists offered by Bennett and Cuomo. The problem is the translation of these lists into a visible, didactic curriculum. The proponents of moral education might reply, with some justice, that they are better able (than, say, Rawls) to articulate a rhetorical consensus because the core values to which they appeal are, as a matter of fact, widely shared and similarly interpreted. Therefore the specific content of these programs can be worked out given the broad consensus on basic values, the potential for controversy is lessened because of this consensus, and any residual conflict is a small price to pay for an important program. At the same time, however, the record for programmatic development and implementation of curricula in moral education has been spotty to say the least. Besides the continued reluctance of school officials to get involved in these touchy questions, there have been numerous problems in getting agreement on what should be taught and how.

Whatever the merits of these objections and replies, there is a more important issue concerning moral education in the public schools. Namely, the question of whether the schools will engage in moral education is moot. The schools have always done so. The reformers' depiction of moral education in the public schools based on programs in values clarification, or on school administrators' claims of neutrality in moral matters, is somewhat misleading. Contrary to being neutral about questions of value and virtue, the schools do engage, often necessarily, in moral education. If we look more carefully at what the schools actually do or at least attempt to do, rather than appealing to an abstract political theory or a list of values, we can see the schools promoting, albeit imperfectly, a range of moral and intellectual virtues. We can discover several strands of virtue "situated" in a variety of ways in the public schools, reflecting some of the consensual values of our society. These set the context for, and make sense of, the narrower academic aims of the school. That the schools engage in moral education in these ways with relatively little controversy indicates that there is some consensus about certain values and virtues as well as about the role of the school as a moral educator. If we consider some of the virtues embedded in school curricula and practice we can develop a more suggestive picture of how the moral aims of a new common school might be achieved.

Moral Virtues

Hobbesian Health Class

The call for schools to teach morals in a didactic way, even "like physics," fails to note that there is already such a course in public schools. It is called health class. It is not usually thought of as teaching morals save when controversies arise, for example, relating to sex education. When we think of health class, we almost automatically think of sex education. This is both predictable and unfortunate. It is predictable because health classes have attracted attention when they have considered issues that spark controversy. It is unfortunate because it distracts us from the fact that health class is the closest thing we have to the style of didactic moral education suggested above. For the most part health classes promote values that are basic, widely shared, and noncontroversial. Therefore that these values are taught in a didactic way almost never strikes anyone as violating students' rights.

What are the values taught in health class? Without pushing the analogy too far, it is reasonable to call them "Hobbesian." First and foremost, they relate to one's physical well-being. Students learn how to take care of the irreducibly distinct, physical self. The primary concern of health class is the care of one's body, and the body is spoken of as a kind of mechanism. Second, the topics covered in health courses appeal directly to self-interest. Students are presented with the consequences of certain kinds of behavior and exhorted to, ultimately, take steps to preserve themselves.[34] Where health class involves didactic teaching regarding concerns such as avoiding drug and alcohol abuse, there is no controversy concerning the teaching of moral virtue(s) (prudence, moderation, and so on). Indeed, we demand that the schools engage in teaching these virtues because they are presumed to reflect important, common values.

The values taught in health class are really only "core" values in the weak sense of being boundary principles. Liberal democratic society, and perhaps any society, is prepared to acknowledge and encourage moral virtues related to self-preservation. We do not question the right of individuals to preserve their physical well-being, and are prepared as a society to encourage young people, in a didactic way, to do so. However, virtues related to self-preservation and satisfying legitimate physical needs are not, however, a complete picture of moral virtue. In the case of health class, recent curricula have tended to try to broaden the range of issues to family and interpersonal relationships. For example, one model curriculum suggests that the "decision-making skills" developed in dealing with personal health may be applied to other interpersonal relations. Similarly, it is often suggested that students recognize in others the stresses and problems they find in themselves.[35] But these extensions of the basic lessons of health class are only carried in directions that are modest and unproblematic. The primary goals of the health class are to remind students of their (self-)interest in bodily health and persuade them to act in accord with moral virtues related to prudence (self-control, moderation). Although these moral virtues are not the only traits of character prized in our society, they are sufficiently widely held and important enough for schools to promote them in a didactic way.

At the same time, these variations in the teaching of "health" indicate the artificiality of distinguishing between "moral" and "civic" (or even "academic") education. Health lessons might seem to be some distance from discussions of the institutional framework of government, the rights and responsibilities of citizens, and so on. Nevertheless, it is extremely difficult to separate education in these virtues from civic education, since these classes address what are obviously problems in public policy. Drug abuse, pregnancy, and sexually transmitted diseases are not wholly "private" matters, and they are arguably some of the most severe policy problems young people face. Teaching students the personal and public consequences of these choices has considerable significance for how, or even whether, students function well as citizens. Health lessons can be extended into civic lessons. There have been several programs that have started out dealing with some specific health issues such as pregnancy prevention but then extended into a range of issues concerning community relationships and service. Finally, and perhaps obviously, the academic enterprise of the school is impossible unless these "health" lessons are taken to heart. To the degree that these lessons foster self-respect and self-control, academic tasks are likely to be easier to accomplish.

The "Hidden Curriculum"

Education regarding moral virtue goes well beyond health or other classes. A powerful, perhaps even the most powerful, way that the school is engaged in moral education is simply in the way that it operates. This is commonly called the "hidden curriculum." At a minimum, it includes the rules and customs of the school as an organization. The school might not offer morality as a subject (beyond health class), but it inevitably teaches by example in the way in which it is organized, rules are set and enforced, and personal relations are conducted between and among the various groups within the school. Much of the literature on "effective schools" notes the importance of the "ethos" that includes a safe and orderly learning environment. Indeed, the term "hidden" is not entirely apt. Good schools typically make clear to students what is expected and why, giving them a stake in creating reasonable behavior in the school.[36] Explaining the rules and the reasons for them is not typically a matter of referring to basic moral principles. Rather, it generally presumes the legitimacy of the school's purposes and tries to enlist--and if necessary demand--student cooperation. Although school administrators often refer to this posture as not teaching morality, it is clear that the schools routinely provide moral guidance concerning civility, tolerance, and numerous other virtues as part of meeting the basic needs of the organization.

The hidden curriculum also extends to the daily instances in which the schools more explicitly encourage or even require students to participate in activities that are valued or praised. The daily rituals of the school (the pledge to the flag) and extracurricular activities promote political and personal values and traits of character. Some schools are experimenting with more self-conscious promotion of student cooperation on an everyday basis, and many states and districts also have community service requirements. What is crucial about these broader aspects of the "hidden" curriculum is that they go well beyond the individualistic lessons of the health class and the necessary rules of school order. They provide instruction concerning core values and virtues, traits of character and citizenship, that are noncontroversial. As one observer rhetorically asks, "Who would raise a question about anti-litterbug posters in the hall or pictures of Martin Luther King on the bulletin board. . . . What about participation in the neighborhood cleanup campaign or afterschool visits to the home for the elderly? Would anyone object to these?"[37] This list could be extended in any number of directions. To be sure, the encouragement of concern for others and public-regarding behavior may not be programmatic in the way that the ordinary academic curriculum is. Nevertheless there are moral lessons being taught that reflect shared values, including many of those found on reformers' lists.

Again, this kind of moral education is not sharply different from civic education. Studies of political socialization usually focus on the schools' effect on specific political attitudes.[38] Discussions of the hidden curriculum suggest that this is only a part of a broader set of moral and political lessons offered by the schools. The variety of school rules and practices, explicit or implicit, is also significant for political socialization broadly understood. Students learn their relationships to various communities both within and outside the school in a variety of ways through the hidden curriculum, including some very visible rules and programs. Specific curricula in civics may be quite worthwhile, but their influence on students' moral and political understandings may be relatively small compared to the implicit and explicit lessons of the hidden curriculum.

Still, one should be cautious about ascribing too much, for good or ill, to the hidden curriculum. It is not clear what exactly it is--"it" is many different things--and it is odd that something hidden is often talked about as if it is well understood. Many observers commenting upon it have seen quite different lessons being taught. Some suggest that the schools have little or no moral impact beyond providing another "consumption experience" for young people; the schools, like shopping malls, have an unfocused, consumer-oriented character. Others have argued that the hidden curriculum expresses organizational needs that are authoritarian and in conflict with the schools' attempt to encourage the development of independent judgment and democratic character. Still another view is that the emphasis on academic performance encourages individualism and moral insensitivity. Thus the hidden curriculum has been variously characterized as strong and weak, authoritarian and individualistic.[39]

It is not crucial to resolve these debates. Many of the competing claims about the hidden curriculum can be consistent with one another. In some ways the school is neutral, in others authoritarian, and so on. The key point here is that many of the basic rules of the organization and the other lessons taught in the hidden curriculum reflect consensual values. The above criticisms suggest that schools have departed from such consensual values in practice, for example, by creating a shopping mall atmosphere rather than encouraging students to be serious about their work. The schools may not always teach these lessons well and sometimes they may not even teach the right lessons. Still, few would deny the schools' legitimate claim on minimal standards of self-discipline, cooperation, respect for others, and tolerance. Similarly, few would criticize formal or informal activities that encourage public-regarding behavior. Where the schools have pursued these aims they have not met with much opposition because the values involved are typically widely shared in the local or larger community. There is considerable agreement about the legitimacy of the schools' promoting certain values and virtues in their everyday activities.

The question then is whether the schools are doing enough in this area to teach appropriate values and whether they can or should do it in a more systematic way. As I will discuss, the schools can and should do more to encourage other- and public-regarding attitudes and behavior. But it is not clear whether a programmatic approach in this area would be more effective. Improving upon the current, implicit pattern of moral instruction is probably more effective than a more direct preaching of some specific values. Exercising moral virtue is not simply a matter of intellectual pronouncement and assent. Practicing these virtues, having them become matters of habit and custom, is more likely to be meaningful to students. This approach is also probably safer from critical scrutiny because, beyond reflecting noncontroversial values, it is not offered in such a systematic, visible, and didactic way that it invites opposition. However, even where schools develop more explicit and visible programs aimed at encouraging students to develop regard for others, they are likely to be safe from challenge to the extent that they do not promote controversial moral stances. For example, one experimental program, the Childhood Development Project, institutionalizes students' helping one another in a variety of ways without provoking community opposition.[40] Although formal, and explicitly moral, this program has broad community support because the values it promotes are basic and widely shared. It is clearly possible that such action-oriented programs can be viable and effective.

It is also important to note that the values or virtues expressed in the hidden curriculum and, to a lesser extent, those taught in health class do not function in same way Rawls' proposed "charter" or some list of didactic values apparently would. They are not "theorems" within a coherent set of intellectual principles from which guidance can be deduced. Nor are they a catechism of values that students must recite as part of some didactic moral lesson. Rather they are more like labels that mark off situations and organizational routines, matters of habit and custom, and categories of concern. Educating students regarding these virtues is less a matter of providing principles or values and deriving consequences intellectually than of getting students to recognize instances in which certain behavior is desirable and act accordingly: moderation or abstention in physical matters, understanding the rules of the school as an organization, seeing and taking opportunities for public-regarding behavior. The validity and importance of the schools' activity here are largely taken for granted because the values and virtues being promoted are widely held to be legitimate, both in themselves and as a proper aim of public education. The overlapping consensus here does not concern theorems but agreements about these values and virtues and the appropriate role of the school in providing instruction concerning them in both word and deed.

Intellectual Virtues

Academic Values

Health class and the hidden curriculum are both instances in which the schools emphasize moral virtues. The goal is action, proper behavior. Having or at least understanding the right reason may be part of the instruction, but the emphasis is on action not thought. The failure to act in accord with these virtues is often immediately visible and problematic. Alcohol and drug abuse, disorder and violence typically require some organizational response from the school. Proper reasoning may be desirable, but proper action is by and large required.

At the same time, schools are also charged with promoting intellectual virtue. Obviously, in some narrow sense, these virtues are part of the thinking skills ideally developed through academic work. But they are also part of broader moral education as well.[41] Developing the abilities to categorize moral concerns, consider relevant evidence and argument, and understand conflict and ambiguity are also part of moral education, properly understood, and arguably core values in our society. One of the failings of values clarification was its apparent discounting of intellectual virtue in favor of the expression of preference or desire. The seeming emphasis on unregulated opinion, a substantively empty process of moral reasoning, prompted calls for a more prescriptive moral education.

The difficulty, of course, with some reformers' proposed emphasis on didactic instruction in core values is that it may encourage an uncritical understanding of these values as well. In its own way a didactic approach also deemphasizes the importance of intellectual virtue and thereby neglects other values that are also basic and consensual. This is an especially significant omission in a liberal democratic society, given that individuals will routinely confront others with different values or who interpret basic values differently. As Irving Horowitz notes, "Moral education for democracy entails the ability to learn how to absorb information about people with different sentiments, values, and interests. This naturalistic vision is the opposite of a notion that moral education is a matter of 'our' teaching 'them' right values."[42] Instead of simply telling students what is right and wrong, what is desirable is an ongoing dialogue about the different ways in which moral virtues and political commitments in our society may be interpreted and understood. Such a dialogue should consider reasons and evidence for and against conflicting, yet plausible, positions.

As in moral education generally, there is some question about whether topics related to intellectual virtue--moral judgement, critical thinking-- should be treated as separate topics or infused into the regular curriculum. Certainly academic subjects are a natural vehicle for teaching moral values and for practicing the intellectual virtues associated with moral judgment. Rather than learning a separate litany or catechism of basic values, students can find moral lessons in their courses. These lessons do not require immediate action by students but can promote thinking about moral categories and concepts. As Diane Ravitch puts it:

> The answer for demands for character development in the schools lies not in the creation of new courses but in recognizing that the school already has powerful resources. . . . Science, properly taught, teaches children the values that are embedded in scientific inquiry: honesty, open-mindedness, critical thinking, and the capacity to withhold judgement in the absence of evidence . . . literature is a potent vehicle for questions of social and personal values . . . history provides limitless prospects for the study of values and ethics. It is a living laboratory in which to consider the relations of ideas, actions, and consequences. . . . As humanistic studies, literature and history inevitably evoke questions of value and inspire questioning about the nature of the good society, the moral attributes of a good life and the qualities of character that awaken our admiration or elicit our contempt.[43]

In using the regular curriculum for moral education, immediate action is less important than the cultivation of intellectual awareness. We encourage students to become aware of the value of open-mindedness, to study the relations of ideas and consequences in history, to consider what we admire and abhor. Academic and moral aims are virtually indistinguishable here; making students thoughtful individuals and citizens is academically and morally valuable.

Unlike health class or the hidden curriculum, the goal is not to produce immediate action, but a kind of intellectual orientation, the cultivation of habits of mind that will then presumably produce a more responsible person and citizen. However, it is also important to note that these intellectual virtues are not independent of the moral virtues just discussed. Rather, they involve the ability to "see" and categorize moral issues, to give relevant reasons and persuasively argue about substantive moral concerns. Intellectual virtue does not guide moral virtue; rather the two are constantly intertwined and interacting.[44]

Critical Thinking

Recently there has some discussion concerning whether critical thinking skills can be defined and taught apart from particular subject areas. Much of this debate is an outgrowth of new speculations in cognitive psychology about the nature of intelligence. On the basis of these theories or on an ad hoc basis, a number of experimental programs and curricular packages for teaching "critical thinking" have been developed ranging from computer-assisted instruction to discussion of the "great books."[45] For present purposes, it is not necessary to sort through the debate between an "infused" or "separate" approach. Rather, what is interesting about both is that they illustrate a consensus concerning intellectual virtue(s) in a liberal society. The discussion revolves around describing the nature of these critical faculties and the most effective way to promote them, rather than whether they are valuable capacities. It is presumed that open-mindedness, sensitivity to evidence and argument, reflective judgment, and so on are intellectual virtues, core values, worthy of promotion by the schools. Again, although the schools often do not do enough to promote these virtues, such findings are typically accompanied by suggestions for reform that would promote critical dialogue. These suggestions are made confidently because they reflect shared values relating to intellectual virtue.

Finally, it is important that there should not be a sharp separation between moral and intellectual virtue. Perhaps the key link between them is, and has always been, civic education. That is, students should not only learn how to be thoughtful concerning moral matters but also understand the role of political institutions in dealing with intellectual and moral disagreement. Certainly students need to develop reasoning skills that help them deal with the intellectual task of applying and interpreting shared values. These skills, however, are not a guarantee of "right" answers, because most social problems involve differences in how shared values are to be applied rather than fundamental differences in values. Students should also recognize the possibility of reasonable disagreement, anticipate the inevitability of political conflict, and understand how political processes can resolve these problems within a broader set of social and political rules and institutions. The traditional teaching of the institutional framework and processes of government and the rights and responsibilities of citizens should presume the inevitability of disagreement and the necessity for mechanisms of conflict resolution. As one curriculum guide puts it, "Even when all sides in a dispute over the application of an accepted civic value to a particular instance are being reasonable, they may still disagree over this application. . . . Our society has procedures for making decisions in such cases."[46] More generally, students should not only understand these institutions and procedures, but how they can act as participants within them.

Culture, Consensus, and Program

To summarize, if we look closely at the various ways in which the schools engage in moral education, we find them promoting (although imperfectly) a range of virtues that reflects core values. Some curricula and practices involve moral virtues concerning right action. The most explicit of these are (Hobbesian) virtues related to one's bodily needs. These are often given a didactic treatment through health classes. Though less explicit, moral virtues communicated through the hidden curriculum derive their legitimacy from organizational needs of the school and widely shared standards of civility and cooperation in social life, including the requirements for good citizenship. Regarding intellectual virtues, the curriculum itself, properly taught, promotes these virtues and provides practice in thinking about and categorizing moral concerns. Programs in critical thinking may serve the same purpose(s).

Taken together, these virtues constitute a core comparable to Mann's "creed . . . accepted by all." They reflect moral and political aims for the schools that serve all students more or less equally. Moreover, they provide the context that makes sense of the academic aims of the school. The goals of the curriculum and the policies and practices of the school as an organization ideally aim at promoting these virtues. Admittedly, these policies and practices can be contested and changed, but in general they do reflect a variety of consensual values. The promotion of prudence and self-respect through health class, the creation of a fair and caring organization that encourages the development of good habits and attitudes, and the provision of a curriculum that produces knowledgeable, thoughtful people are all worthy aims for schools.

But even this description makes the idea of moral education in a new common school sound more programmatic or theoretical than it is. This "creed" is not a set of fixed and organized principles but a "culture" or "ethos," a set of beliefs, attitudes, and dispositions that is institutionalized in policies and practices. As Gerald Grant puts it, "A school with a strong positive ethos is one that affirms the ideals and imparts the intellectual and moral virtues proper to the functioning of an educational community in a democracy." It "represents the enduring values or character of the schools community: the spirit that actuates not just manners, but moral and intellectual attitudes, practices, and ideals."[47] Or in Gilligan's terms at the beginning of this chapter the aims of moral education should be seen as more "contextual and narrative rather than formal and abstract." The schools' "narrative" should involve and encourage "the activity of care" and the "understanding of responsibility and relationships" embedded in the activity of schooling.

One way to see the difference between this notion of moral education and a more programmatic perspective is by looking at the problems associated with Lawrence Kohlberg's developmental approach to moral education. Kohlberg offers a programmatic means for charting moral development through three levels, each of which includes two stages. The earliest, "preconventional" stages are characterized by compliance based on authority and self-interest, while the middle, "conventional" level involves judgments in response to the opinions and expectations of others or the rules or customs of some larger reference group. At these levels, moral standards typically come from some external source. At the highest, "postconventional" level, moral reasoning is based on internalized, self-chosen, universal principles of reciprocity, justice, and equality. As Gutmann puts it, "Moral autonomy means doing what is right and good *because* it is right and good and not because teachers or any other authorities demand it." Not surprisingly, Kohlberg invokes Rawls' principles as a model of the "highest" form of reasoning.[48]

Leaving aside the question of whether there is a sound empirical basis for Kohlberg's claims, there is considerable room to criticize them as giving undue moral priority to certain kinds of reasoning or principles. One of the most telling critiques of this approach is Gilligan's criticism of its "male" bias. Kohlberg's hierarchy places impersonal, formal, and legalistic analyses of moral positions above a more "female" orientation toward cooperative and personalized solutions of moral dilemmas. It places the "morality of principles" or an "ethic of justice" above "the morality of associations" or an "ethic of caring."[49] Gilligan's criticism may be recast in terms of a variety of moral and intellectual virtues that must be situated in an institutional setting such as schools. The "different voice" that she notes does not seek the resolution of moral conflicts through philosophical appeals to theoretically structured principles. It takes seriously more local and contextual considerations, as well as the importance of interaction in resolving conflict. Similarly, Gilligan's position allows the possibility of plurality of primary moral claims such as those rooted in a "morality of associations." It is thus doubtful that Kohlberg's highest stage of moral reasoning reflects consensual positions, either about the structure or substance of moral reasoning. Or it can do so only by overriding other moral commitments that have claims to legitimacy, such as those raised by Gilligan.[50] The expectation that moral reasoning must, like a good theory, be based on a few hierarchically ordered principles may not be an attainable or appropriate aspiration, and particularly not one for guiding a program in moral education.

Improving moral education in the schools, then, may be less a matter of introducing a catechism of core values or a theoretically guided program such as Kohlberg's than of self-consciously doing better what is already being done--or at least what is (rhetorically) agreed ought to be done. Schools should build on the varied points of this broad consensus. First, they must promote students' physical well-being and provide a safe and orderly environment for learning with reasonable rules fairly enforced. Ordinary procedures and classroom practices should be used to encourage cooperative and other-regarding behavior. Much of the hidden curriculum needs to be scrutinized to avoid sending many of the wrong messages noted by critics. The academic curriculum can present more of an intellectual challenge generally, and on moral issues in particular. Finally, the schools can develop more relationships with the community and encourage civic involvement through service requirements or curricula that address local problems.

Again, many schools do too little, if anything, to promote these virtues. Disorganization, discipline problems, the teaching of subjects in a rote manner rather than to promote critical understanding are all familiar criticisms of the schools. At the same time, there are also many schools in which the range of moral and intellectual virtue is encouraged. Their success in actually promoting these several strands of virtue is less important than the fact--as indicated by the ongoing criticisms of the schools--that few would disagree that these are virtues and values the schools should promote. Imperfectly realized though they may be, these values are arguably a more complete and practical representation of an overlapping consensus. Insofar as the schools provide a practical means for promoting agreement on widely shared values, the core values they embody and the means for promoting them are richer, more complex, and more varied than those provided by some more didactic or theoretical program. This consensus reflects a common culture, with all its complexities and tensions, rather than a theoretical or programmatic approach to moral education.

It might be wondered whether this list of virtues is merely rhetorical or symbolic. On the contrary, the point is that any or all of these tasks can, and are, being pursued in concrete ways in good schools on a day-to-day basis. Doing more by way of moral education simply means being more self-conscious about, and active in pursuing, the opportunities for moral education within the current institutional setting. That is not to say that such pursuits might not take a more programmatic form. For example, projects like the Child Development Project revise the hidden curriculum by creating more cooperative classroom relationships without generating problems or opposition. Similarly, there has been increased interest in service requirements, and several states now require some form of community service as a graduation requirement. Much of the thrust of the pedagogical approach of the Coalition of Essential Schools and similar efforts at restructuring forge links with the community as a means of encouraging thoughtful involvement in practical issues, thereby linking moral and intellectual virtue. Whatever the strengths and weaknesses of these programs, the point here is that they are not and cannot be separated in any way from the everyday operation of the schools. Although these projects and programs do not have the sweeping quality of some reformers' pronouncements about moral education, they are probably a more practical means of translating the elements of rhetorical consensus into reality. This is probably a better strategy, one more in keeping with consensual principles, than a more theoretical approach. Rather than listing values as if they were intellectual principles to guide action, these projects act upon shared values in an institutional setting.

Finally, it might be objected that thinking in this way about the moral aims of a new common school does not directly address the many academic and curricular disputes such as the debate about multiculturalism. Certainly, it does not solve such problems since they are manifestations of deeper problems in liberal democratic ideology. But it does put such arguments in a wider context by suggesting that curricular issues and issues of schooling generally be evaluated in terms of some common moral purposes, the promotion of virtues discussed above. Though such conflicts about curricular matters are inevitable, they can be more readily evaluated by asking how proposed programs promote the kind of moral and intellectual virtues we wish to foster in all students. For example, the traditional one-dimensional history of the United States is unlikely to encourage the development of tolerant attitudes toward others, let alone intellectual civic skills of evaluating institutions and policies. But then neither will a particularistic account that gives an equally one-sided view from the perspective of one or another historically oppressed group. Rather, schools should encourage the genuine self- and mutual respect that comes from recognizing diversity within a broad moral consensus concerning tolerance, cooperation, and open and truthful intellectual inquiry--the common ground in our otherwise pluralistic society. It is this broader moral mission that makes sense of otherwise disembodied claims for academic excellence or cultural representation. Ultimately, public education cannot and should not attempt to separate its academic purposes from its moral ones.

Other Difficulties, Other Themes

The previous discussion of problems and prospects of the common school theme assumes that the aims of the school are within reach of, and apply more or less equally to, all students. The issues raised above all occur within the general understanding of a modernized version of the common school. For example, the core problem would confront any variation on the common school theme independent of other goals the schools might pursue.

Of course, other goals pose different kinds of challenges, including challenges to the ideal of commonality itself. In the broadest terms, it might be objected that, beyond the most basic skills, it is not clear why there should be a "one size fits all" curriculum or program. Even if we allow the notion that a common school will accommodate a broad range of subjects and viewpoints, it still might be wondered whether there is one curriculum or approach that can possibly be appropriate for the various individual backgrounds, talents, and aspirations. Students have widely varying abilities and interests that may not necessarily be well met by a common curricular approach. Can there truly be a common curriculum that suits students from rural and urban areas, different family backgrounds, cultures, and religions? Is not the very existence of the core problem a signal that commonality may not always be desirable in a diverse society? In general, then, this objection raises the notion that somehow educational policies and practices should be more cognizant of individuals' different characteristics.

A more specific form of this objection points to the economic implications of schooling and another major theme in public education. In emphasizing a common curriculum, it might be argued, the schools will probably give less attention to particular individual skills and needs at either end of the spectrum. An individual student who is talented in, say, math may not find room to develop his or her gifts, even with the room allowed for some electives. The student who is not academically inclined might find less value in struggling with academic subjects that seem irrelevant to his or her plans. What may be relevant from the standpoint of general education may not be quite the same as what is relevant to an individual student and his or her career aspirations. More generally, any individual student's desire to find personal instrumental value in public education is less easily accommodated under any proposed common school than under current practices.

This in turn raises the issue of whether the general education called for in these proposals provides either adequate training for students to enter the job market or sufficient economic opportunity for the disadvantaged.

In terms of collective welfare, general education might bring students across a threshold of minimal or functional literacy, but it might be wondered whether this is sufficient in a more technically complex society. A program of general education that is less conscious of preparing students for the world of work, it might be argued, can neither provide for the nation's economic needs nor provide individual students with the opportunity and skills to advance economically. It is precisely this type of problem that has, historically and in the recent literature, led to calls for educational reforms more specifically geared to individual achievement and economic productivity. These types of claims are part of the "human capital" theme, to which we now turn.

Notes

1. Blest be the tie that binds/Our hearts in Christian love;/The fellowship of kindred minds/Is like to that above .../We share each other's woes,/Each other's burdens bear,/And often for each other flows/The sympathizing tear./John Fawcett, 1782.

Fawcett's hymn celebrates the tie that binds an ideal Christian community. Whatever differences there might be among its members, they share a common faith, the "fellowship of kindred minds," and a concern and love for one another ("share each other's woes, each other's burdens bear"). The virtues of Christian faith and charity define and guide the community. They are simple, yet powerful, values that override other differences between or among individuals. The separate identities of individuals are less important than their shared faith and love as Christians.

Ideals expressed in song often bear little relation to reality. The rise of liberalism as an ideology is explainable in part by the fact that Christian communities failed to find or maintain any such tie. The resulting religious wars and persecution suggested that if there were to be ties at all, they had to admit a fair measure of pluralism. The problem for liberal democracies, and public schools within them, is to find some ties consistent with this pluralism.

2. Even in the most radical proposals for school choice there is provision for the setting of standards that would apply to all schools. This issue will be discussed in Chapter 5.

3. See Carl Kaestle, *Pillars of the Republic: Common Schools and American Society, 1780-1860*. New York: Hill and Wang, 1983.

4. Michael Katz, *The Irony of Early School Reform*. Cambridge: Harvard University Press, 1968.

5. R. Freeman Butts, *Public Education in the United States: From Revolution to Reform*. New York: Holt, Rinehart, and Winston, 1978, p. 75.

6. On the inequalities generated by tracking, see Jeannie Oakes.*Keeping Track: How Schools Structure Inequality*. New Haven: Yale University Press, 1985.

7. Robert Hampel, *The Last Little Citadel*. Boston: Houghton Mifflin, 1986.

8. George Counts, *Dare the Schools Build a New Social Order?* New York: Arno Press, 1989 (reprint of the 1932 edition); for a more recent example, see Henry Giroux and Peter McLaren, eds., *Critical Pedagogy, the State, and Cultural Struggle.* Albany: SUNY Press, 1989.

9. Hampel, *The Last Little Citadel.*; on the notion of "treaties," see Arthur Powell, Eleanor Farrar, and David Cohen, *The Shopping Mall High School.* Boston: Houghton Mifflin, 1985, Ch. 2.

10. These two questions will be raised with regard to the other two themes discussed in Chapters 4 and 5.

11. Some argue that there is a clear distinction between civic and moral education. For one version of this argument, see Jack Nelson, "The Uncomfortable Relationship Between Moral Education and Citizenship Instruction," in Richard Wilson and Gordon Schochet, eds., *Moral Development and Politics.* New York: Praeger, 1980, pp. 256-285. The suggestion here is that any such distinction is artificial, based on a narrow view of what moral education entails.

12. National Commission on Excellence in Education, *A Nation at Risk.* Washington, D.C.: U.S. Department of Education, 1983, p. 24.

13. Some examples include Ernest Boyer, *High School: A Report on Secondary Education in America.* New York: Harper and Row, 1983; Theodore Sizer, *Horace's Compromise: The Dilemma of the American High School.* Boston: Houghton Mifflin, 1984; E. D. Hirsch, *Cultural Literacy.* Boston: Houghton Mifflin, 1987; William Bennett, *James Madison High.* Washington, D.C.: Department of Education, 1988; Theodore Sizer, *Horace's School.* Boston: Houghton Mifflin, 1992.

14. Boyer, *High School,* p. 126.

15. See George Madaus, "The Effects of Important Tests on Students: Implications for a National Examination System," *Phi Delta Kappan.* 73 (November 1991), pp. 232-239. There are several other articles in the same issue that discuss the pros and cons of national testing.

16. Some reformers implied that it was also a misguided egalitarianism that contributed to this decline. However, it is important to distinguish the legitimate aspirations of an effective, equal common school and the moral and curricular relativism that has negative effects on education in any form.

17. Powell, Farrar, and Cohen, *The Shopping Mall High School,* Ch. 1.

18. Thomas Toch, *In the Name of Excellence.* New York: Oxford University Press, 1991, p. 4.

19. Sizer, *Horace's Compromise,* pp. 84-98.

20. Hirsch, *Cultural Literacy,* especially Ch. 1.

21. Bennett, *James Madison High;* Mortimer Adler, *The Paideia Proposal.* New York: Macmillan, 1982.

22. Sizer, *Horace's School,* p. 232.

23. It is important to note that the drive for national, presumably standardized, tests may not be consistent with excellence as understood by proponents of a new common school, such as the Coalition of Essential Schools. On this "paradox of standardized testing," see Toch, *In the Name of Excellence,* Ch. 6.

24. Task Force on Minorities, Equity, and Excellence, *A Curriculum of Inclusion.* Albany: New York State Education Department, 1989.

25. See Diane Ravitch, "Multiculturalism," *The American Scholar.* 3 (Summer 1990), pp. 337-354.

26. "A Glaring Omission in History Texts,"*Christian Science Monitor.* January 23, 1989, p. 18; "Schools Tackle Lessons on Religion,"*Christian Science Monitor.* September 23, 1991.

27. Ravitch, "Multiculturalism," p. 340.

28. William Bennett, "Moral Literacy and the Formation of Character," address to the Manhattan Institute, New York, October 30, 1986; see also William Honig, *Last Chance for Our Children.* Reading, Mass.: Addison Wesley, 1985, Ch. 5.

29. On values clarification, see Louis Raths, Louis, Merrill Harmin, and Sidney Simon,*Values and Teaching: Working With Values in the Classroom.* Columbus, Ohio: Merrill, 1966. Second edition, 1978; see also Jonathan Friendly, "Ethics Classes Avoid Teaching Right and Wrong," *New York Times.* December 2, 1985.

30. Bennett, "Moral Literacy and the Formation of Character," p. 2.

31. Mario Cuomo, remarks at the Newsday Education Symposium, SUNY College at Old Westbury, March 4, 1987, p. 6.

32. Gerald Grant, "The Education of Character and the Character of Education," *American Education.* 18 (1982), p. 41.

33. Maryland is one of the states where several systems have adopted lists of values to be taught. For example, see Mary Ellen Saterlie, "A Community-Based Values Program," *Educational Leadership.* 45 (May 1988), pp. 44-47, for Baltimore County; also, "School Board Approves 18 'Values' to be Taught in Howard County," *Baltimore Morning Sun.* November 21, 1990, p. 5B.

34. See Kerry Redican, Larry Olsen, and Charles Baffi, *Organization of School Health Programs.* New York: Macmillan, 1986, especially Chs. 14, 15; John Seffrin and Mohammed Torabi, *Education in Healthy Lifestyles: Curriculum Implications.* Bloomington, Indiana: Phi Delta Kappa, 1984.

35. Quest International, *Skills for Adolescence.* Gainesville, Ohio: Lions Quest, 1988. This approach may also be seen as "Hobbesian" in its dependence upon introspection.

36. But instruction in this "curriculum" is not primarily academic or formal, even as it might be expressed in explicit rules and expectations. Rather, it requires numerous judgments in context as to how to best enlist the cooperation, support, and endorsement of students for the norms and values of the school. As Sizer puts it, "The expression of decency and efforts to persuade younger folk to adopt the school's values involve judgment and are not matters that can be turned into readily disseminated 'rules.' The sought for decency will emerge only when students as well as faculty want it, when the local definition is 'theirs' and they have 'ownership' of it." *Horace's Compromise*, p. 125.

37. Philip Jackson, "The School as Moral Instructor," in Fred Schulz, ed., *Education 90/91, Annual Editions.* Guilford: Dushkin, 1990, pp. 97-98.

38. See R. D. Hess and J. V. Torney, *The Development of Political Attitudes in Childhood.* Chicago: Aldine, 1967; M. K. Jennings and Richard Niemi, *The Political Character of Adolescence.* Princeton: Princeton University Press, 1974. For more recent findings, see Orit Ichilov, ed., *Political Socialization, Citizenship Education, and Democracy.* New York: Teachers College Press, 1990.

39. See respectively, Powell, Farrar, and Cohen, *The Shopping Mall High School;* Richard Merelman, "Democratic Politics and the Culture of American Education," *American Political Science Review.* 74 (1980), pp. 319-337; John Goodlad, *A Place Called School.* New York: McGraw Hill, 1983, "It is difficult to be sanguine about the moral

and ethical learnings accompanying many of the experiences of schooling. My perception is that the emphasis on individual performance and achievement would be more conducive to cheating than to the development of moral integrity. I have difficulty seeing how much of what goes on in classrooms would contribute to understanding and appreciating the contributions of others." pp. 241-242. For a general review of theories of the hidden curriculum see Kathleen Lynch, *The Hidden Curriculum*, New York: Falmer Press, 1989, Ch. 1.

40. For a description of the project, see Eric Schaps, "A Program that Combines Character Development and Academic Achievement," *Educational Leadership.* 43 (January 1986), pp. 32-35.

41. The term "intellectual virtue" here is concerned primarily with *phronesis*, or practical wisdom, rather than with the more abstract pursuit of knowledge for its own sake (dianoetic virtue). Of course, both are proper aims of the school especially, as is mostly the case, when they overlap with one another.

42. Irving Horowitz, "Moral Development, Authoritarian Distemper, and the Democratic Persuasion," in Wilson and Schochet, eds., *Moral Development and Politics*, pp. 16-17.

43. Diane Ravitch, *The Schools We Deserve.* New York: Basic Books, 1984, pp. 22-23.

44. For example, Robert Liebert, in a critique of Lawrence Kohlberg's approach, notes a gap between cognition and behavior. He cites an experiment in which theological students on the way to give a lecture on the Good Samaritan were confronted by someone in distress. "Most of the seminary students did *not* help the victim in this situation, and neither the topic on which they were to lecture nor the value they placed on religious commitment was associated with helping." (The same gap might occur in the didactic program envisioned by Bennett and others.) "What Develops in Moral Development?" in W. Kurtines and J. Gewirtz, eds., *Morality, Moral Behavior, and Moral Development.* New York: Wiley, 1984, pp. 177-192, p. 187. More generally, Betty Sichel discusses some of the criticisms of Kohlberg's theory as wrongly separating form and content, judgment and behavior. She also provides a useful list of "suitable intellectual virtues" that may help bridge these gaps: "The ability to discern what the problem is; analytical abilities to discern what moral excellences are involved with the various dimensions of the problem and with alternative solutions of the problem . . . data collecting skills to choose which information and data relate to the problem and . . . to the agent's moral excellences; imagination and creativity to envisage the problem in a different way . . . to foresee the success or failure of various solutions . . . and how these solutions might affect the agent's moral excellences; reasoning ability to discern and evaluate . . . presently held moral excellences and then possible implications for moral judgement and action."*Moral Education: Character, Community, and Ideals.* Philadelphia: Temple University Press, 1988, pp. 260-261.

45. On the question of "generic" thinking skills, see Lauren Resnick, *Education and Learning to Think.* Washington, D.C.: National Academy Press, 1987; on multiple intelligences, see Howard Gardner, *Frames of Mind.* New York: Basic Books, 1983; Robert Sternberg, *Intelligence Applied.* New York: Harcourt Brace, 1986; for a curricular approach, see Joan Baron and Robert Sternberg, *Teaching Thinking Skills: Theory and Practice.* New York: Freeman, 1987.

46. New York State Education Department, "Education for Values," item for discussion with the Board of Regents, April 9, 1987, p. 2.

47. Gerald Grant, *The World We Created at Hamilton High*. Cambridge: Harvard University Press, 1988, p. 188.

48. Lawrence Kohlberg, *The Philosophy of Moral Development*. San Francisco: Harper and Row, 1981; for a succinct summary, see Amy Gutmann, *Democratic Education*. Princeton: Princeton University Press, 1988, pp. 48-64.

49. Carol Gilligan, *In A Different Voice: Psychological Theory and Women's Development*. Cambridge: Harvard University Press, 1983. On the use of narratives in moral education, see Paul Vitz, "The Use of Stories in Moral Development: New Psychological Reasons for an Old Method," *American Psychologist*. 45 (June 1990), pp. 709-720.

50. Evan Simpson makes the point against a "rationalist" approach such as Kohlberg's in a more general way: "If gentleness, humility, generosity, and kindness are considered moral qualities, then the rationalist [Kohlberg's] account faces a more severe complaint than narrow and arbitrary classification [of moral terms]. These virtues are not only approved without reference to principles but are also foreign to a principled approach . . . virtue cannot be generally represented as conscientious adherence to principle. The norms typical of many virtues require the use of judgment in order for us to know how to respond appropriately to the particularity of a situation not adequately governed by rules." *Good Lives and Moral Education*. New York: Peter Lang, 1989, p. 10.

4

Schools, Scapegoats, and Skills: Educational Reform and the Economy

The difference of natural talents in different men is, in reality, much less than we are aware of; and the very different genius which appears to distinguish men of different professions, when grown up to maturity, is not upon so many occasions so much the cause, as the effect, of the division of labor. The difference between the most dissimilar characters, between a philosopher and a common street porter, for example, seems to arise not so much from nature, as from habit, custom, and education. When they came into the world, and for the first six or eight years of their existence, they were, perhaps, very much alike, and neither their parents nor playfellows could perceive any remarkable difference. About that age, or soon after, they come to be employed in very different occupations. The difference of talents comes then to be taken notice of, and widens by degrees, till at last the vanity of the philosopher is willing to acknowledge scarce any resemblance.

--Adam Smith

To begin, there can be no denying that the skills of literacy and critical thinking that are properly associated with effective school programs are essential to a modern economy and that the schools ought to be held accountable for nurturing those skills in all children. The continued advance of those skills through the entire population will undoubtedly aid the development of the American economy. Nevertheless, American economic competitiveness with Japan and other nations is to a considerable degree a function of monetary, trade, and industrial policy. . . . Therefore to contend that the problem of international competitiveness can be solved by educational reform defined solely as school reform, is not merely utopian and millenialist, it is at best foolish and at worst a crass effort to direct attention away from those truly responsible for doing something about competitiveness and to lay the burden instead upon the schools.

--Lawrence Cremin

The common school theme is strongly egalitarian. It embodies the moral equality of all individuals and their equal status and rights as citizens. As discussed in Chapter 3, the notion that all individuals have some claim to an equal basic education has always been an important theme in public education in the United States. In the nineteenth century the common school attempted to minimize cultural and other differences in order to establish a shared foundation for citizenship. Ultimate differences in status and attainment derived mainly from sources other than the schools, in Adam Smith's terms, from "habit" and "custom" associated with one's social class. Further differences might be created by "education," but mainly through private academies that confirmed rather than conferred status. It was not seen as the primary function of the public schools to mark the "different genius" of individuals. Larger social forces embodied in class and status, rather than "natural talents," were primarily responsible for these apparent differences.[1]

This egalitarian ethos, however, has never meant that the schools can or should ignore differences between and among individuals. Part of the respect for the individual in liberal democratic ideology has been the recognition of differences in talents and achievement. Even before the development of the common school it was recognized, rhetorically at least, that public education might have legitimate meritocratic purposes. For example, even as he advocated a system of free public schools that provided a common, basic education, Thomas Jefferson also proposed that the schools "rake out the rubbish" and select the best students for further education for leadership. Similarly, Horace Mann claimed that public education would be a mechanism for social mobility, "the great equalizer of the conditions of men, the balance wheel of the social machinery." By putting all children on an equal footing, educationally at least, the common school would provide the opportunity for children of all classes to advance socially and economically. It would give everyone the chance to obtain the knowledge and skills necessary to participate and succeed in the larger world according to their abilities and accomplishments. Then, as now, equal education would supposedly provide equal opportunity.

The problem is deciding how precisely the schools can and should embody a commitment to merit and equal opportunity. On the one hand, the schools might be seen as Mann's "equalizer," giving all children pretty much the same education regardless of their different backgrounds or even their different abilities. In terms of the metaphor of a race, the schools would create a common starting line from which individuals could then proceed to pursue their goals. The determination of the winners and losers in the race, the "raking out," would take place elsewhere in the larger economy and society. On the other hand, the Jeffersonian position makes schools part of the race itself. Differences in educational attainment (merit) translate into differences in opportunities. This tension between commonality and individualism, equality and merit is an inevitable part of liberal democratic ideology. The egalitarian ideal of treating people equally may not mean treating everyone the same. It can and perhaps even should mean providing different and perhaps unequal services (for example, remediation) to give everyone a fair chance. Similarly, it also implies recognizing differences that may lead to unequal rewards in terms of wealth, status, and power. Equal opportunity in a liberal democratic society suggests both the need for compensatory policies and the opportunity to pursue unequal outcomes.

The clearest manifestation of these tensions has been in the relationship of the schools to the economy. For example, Mann's construction of coalitions in favor of tax-supported schools depended in part on his ability to convince business groups that public education would enhance the labor force. It would guarantee basic literacy and, perhaps more important, good habits and attitudes toward work. All students would be brought to the starting line of life's race prepared for work. This economic benefit was seen as a natural extension of the cultural and political aims of the common school. However, as the high school developed in the latter part of the nineteenth century there was a shift toward the notion that schools' economic role should vary as students' abilities and interests varied. The schools would not provide the same education to all, but prepare students for different economic roles appropriate to the division of labor in an industrial society.[2] The secondary schools thus became involved, as they certainly are still, in sorting students and directing them toward different options after school. The economic race was thus moved inside the school, and meritocracy, equal opportunity, and academic performance became bound up with one another.

The shift toward differentiated curricula that occurred as secondary schools developed marks the emergence of a second major theme in public education, the "human capital" or "productivity-achievement" theme. This theme clearly has a more individualistic emphasis than the common school theme. Schools provide an arena for the development of individual capacities and assume that people will differ in their ability to achieve. By tailoring curricula to individual talents and interests, the schools can better prepare students for life after school, especially in their capacity to be productive workers. Schools become arenas for the development a more specialized human capital. The meaning of equality is thus shifted from the the more egalitarian notion of the common school theme to one more concerned with equal opportunity. The latter notion requires the schools to play a more prominent role in determining students' future economic roles. Equal opportunity understood in this fashion not only respects individual differences and talents, it also serves collective interests by developing students' productive potential.

There can be little doubt that the human capital theme has played and continues to play a major role in our understanding of the purposes of public education. Our notions of merit and equal opportunity are heavily dependent upon educational performance. The differentiated curricula and ability grouping produced in response to this understanding have been institutionalized in most public schools, especially at the secondary level. Moreover, the schools have and continue to be seen as an important factor in our economic prosperity. In the recent reform movement, when the nation was said to be "at risk" few doubted that what was primarily meant was economic risk. Few discussions of educational reform since the "at risk" report are without explicit or implicit references to the schools' role in enhancing productivity and competitiveness. Certainly the human capital theme has had its critics, including persistent advocates of the common school, critics of the "equal" opportunity promoted by different curricula and standardized testing, and those like Lawrence Cremin who doubt the schools' economic significance.[3] Nonetheless, the idea that schools have an important role in serving both individual opportunity and collective economic aims has had and still has considerable force in both educational rhetoric and school practices.

In this chapter I discuss the evolution of, and variations on, this theme and some of the current problems and controversies surrounding it. A brief history of the emergence of this theme suggests that the creation of the "comprehensive" high school involved two kinds of compromises. One was a compromise with the previous theme of the common school. The high school would sort students and offer them different, if overlapping, curricula within a common setting and with some common activities. The other, related compromise occurred between the two variations on the human capital theme, one technical and the other liberal. The schools would provide a mixed program of technical and liberal education as a way of keeping fairly open a variety of opportunities for students. As with the variations on the common school theme, there is some tension between these two variations and each has maximum and minimum versions that pose the dilemma of excess and deficit. On the one hand, the schools can, as they currently are, be charged with doing too little to serve the economy. On the other hand, in pursuing these goals more aggressively they may be charged with overstepping the bounds of state authority, especially with regard to providing equal opportunity for all individuals.

In whatever manifestation, one key problem with this theme is indicated by Cremin's comment, namely, that the economic significance of the schools is often overstated. The evidence for the schools' role as enhancer of competitiveness (macroeconomic) or productivity (microeconomic) is relatively shaky. There is a great deal we do not know about these relationships, and what we do know does not suggest that the schools can or will be the primary engine of economic revival. This in turn implies that we have yet to adequately answer the knotty conceptual and moral questions of equal opportunity and its relationship to schools and academic credentials. These problems of equal opportunity simply highlight the continuing tension between this theme and that of the common school. The suggestion here is that the human capital theme has been overstated, even on its own terms, and what is valuable within it, both in theory and practice, is probably best understood in terms of other themes.

"Head" and "Hand": The Comprehensive School

The development of public secondary schools in the latter half of the nineteenth century posed some new challenges for the ideal of common education. In simplest terms, the issue was what schools would do with students who had presumably already received a basic, primary education. The first answer offered by some educators was to do what the private secondary academies had done. They would offer some modernized version of traditional liberal education as then understood--classical languages, arithmetic and geometry, music--the stuff of trivium and quadrivium. In 1893, a report of the Committee of Ten, a group of college presidents and educational administrators, sought to codify this notion and make it more up-to-date and suitable for mass consumption. For example, the classical curriculum would be augmented by such "new" subjects as chemistry and other sciences. The particulars of this proposal are less important than the general notion that the emerging high school's focus should be academic or "liberal" and that such continued academic training was valuable to all: "training the powers of observation, memory, expression, and reasoning . . . serves to broaden and cultivate the mind . . . they counteract a narrow and provincial spirit . . . they prepare the pupil in an eminent degree for enlightened and intellectual enjoyment in after years . . . and they assist him to exercise a salutary influence upon the affairs of his country."[4] The secondary school would thus be an extension of the common school with an emphasis upon a common curriculum appropriate for citizenship. General, liberal education would do for all what had previously been reserved for the few.

Initially, the concessions to "modern" subjects were attacked as corrupting the purity of classical education. Ultimately, however, the Committee of Ten's proposals were defeated, or at least significantly modified, because they were seen as not being modern enough. Many groups, including some educational progressives, attacked the proposals as elitist and irrelevant to the concerns and futures of a majority of students not bound for colleges or professions. Different, less academic students, it was argued, needed different curricula more suited to their needs and more directly aimed at preparing them for their future roles in society. This criticism was further advanced, rightly or wrongly, by emerging pedagogical theories that emphasized the importance of student-centered instruction and the need to make subjects relevant to students. Following a perennial distinction, it was argued that the curriculum should be less "academic" and more attuned to the "real world" that students were facing.[5]

This debate over secondary education also reflected a reaction to the larger social forces of immigration and industrialization. The achievement of commonality would be more difficult (and perhaps less appropriate) in a large-scale, diverse, urbanized, and industrialized society. Immigration made the "Anglo conformity" of the common school, especially with its religious overtones, less acceptable and suggested a more secular understanding of public education. Many immigrant groups could not see the point of "liberal" secondary education and demanded something more practical. Emerging large-scale industrial enterprises provided both a model for a more efficient, central organization of education and a source of demands for more practical, specialized instruction. A broad coalition argued that "social efficiency" should be reflected in both the aims and organization of the public schools. This required greater standardization and efficiency in school organization and practices coupled with a recognition of differences among individual students.

The turning point in developing the logic of secondary education was a policy debate concerning vocational education in several states before World War I. A number of business groups proposed that secondary vocational schools be established for job training so that America would be more economically competitive, especially with Germany. This proposal took various forms, the most controversial being that public monies would be disbursed to businesses to set up and run these schools. Business was opposed in this quest by a coalition of labor groups who feared increased business power via the schools, by educators who both wanted to maintain control of the schools and believed that the segregation of some students from others was undemocratic, and by middle class progressives who had fought to insulate the schools from political patronage and were reluctant to see them turned over to another special interest. The question of vocational education focused attention on a dilemma concerning the purposes of secondary schools. On the one hand, the extension of the logic of the common school to secondary education, particularly in an academic way, seemed inappropriate for students who apparently had different abilities (and likely futures). On the other hand, the idea of differentiating and segmenting schooling, or worse parceling it out to private interests, seemed to contradict the basic egalitarianism of public education. It threatened to institutionalize class differences and compromise equal opportunity.[6]

The compromise position that emerged from this debate was that publicly controlled high schools would be comprehensive. That is, they would provide differentiated curricula that reflected students' varying abilities and needs but do so in a common setting. The high school would be a hybrid, combining several kinds of overlapping academic and vocational curricula in the same building. Evaluation of students' talents, aided by emerging, professionally guided practices of testing and counseling, would lead to curricula tailored to students' needs and appropriate for their likely futures. In its crudest form this was often expressed as distinguishing between "head" and "hand" students. The former would receive a rigorous academic curriculum with some limited vocational courses and the latter would be given the reverse. This position, consolidated in the *Cardinal Principles of Secondary Education* in 1918, reflected a distinct shift in emphasis away from the principles of the Committee of Ten. An emphasis on "health, command of fundamental processes, worthy home membership, vocation, citizenship, worthy use of leisure, and ethical character," clearly implied a more comprehensive mission. This mission involved meeting the distinctive needs of various clientele both within and beyond the school. Such an education was less directly academic in that it took a broader, more student-centered view of what could and should be offered in the schools.[7]

The development of separate, if overlapping, programs tailored to students' needs represented a different interpretation of the common elements in public secondary education. Beyond sharing a common identity in the school and its activities and the continuation of basic education through adolescence, what was now shared by all students was an equal opportunity to display one's talents. Individual opportunity for achievement not only conformed to notions of meritocratic fairness, it also served collective interests as well. Preparing students in appropriate ways would make them more productive economically. As David Tyack and Elizabeth Hansot put it, "All children, according to the theory of the administrative progressives, should be given through public education a fair chance to acquire the knowledge and skills necessary in a specialized, credential-oriented society." Advocates of a modernized common school such as Dewey dissented, pointing out that differential, competitive, and vocationally-oriented education would reinforce class differences. Nevertheless, the establishment of varying curricular expectations in public secondary schools represented a clear break with the notion of a common curriculum.[8]

One of the great ironies about the development of the human capital theme is that it has generally led schools to be more, rather than less, academic. The comprehensive school became self-contained even as it purported to offer curricula and programs that would smooth the transition to life after school. Despite the emphasis on the transition to the real world, the schools in this century and even now have been relatively insulated from society in general and the economy in particular. For example, during the Great Depression the schools were not given much of a role, even rhetorically, in dealing with a severe economic crisis. Student-centered pedagogy was typically not interpreted as engaging students in real-world problems, but in things of immediate interest to them. Similarly, as a relatively autonomous professional organization, the school simply assumed that by sorting students in accord with their talents it was doing what it needed to do to serve the economy and larger society. This also incidentally served to free the schools from the real or imagined threat of political interference. Overall, then, the emergent high school broke less with conventional academic study than some more focused economic role might imply.[9]

The rough sorting of students into head and hand students had, and to a large extent still has, some peculiar results. The top academic ability group has become a college-bound track. Students are not prepared for any specific job or even given skills that are clearly and directly applicable to specific jobs. Rather, they are prepared for more education. The schools train these students to continue to be students. At the other end of the scale, vocational education programs have usually sought to make explicit ties between schools and jobs. However, the range of occupations is rather narrow and has often been limited to occupations in which training is not expensive and technology does not rapidly shift, such as auto mechanics or cosmetology. Thus at the extremes the sorting of students by academic ability has not and does not seem to relate directly to the larger needs of the economy. Students either receive standard academic training or training for occupations that are mostly routine and "low tech." There might be doubts about the larger economic significance of either. These doubts are deepened in the latter category because such jobs seem to be both scarcer and less well-paying.

An even bigger problem with this grouping of students has always been how to deal with the majority between the extremes. The schools have never seemed certain of what students who are neither best nor worst academically should be doing. Their needs were at least in part the inspiration for the idea of "life adjustment" education that would focus on the practical skills needed to get on in the world. Although it moves away from conventional academic work, such an approach is not vocational either. Indeed, how to deal with this group remains both a bit of a mystery and an embarrassment. Even in the current reform movement field studies have typically noted the ambiguous position of the middling students who do not seem to have the clear direction of some of their counterparts "above" and "below" them. One study refers to this group as the "forgotten half."[10] An alternative increasingly available to these students is the expanding community college system. It combines both liberal postsecondary education with a wider range of vocationally relevant curricula, for example, in professional or quasi-professional occupations. Similarly, given the decline of the college-age population, admission to regular colleges, expanded to accommodate the baby-boom generation, is much easier for this group. But if admission is relatively easier, getting a degree from a four-year institution seems somewhat less so. Nearly forty percent of those who begin a four-year program do not graduate within five years, a "dropout" rate that is higher than that for public secondary schools.

Thus, although the formation of the comprehensive high school was prompted by economic concerns, its relationship to these tasks has been rather ambiguous. To be sure, school performance has economic significance for individual opportunity. There has been a steady increase in the educational credentials required for most jobs. Those with the most educational credentials have reaped significant, and recently growing, economic benefits. But the direct relationship of educational programs to collective economic performance is unclear, to say the least. For the top students schools are primarily preparatory for college entrance, and college is merely the gateway for further professional education or training. Students involved in vocational education are receiving some more direct, economically relevant training, but it is not much related to the larger issues of economic productivity and competitiveness. The great body of middling students drift in between, and the economic significance of their curriculum is vaguer still. Far from bridging the gap between the academic and real worlds, the schools seem to be ambiguously related to the outside world, both economically and in other ways.

Despite these ambiguities, the idea that the schools could serve some economic purpose has been a persistent theme in contemporary education. The current emphasis on the implications of poor educational performance for our international competitiveness has clear historical precedent. For example, in the wake of Sputnik, there was much discussion of how the schools could be mobilized to develop the economic and technological superiority necessary to win the Cold War. James Conant, perhaps the most visible spokesman for that period's drive for reform, was primarily concerned with ensuring that the top students were given rigorous academic challenges, especially in math and science. The elite students needed to be separated and given the rigorous curriculum that would permit them to meet the political, economic, and technological challenge posed by Communist countries. Improving academic performance, particularly among these students, would presumably gain the United States supremacy in the global struggle.[11]

This global challenge required the schools, of course, to set more and higher academic standards as well as to try new ways of instruction. For example, the "new math" would teach students how to think like mathematicians. However, perhaps the greater and more lasting effect of that period's reform efforts was on the postsecondary system. The federal government undertook the support of students, for example, through loans under the National Defense Education Act, and institutions, through agencies like the National Science Foundation. The government also engaged in more direct contracting to support higher education and targeted technical and military projects. These programs probably did more for generating scientific talent than the "new math."

As the Cold War has disappeared, what Joel Spring calls the "SONY War" has intensified and been a major theme of the current reform movement. The schools are now to develop human capital to respond to an economic rather than military threat. For example, the "at risk," report suggested that our international economic competitors' successes signified "a redistribution of trained intelligence throughout the globe." Our students were not developing the skills necessary to live and work in a technologically changing, economically competitive world. Similarly, the very first section of *America 2000* is titled "America's Skills and Knowledge Gap." It expresses concern about the educational achievements of our "international competitors and trading partners" as well as claiming that "our employers cannot hire enough qualified workers."[12] There have been a number of studies prepared by government agencies or supported by them that variously explore the "workforce crisis," discuss the desirability of "investing in people," and pose the stark choice of "high skills or low wages." One Labor Department SCANS report puts the matter rather bluntly in its title, "What Work Requires of Schools." It is either stated or implied that schools play an important role in improving our economic competitiveness--and have not been doing their job well.[13]

The discussion of the relationship of educational reform to economic competitiveness has undergone an interesting shift as the reform movement has proceeded. This shift further underscores an ambiguity between direct and indirect economic significance of education, between technical training and general education. Initially there was considerable discussion of the skills needed for a technologically sophisticated workplace and specifically training in math, science, and computers. At the same time there was also the recognition that not all students would be able to develop these high-tech skills and that competitiveness might depend as much or more on "ordinary" workers. Therefore we need to attend to the development of basic skills across the board. As the "at risk" report put it, "we are trying to raise the floor and the ceiling." More recently, however, a new emphasis on critical thinking or "learning to learn" has emerged in several reports. Instead of emphasizing specific technical skills, these reports emphasize some general intellectual skills that must be developed by all students (or as many as possible). In a world economy that is based more on information-based services and less on high-volume, capital intensive production, the nations that succeed will have well-educated workers at all levels. The struggle in the international economic arena requires the development of critical thinking skills for students across the board.

The importance of education in improving economic performance is thus an article of faith in the current reform movement and a central proposition of the human capital theme. However, as will be seen, there are some serious questions about the schools' role in enhancing economic competitiveness and whether the current reform movement is likely to help them do so. Specifically, there are difficulties in assuming strong links between schools and the economy, particularly given our limited understanding of the relationship between education and job skills. Indeed, one need not look much farther than the several reports that were done or supported by the government to discover some of these difficulties. Moreover, and perhaps more important, the current public discussion of the relationship of education and the economy has, wrongly, tended to ignore or treat as settled significant pedagogical and institutional questions about skills and critical thinking and about the schools' relationship(s) to other institutions. Finally, these problems with the human capital perspective are not merely empirical issues. Rather they suggest some deep conceptual and normative problems concerning the idea of equal opportunity and the role of educational credentials in relation to it. There is a continuing tension between this theme and the egalitarian thrust of the common school theme. It raises basic policy issues about what aims, including economic aims, the public schools can and should pursue and how to best pursue them. Before exploring these problems it is useful to review the variations on the human capital theme, especially as they pose the dilemma of excess and deficit.

Variations on a Theme: Training and Thinking

The original debate about the economic functions of secondary education revolved around the location and control of technical training. Although those interests that wanted to create separate apprenticeships and vocational schools lost the political conflict concerning institutional control, they did in a sense win the debate about the value, or lack thereof, of various kinds of education. Most simply, they established that advanced academic or liberal education was really not appropriate to all students. The schools could and should develop some more direct, economically relevant education for those students that were not likely to profit by further academic pursuits. (This, again, squared with supposedly "progressive" pedagogical notions about fitting education to needs and abilities of the

	Technical	Liberal-General
Maximum	Apprenticeships, direct training Vocational education	Critical thinking Academic education
Minimum	Shifting, "basic" skills	Basic literacy, numeracy

FIGURE 4.1 Variations on the Human Capital Theme

child.) Certainly, academic education was still valuable for those who would go on to further education or who would be otherwise engaged in "head" work, but its value was seen as indirect. This also left unanswered the question, one that still troubles American education, of what to do with the many students who fell in between.

Implicit in this debate about vocational education and the development of the human capital theme, then, is a distinction between two types of education for the economy (see Figure 4.1). The first and most obvious variation on the theme is that the schools serve as trainers preparing students for the workplace. Minimally this means that the schools provide basic literacy and numeracy. There may be shifts in what are seen as basic skills that might also include specific, job-relevant skills such as keyboarding. This definition also involves basic habits and attitudes toward work such as punctuality, responsibility, and so forth.[14] One of Mann's arguments for the original common school was that schools would produce willing workers with basic skills for developing industries. The more ambitious version of this theme would be that the schools might train students for specific occupations or develop skills that are clearly transferable or applicable in actual job settings. For example, the schools might provide training in computer programming or they might, as in Germany, mandate certain apprenticeships or other forms of job training as part of public education.[15] There is obviously a continuum of possibilities for training between the minimum and maximum.

The great difficulty with the notion of schools as trainers, at least as they are configured in the United States, is that schools are generally not well-equipped to do training. They can hardly cover the range of possible job categories, and they are very unlikely to be able to keep abreast of changing job requirements and technologies. For example, despite the persistent talk about the importance of computers in the workplace, it is doubtful that the schools could provide much beyond the elementary training in the job-related use of computers because the technologies involved change so rapidly and dramatically. In general, the training mission of vocational education has never gone beyond relatively stable, often low-level technologies requiring little capital investment. Without a dramatic restructuring or much more systematic institutional ties to employers and apprenticeships it is extremely doubtful that schools could take on a more robust training mission.

Leaving aside the practical question of how readily the schools could take on direct training missions, there is also the normative issue of whether doing so would compromise equal opportunity. Clearly, the current system of differentiating students raises questions about whether all students are being given a fair chance at higher-paying, higher-status occupations. A more aggressive program of using the schools for training for the economy would probably make these differentiations sharper. The German system makes early judgments as to who will go on for further academic education and who will be offered a more limited academic program with specific occupational training. That system, whatever its virtues for enhancing economic productivity, is not likely to be consistent with American notions of equal opportunity. The American system is looser. It allows more possibilities for obtaining educational credentials for a range of occupational options. It is generally felt that access to such credentials should be open to as many individuals as possible for as long as possible.

The continual expansion of the postsecondary system, including the growth of community colleges, indicates an expansive notion of equal opportunity. The educational "race" continues for more years here than in many other countries. If the state attempted to play a more direct, aggressive role in determining these economic outcomes through the schools it would likely be charged with overstepping its authority and compromising equal opportunity. This might be especially true if playing this role led to the reinforcement of current social inequalities, for example, if the poor and minority students were disproportionately singled out, even more than they currently are, for nonacademic training.

The compromise that produced the comprehensive high school limited the schools' role as job trainer. The schools would primarily serve the economy more indirectly through general or liberal education rather than job-relevant training. They would provide academic skills that would prepare students for the world of work, but these skills would be more or less generic. Again, the minimal variation on this theme is the provision of basic literacy, numeracy, and appropriate habits and attitudes. The more ambitious version of this theme would have the schools provide more advanced intellectual skills. Students would need these as they advance to further education or to jobs that would call upon these broader academic skills. For example, the writing and critical thinking skills that one might find in the study of literature or history would transfer to the practice of law or the profession of teaching. Other white-collar jobs would likewise require academic skills related to mathematics or writing, as well as the ability simply to think clearly. This more indirect service to the economy primarily involves sorting rather than training. It puts students into broad categories that signal educational institutions and employers what kinds of abilities students possess.

As in the discussion of the common school theme, we can see that in this theme there are tensions between its variations and between the maximum and minimum versions of each. Direct, more or less specific job or technical training is different from academic instruction, as indicated by the difference between Germany's dual system and our own. Moreover, within each variation we again see a version of the dilemma of excess and deficit. The more ambitious the schools become about training and/or sorting, the more they risk the charge of doing too much to determine students' economic futures, thus compromising equal opportunity. Academic sorting continues to be both widely practiced and widely criticized.[16] Nonetheless, the schools do not engage in the sharper winnowing found in other systems. As in the common school theme, it is politically safer to pursue something less than the maximum aim(s) of this theme. Pursuing the more minimal versions can lead to the criticism, as in the current reform movement, that the schools are doing too little to promote economic growth. Finally, although these are tensions within the human capital theme itself, there are similar conflicts between this theme and that of the common school. The comprehensive high school, then and now, does not provide the same education for all students through secondary school.

The rhetoric of the reform movement, especially recently, suggests that these various tensions can be resolved by an emphasis on "higher order" or "critical thinking" skills. All students, it is argued, need to develop these skills to be able to function in the workplace of the future. This workplace will have flatter hierarchies and depend upon workers to be flexible, adaptable, and able to exercise discretion in doing their jobs. On this view, the distinction between education for critical thinking and for job training evaporates because general education *is* training for the new economic order. Although there has not been a direct assault on vocational education, this new approach implicitly suggests that job-specific training is at best an artifact of old economic thinking. As Robert Reich puts it, "The old system of education mirrored the old system of production: Most people spent eight to twelve years of their childhood training for cog jobs, while a few were propelled toward top policy and planning positions. The new system must prepare far more people to take responsibility for their continuing education and to collaborate with one another so that their combined skills and insights add up to something more than the sum of their individual contributions."[17] Students must be able to think on the job, it is argued, if we wish to remain competitive in this new economic world. There simply will not be good-paying jobs that require only a willingness to work and a strong back. Since all students need these skills, there is apparently less tension, at least potentially, between common and differentiated education.

On whatever variation, the notion that schools have an important economic role to play has been a standard feature of American educational rhetoric in the twentieth century and quite prominent in the current reform movement. These variations suggest that the schools can provide either direct training or a more indirect service to the economy through general education. However, these arguments depend upon some empirical claims about education and the economy and, more specifically, how education can best serve the economy. A closer examination of these claims raises some doubts about how readily schools can perform the tasks suggested by this theme. There is much we do not know about the relationship between education and the economy, between schools and skills, and what we do know is not strongly supportive of the claims implicit in the human capital theme. This in turn suggests that some of the compromises forged between these variations may not be serving students or the economy well. It also raises persistent, difficult questions about equal opportunity and educational credentials.

Education and Macroeconomics: Levers, Supply, and Demand

At some level the proposition that educational achievements will have economic impacts is indisputable, just as it is indisputable that our educational achievements are not what they should be. Still, the rhetoric about education and the economy often conflates or compresses together a variety of claims concerning the variations described in Figure 4.1. On the one hand, this makes analysis more difficult, since it is not clear what exactly is being claimed and what it implies for policy. On the other hand, consensus of a sort is made easier. Both liberals and conservatives can readily agree to some general, rhetorical proposition(s) relating education and the economy.[18] Nevertheless, we need to disentangle the various claims about education and the economy, asking whether and in what ways this vague consensus and the policy implications drawn from it are justified.

Perhaps the simplest way to begin to sort these claims is by distinguishing "macro" from "micro" arguments in the two variations on this theme. Much of the rhetoric linking education and the economy treats educational performance as a kind of macroeconomic lever analogous to taxes, spending, or the money supply. Raising educational performance, whether with regard to technical skills or general academic achievement, will enhance competitiveness. This claim, taken historically, may be taken to imply that schools were a factor in America's relative economic decline in recent years. This impression may be reinforced by the fact that the beginnings of both our economic and educational problems are often traced back to the early 1970s.[19] Taken prospectively, our economic problems will, it is argued, be exacerbated by the schools' poor performance. Any economic revival must include significant educational improvement.

This argument is most intuitively plausible with regard to the most basic skills. Basic literacy and numeracy are obviously essential to any industrial (or postindustrial) economy. Over the long run if a significant percentage of our workforce has basic skills comparable to those found in less economically developed societies, we will have difficulty competing in what William Baumol calls the "club" of advanced industrial societies. A well-developed secondary and postsecondary system of education is characteristic of this club. It is believed to help advantaged nations develop or absorb technology and discover other ways of increasing productivity.[20] At some gross level, then, it seems to be a truism that educational levels in a society are correlated with, and contribute to, economic growth and productivity.

Nevertheless, it is difficult, save in the most general terms, to place blame or draw specific policy inferences from these gross correlations. Even those who do aggregate analyses caution against such inferences. There are numerous methodological problems such as the common problem of correlation versus causation, especially in comparative studies. If more prosperous nations have greater educational attainment it may be because they have more to spend on education, rather than that they have more to spend because they are more educated (and therefore more productive). Perhaps the most that can be said here is that there is some evidence that levels of education and productivity and growth are positively related, again in the aggregate, and that lagging educational attainment over the long run could have effects on our economy. This is quite different from saying that recent declines in educational achievement have significantly contributed to the relative decline in America's economic competitiveness. Similarly, it is not clear, current rhetoric to the contrary, that educational reform is the key factor in an economic revival, save in some very long run.

There are both intuitive and empirical objections to the idea that educational performance was a significant factor in our recent economic difficulties. As Cremin suggests, there are many factors--the trade policies of various governments, government policies on taxes and spending, exchange rates, investment and savings decisions, ways of organizing the workplace, patterns of union-management relations--that seem more important in the decline of American industries than the academic achievements of the workforce. Just intuitively, it would seem that government and business policies have had more to do with how our economy has fared internationally than whether scores on the SAT (Standard Achievement Test) rise or fall.

More specifically, any aggregate evidence about the relationship of educational and economic decline in this period is mixed. The drop in productivity was very sharp after 1973 but the decline in achievement scores was more gradual, indicating that the latter is probably not the cause of the former. Indeed, as Andrew Hacker points out, the generation with the most influence on economic matters was educated when the schools were supposedly doing their job well. On a slightly different note, one aggregate study suggests that only educational attainment and favorable weather conditions for farmers contributed *positively* to growth in the 1970s, and years in school have actually increased as the economy has declined. It is very difficult to suggest, then, that declining educational achievements were a major factor in recent losses in productivity and competitiveness.[21]

Perhaps a more common and more prospective "macro" argument suggests a growing gap between the skills demanded by the American economy and the supply of skills students have as they emerge from the schools. Whatever the source(s) of our previous economic woes, it is claimed that education will play a significant role in any economic turnaround, and the signs are not promising. The "knowledge and skills gap" referred to in the *America 2000* report concerns both general and technical skills and foresees significant shortages in each. Business cannot find students who have the technical skills for the new workplace in which computers and other new technologies play a major role. For less-skilled jobs, applicants lack basic skills of literacy and numeracy, let alone higher-order skills of critical and independent thinking. These failings are compounded by bad attitudes and work habits. Schools, it is claimed, are simply not producing the human capital business needs, creating a workforce crisis. This crisis can only get worse as low-skilled jobs go abroad or disappear altogether and as requirements for the remaining jobs inevitably increase. One widely cited report predicts, "Overall the skill mix of the economy will be moving rapidly upscale."[22]

It is important to note here that any current or future gap of this sort is likely more a function of changes in demand than supply. Declines in educational achievement have pretty much bottomed out. There has not been any significant downward shift in nearly a decade, and there are some areas of clear improvement, for example in the scores of minority students. One recent national "report card" grudgingly admitted that achievement levels now roughly match those of 1970. Another study suggests that the most significant declines in standardized measures like SAT are attributable to students in the higher academic groups who are simply not scoring as well as previous generations.[23] These indicate that for some basic skills, things are not as bad as common rhetoric might lead us to believe. The supply of these skills has remained rather steady, even as there have been declines in average overall achievement.

Thus the argument for a skills gap mainly rests upon claims of a shift in the composition of the demand for labor away from the lower-level skills adequate for a high-volume, standardized production economy. The service sector has expanded and manufacturing jobs have declined. Students without the skills to compete in this sector will no longer have recourse to reasonably well-paying jobs on an assembly line. It is doubtful that the significant minority without a high school degree have much hope in the labor market, especially if, as claimed in recent reports, job requirements for basic skills, independent thinking, and adaptability are constantly increasing. These shifts mean the schools must do a better job in providing higher levels of both technical and general education.

Not only has the general demand for skills increased, the shift in the nature of the workplace itself, it is argued, will demand still higher skill levels. There will be increased need for workers with technical skills to work with new technologies in production, particularly those involving the use and handling of information. For example, a line worker in an auto plant will need to know how to deal with, adjust, and perhaps even repair a robotics painting system. Perhaps more important, the evolving workplace will demand higher order skills and abilities in all workers, "thinking skills--thinking creatively, making decisions, solving problems, seeing things in the mind's eye, knowing how to learn, and reasoning."[24] These skills will permit workers to be able to acquire and use information, work with changing technologies, work better with others in a team setting, and allocate and use resources productively in the "high performance workplace." Whether seen as providing technical or general education, the schools are urged to do more to prepare workers for the workplace of the future.

Again, the schools may not be performing as well as we might desire. Nevertheless, there are a number of questions about the nature and future of the "skills gap" in its various forms and the relative roles of schools and businesses in closing the gap. In some areas, most notably those involving specific technical skills, the problem of a skills gap has been more one of anecdote and anticipation than a documented shortage. For example, there is relatively little evidence that the schools are not producing the students with the ability to enter technical and scientific fields, especially those involving computers. Surveys of businesses have not shown shortages of qualified people for technical and engineering kinds of jobs. Indeed, one study suggests that the only real labor shortages are in the health care field and for Roman Catholic priests, hardly the cutting edge of economic competitiveness. Moreover, it is commonly noted that while the so-called "high-tech" fields are the most rapidly growing in percentage terms, the absolute number of high-tech jobs is small compared to certain lower status and skill service categories.[25]

The issue then is not a skills gap with regard to technical training but concerning more general skills. Here too, however, there are reasons to doubt the nature and significance of the alleged skills gap. First, there is the issue of how "upscale" the future demand for skills will be. Projections of absolute job growth suggest that a "very large number of jobs will be created in medium to low skilled fields" such as marketing and sales (mostly cashiers) and service jobs including "cooks, nursing aides, waiters, and janitors."[26] Even so, it is difficult to project what the skill requirements of job categories like these will be. Much depends upon the way in which new technologies are deployed or the point in a cycle in which the use of a technology is either new or has become routinized. Similarly, there is no obvious gap in terms of educational credentials, even granting that requirements for such credentials are increasing and will probably continue to do so. Educationally, at least, Americans are overqualified for their jobs. Currently, 70 percent of jobs only require a high school degree or less, but half or more of young people attend college.[27] Finally, although surveys reveal business dissatisfaction with the skills of potential workers, it also seems that employers are often less concerned with specific job skills than habits and attitudes such as punctuality and a willingness to take on responsibilities. Overall, then, there is not a clear and compelling skills gap, save for those individuals with few educational credentials who can no longer compete because less-skilled manufacturing jobs are disappearing.

Certainly the shift from manufacturing to services requires schools to do better at the basic tasks of literacy and numeracy, and there is room for improvement here. For the sake of argument let us also suppose what is plausible, although not totally beyond question, that the workplace will be upskilled rather than deskilled such that there may be a gap between worker skills and job requirements. Even granting this, there still are questions concerning the relative roles of schools and businesses in closing these actual or potential gaps. First, it is typically noted that gains in productivity from on-the-job training are twice those attributable to formal education. At the same time various reports on the workforce note that businesses provide systematic training for only about a third of the workforce, and the majority of that training is concentrated in the professional and managerial ranks. Comparatively, American businesses invest in human capital at considerably lower rates than other nations.[28] Most of the recent reports recommend businesses increase their investment in training, as well as suggesting tax credits to encourage them to do so. It is important to note that these decisions and policies about training, decisions that are important for productivity, are independent of what goes on in the public schools. Moreover, one would think that, given common perceptions of school performance, the impulse to invest in training would be even greater. However, there seems to be a training gap here and the training that is provided is not directed at those who seem to need it most.

Besides training, there are questions about the ways in which the workforce is managed. Much is made in recent reports about the new workplace having flatter hierarchies with greater discretion for employees. The recent reports emphasize how workers must be critical thinkers who can make decisions, solve problems independently, and be adaptable and flexible, adjusting to the inevitable and rapid changes on the job. It is also noted, however, that most businesses are not organized to give their employees this kind of discretion or flexibility. The reorganization of the workplace may be necessary and desirable, but most businesses, perhaps 90 percent or more, have yet to create the organizational environments of the "high performance workplace."[29] That is, even if the schools were performing perfectly, businesses are not currently set up to develop or use those generic skills, however vaguely defined, that are supposedly vital to the modern competitive organization. Whether this is a vicious circle--in which business does not adjust because it lacks confidence in potential employees coming out of schools and schools remain unsure of "what work requires"--is less important than the fact that changes in training and management must accompany school reform.

Given our apparent loss of economic competitiveness and the relative slowness of business to respond to the challenges posed by our competitors (for example, in matters of training and organization) one could easily imagine a National Commission on Excellence in Business criticizing corporations and demanding reform. One might also imagine comparable critiques of government policies, most notably concerning infrastructure and debt. Schools have borne more than their share of criticism for our economic difficulties. The important issue here, however, is not the relative distribution of blame for our economic woes. Rather, the point is that in treating schools as a kind of macroeconomic lever (whether in terms of overall performance indicators or quality of labor supply) we tend to downplay the importance of other factors more obviously related to economic performance that involve government and business decisions. We also de-emphasize what are probably more important factors--training and workplace organization and the deployment of technology--in enhancing productivity. Most important, we fail to ask more "microscopic" questions about how students develop skills relevant to the workplace and what schools can and should do in this regard.

Microeconomics: Skills, Schools, and Dollars

There can be little doubt that the schools serve the economy by providing students with basic skills, particularly literacy and numeracy. We can therefore make the general assumption, as Cremin suggests, that education is important for an economy and that schools must play this role in creating an appropriate labor supply. However, this still leaves us with critical questions regarding how schools can (or should) develop other job-related skills. That is, what role do schools play in preparing students for the world of work? What kinds of skills might schools help students develop? Are these, as the variations on this theme suggest, mainly technical skills or more general, transferable ones? Examining these issues reveals one central fact, several competing theories, and admissions that there are many things we just do not know. Overall, such an examination again suggests that the empirical evidence about the schools' role in the economy is not strongly supportive of the human capital theme.

The one unassailable, widely agreed upon fact in the field of education and economics is that there is an economic return or premium attached to education. Educational attainments typically have tremendous economic significance for the individual, and this significance has increased recently, especially for black males.[30] It is important to note here the normative corollary of this fact, namely that educational institutions are seen as primary vehicles for equal opportunity. It is crucial that all individuals have a fair chance to develop skills and accumulate educational credentials that allow them to compete in the labor market. The public schools are seen as vehicles for social mobility, for entry into higher-paying and higher-status positions.

The key problem, of course, is what to make of this fact, how to interpret the relationship of education to individual mobility. For better or worse, the original and still most prominent school of thought, the human capital approach, is firmly rooted in economic models and reasoning. An individual "invests" in education expecting that increased knowledge and skills can command higher wages. There will be a return on the investment in education that exceeds both the costs of the education and the earnings forcgone in obtaining it. Rates of return for different levels of educational attainment can then be economically analyzed. Other analyses can use assumptions and measures borrowed from other parts of economic theory concerning rational investments, measures of productivity, and so on.[31] It is both rational for individuals to invest in education and for employers to hire educated employees in the expectation that they will be more productive.

There are certainly problems with this approach to relating schools and skills. At its worst it can involve a grand tautology. As Arne Kallerberg puts it, "If better educated people earn more than others, one argues, it is because they are more productive in the eyes of rational employers; and we know they are more productive because they are better paid."[32] Alternatives to the human capital approach suggest that it has misread the significance of the correlation of wages and schooling. In general these alternatives share the view that schooling itself may not be a primary factor in enhanced productivity. Perhaps the most proximate departure from this approach is the screening or signaling hypothesis. In this view, schools do not make individuals more productive, rather they signal employers concerning who are likely to be productive workers. What precisely is signaled--habits and attitudes, general intelligence, ability to work with others, specific skills, or some mix thereof--is somewhat unclear. A less benign version of this approach is offered by radical critics who assert that what is being signaled through the schools is class rather than skills. The function of the schools is to reproduce class relations and mimic the hierarchical structure of the workplace and larger society. The "cultural capital" of education is hoarded by dominant groups and passed along to their offspring through the schools. Finally, there is a kind of null hypothesis about the relationship of education to productivity, namely, that formal schooling is largely irrelevant to job performance. There are much better predictors of performance, especially experience, and the links we have forged between education and jobs, at its worst, reflects a mindless credentialism.[33]

Like many debates in the social sciences, the issue of schools and skills remains unsettled. In terms of educational policy, however, we seem to have a mixed program that involves both thematic variations. We can find examples consistent with the several competing theories concerning the relationship of education and the economy. Vocational training and the expansion of vocationally relevant curricula through community colleges exemplify a human capital approach with an emphasis on training for specific skills and jobs, although there is considerable dispute about whether such training makes much difference. Recently there have been suggestions that, as in Japan and other countries, school records should be shared between schools and employers as a way of signaling (to both students and employers) the importance of school performance. Other suggestions involve certificates of various kinds that would guarantee employers that students had achieved certain levels of skill; developing meaningful educational credentials might have special significance for students who are not going on to further academic study. Similarly, programs for greater school-business cooperation, including programs that take students into the workplace as part of their regular studies, seek to break down the wall between academic and other work. Academic exercises can then have some meaning beyond the mere assembling of credentials. Finally, there can be little doubt that educational credentials, particularly advanced degrees from prestigious institutions, have considerable economic value even if such formal education does not actually enhance productivity. Recent years have seen a significant and growing gap between the earnings of those with such advanced credentials and those without.

Recently there has been an interesting turn in the discussions of education and the economy, one that has seemingly transcended these academic debates. There has been some rhetorical convergence around a broad orientation associated with the theme of general education. This convergence emphasizes the importance of education in providing analytical skills--"critical thinking," "higher-order thinking skills," "learning to learn," and so on. In this view, schools do (should) not impart specific skills that make individuals more productive. Rather, they (should) develop generic abilities to acquire skills on the job that in turn enhance productivity. The ability to see the relations within a system, to adapt to varying settings and situations, and to react to specific circumstances and solve problems are the skills needed in the new workplace. A number of recent reports emphasize this academic variation on the human capital theme, that general education should produce high-level, generic skills that can be applied in a variety of settings. For example, the SCANS report lists five competencies that "differ from a person's technical knowledge" and involve such skills as "organizes and maintains information . . . knows how social and, organizational, and technological systems work and operates effectively with them."[34] In the "high performance workplace," there is a premium on thinking and problem-solving skills that go well beyond simple literacy and numeracy.

This emphasis on critical thinking is attractive because, superficially at least, it is consistent with the variety of (empirical or normative) positions on the schools' role in the economy. In this view, there is no real difference between general education and training, given the development of the new workplace. The difference, and potential tension, between training and education dissolves. There is only one variation on the theme which involves developing thinking skills, broadly and generically defined. Either the more orthodox human capital position or its rivals can accept the idea of an indirect relationship between education and productivity, although they would obviously interpret it in different ways. General education develops the most important form of human capital, higher-order thinking skills. Even if one doubts that education of this sort (whatever it ultimately is) is really directly related to job performance or economic competitiveness, focusing on some tasks (like critical thinking) appropriate for schools is preferable to trying to make the schools directly responsive to economic needs.

Similarly, different political groups can readily endorse this orientation, although, as in the academic debate, for different reasons. The traditional conflict between excellence and equity dissolves because all students will develop similar skills in preparation for their economic lives. Liberals can endorse the equity implied by making all students critical thinkers and conservatives can welcome the demands for excellence implied in upgrading basic education. The traditional tension between the civic and economic aims of education, the common school and human capital themes, apparently disappears. As Susan Berryman puts it, "perhaps for the first time in our history the different objectives of education seem to imply similar curricula and pedagogy. In other words, we may not have to choose--the education needed to to function effectively in both high and low skill jobs looks similar to that needed to participate effectively as citizens. . . . The educative challenge common to these disparate activities is to prepare individuals for thoughtful choice and judgement."[35]

There is undoubtedly a kind of "have your cake and eat it too" attraction to this argument. We can simply direct the schools to do (better) what they are supposed to be doing anyway and what they are likely to be most capable of doing. Certainly there is some recognition that pedagogical changes will be required to make the schools promote critical thinking. Discussions of restructuring schools often speak of the need to make schools look more like the new workplace if not reflect workplace issues. Still, it is claimed that there are or can be fundamental continuities between school and job skills. The various educational (civic, economic) functions of schools can all be well-served by an emphasis on critical thinking.

This rhetorical consensus shifts the focus of discussion from the issue of different types of training for groups of students to an emphasis on generic skills for all. However, making this shift treats as settled a number of issues about which we have relatively little conceptual clarity, let alone compelling empirical evidence. For sake of convenience, we can divide these issues into two categories. One is pedagogical, concerning critical thinking and related notions, and the other is institutional, concerning how schools and businesses are (or are not) related to one another. Although these problems primarily confront the attempt to equate education and training, they confront the idea that schools can act as trainers as well. Taken together, they cast doubt upon the claimed reduction of training to general education. They also suggest that neither the academic nor the political disagreements about schools, skills, and institutional purposes can be so readily avoided. There are continuing tensions between the variations on the human capital theme (between training and general education), and between this theme and the common school theme as well.

Critical Thinking and Job Skills

The current discussion often envisions schools as ideally producing critical thinkers, individuals with certain generic skills and competencies, who can step into a job situation and develop the more specific skills required by the job. They can readily change and develop their skills as job requirements shift or even as they move on to new jobs altogether. Someone who is a problem solver, who has "learned how to learn," will be able to deal with the rapidly shifting workplace and be a continually productive worker. The image here is of a kind of renaissance employee, a worker for all seasons.

Attractive as this image is, it does not have much clear empirical support. Part of the problem is the relative lack of definition on both sides of the equation. It is fairly easy to list some of the desirable qualities in an employee of a "high performance workplace" and some of the characteristics of critical thinking. But in neither case do we have a very precise understanding of these traits, let alone how the two are related. For example, a list of job-relevant skills might include several dimensions: cognitive, communication, physical, and interpersonal skills, as well as personality traits and attitudes. Similarly, critical thinking has many components, and it has been recently suggested that there may be several "intelligences" beyond the analytic skills so crucial in school.[36] Conceptual difficulties aside, there is simply a paucity of empirical work connecting education and skills in a direct fashion. For example, a background paper to one of the recent reports notes, "Not a lot is known about how best to train workers for new technologies," and another puts the matter more generally, "Existing evidence on the demands of work is not adequate for formulating policies on education and training."[37] This kind of problem arises for either general education or training, as thematic variations, or attempts to eliminate the distinction between them. We simply do not have the kind of general, hard evidence that would tell us how workers educated in a certain way are able to perform certain jobs better because of their education.

Indeed, what empirical evidence there is tends to be negative or suggest a picture quite different from the one predominant in the current rhetoric. As Linda Gottfredson points out, "Existing evidence about the functional value of education has been quite damning" to the notion that formal education enhances skills. Similarly, Ivar Berg's seminal study of "the great training robbery" points out that even directed, but still "academic," training did little to enhance productivity.[38] Perhaps more important from a policy perspective are findings about the value of experiential or on-the-job training. Beyond the estimates that such training contributes far more to productivity than formal education, there is also evidence that the most effective training is not generic but context-dependent. For example, Thomas Sticht notes that the military has had success with low-scoring students through "functional context" training that does not attempt to impart generic skills but rather is rooted in "authentic activity." Training is clearly connected to actual job tasks. Admittedly, the military has considerably greater control in its program than either schools or businesses, but this finding does remind us that the more general issue of whether critical thinking is context-dependent is far from settled. It may be that the currently popular hypothesis requires a view of the transferability of skills--vague, generic ones at that--that may not be empirically supportable.[39]

The current emphasis on critical thinking, then, is considerably more demanding and less intuitive than it first appears. It requires us to assume that there is a continuity between schools and workplaces, that school work and job tasks call upon the same set of generic skills. Besides conceptual difficulties and the paucity of empirical support, this view is somewhat counterintuitive. As Lauren Resnick points out, there are a number of differences between learning "in" and "out" of school (for example, "Pure mentation in school versus tool manipulation outside." "Symbol manipulation in school versus contextualized reasoning outside school.").[40] This is recognized not only in the students' common perception of a gap between school and the "real world," but in many of the discussions of restructuring that have suggested, however vaguely, that schools ought to be more like workplaces or have specific connections to businesses. Similarly, the SCANS report admits that "the most effective way of learning skills is 'in context' " but then goes on to talk about "competencies [that] span the chasm between the school and the workplace."[41] It recognizes the transfer of skills problem and the effectiveness of learning "in context" but then describes generic, allegedly transferable skills ("knows how social, organizational, and technological systems work") that the schools are somehow supposed to impart. Once it is admitted that, so far as we know, the most effective way of developing skills is "in context," then creating lists of generic skills and competencies is probably more a rhetorical than practical exercise. In short, it may simply be that there are limits to the degree that the tasks of education and work, schools and businesses, are continuous with or analogous to one another.

It is puzzling and disappointing that we do not know more about the relationship of education to skills and that this issue has not been at the forefront of discussion about education and the economy. This is particularly ironic in light of the current emphasis in public rhetoric on educational assessment. We are closely examining assessments of academic outcomes but have largely taken for granted the linkage of educational performances to economic results. Nevertheless, even if we cannot answer the question of how and to what extent (if any) schools enhance skills and raise productivity, some more or less explicit institutional response to this question is inevitable. That is, current or proposed policies or institutional arrangements will create some relationship(s) of schools to the economy, raising further questions of how the two can or should be connected.

Institutional Design and Purpose

When we look at the educational systems of America's economic competitors, we find considerable variation in what might be called institutional design. For example, Japan and Germany have very productive economies but very different systems. The former emphasizes, as does the United States, general as opposed to vocational education for almost all students and the latter has a strong vocational component and differentiated tracks in its dual system. There may be a number of ways of dissolving this apparent paradox, not the least of which is to see it as still further evidence that the schools may not play the powerful economic role often rhetorically attributed to them. There can be more than one way to structure a school system to support a productive economy. It might also be argued that there are critical respects in which these two systems are the same. Both make heavy demands and achieve good results in basic reading and math skills. They score higher than the United States does and the variability in their scores is lower. Also, there are always catch-all explanations in terms of cultural similarities such as attitudes toward school or work, or family involvement in education, or even more mundane factors such as more school days per year.[42]

Without denying any of these explanations, it is equally important to note ways in which the "shape" or "design" of the American system differs from either of these others. Again, unlike Germany's, the American configuration emphasizes general (liberal?) education at the expense of more direct ties to the economy, save for a small vocational component that serves a very limited range of jobs. Moreover, general education in the United States goes on for a longer period without the clear winnowing of the Japanese examination system. The American system provides numerous "second chances" for education, for example through community colleges and adult education. The formal ties between schools and businesses in the United States are more ad hoc, varied, and generally looser than the more structured path from school to work in either Japan or Germany. The United States also lacks comparably firm or formal points at which some students are advanced and others are not. It has a more open, gradual, and less formal system for channeling students into different work or educational settings.

Officials and observers have generally praised the "deliciously messy" American system as providing a greater measure of opportunity to the economically disadvantaged and linguistic or racial minorities, as well as to older students and workers.[43] The United States has a mix of ongoing opportunities for general education and training that are fairly widely available. Almost everyone who completes high school can get into some four-year program, and the community college system provides an array of programs that mix general with technical or quasi-professional education. The current emphasis on critical thinking for all students does not pose any challenge to this configuration. Rhetorical phrases like "lifelong learning" or "learning to learn" reinforce the notion of prolonged general education in a relatively open system. Thus, it is implied that the United States can do what it needs to do within the current institutional configuration, despite its differences (if these are noted at all) from major economic competitors.

Here, as in the discussion of critical thinking, the predominant view neatly leaves current ideological and institutional predilections intact. The United States can have both excellence and equity and can maximize educational opportunities as well as educational achievements that will enhance competitiveness. But not all "mixed programs" represent sensible compromises. It may be that this institutional configuration, supported in part by the current celebration of critical thinking, is a peculiar sort of combination, one that seems less a hardy hybrid than the worst of both worlds. America's mixed program has provided neither the high quality, general education for all students through secondary school, as in Japan, nor specific apprenticeships, job training, and skills, as in Germany. The institutional combination of training and education in the United States also apparently produces other undesirable results. The emphasis upon a prolonged general education leads to the departure of a significant minority, perhaps as much as twenty percent or more, of students who cannot or will not continue formal education through age eighteen. They then have almost no institutional alternatives in a society that places a premium on educational credentials. Even given the numerous "second chance" institutions, this seems a curious expression of equal opportunity, not to mention a potential economic liability. Similarly, in America's "messy" system, the school-work transition, so clearly orchestrated among its economic competitors, is something of an institutional orphan. The relatively weak ties between schools and businesses render them unable to easily assist one another (even when they are willing, which may not be very often) let alone provide any kinds of incentives for student performance or services to assist the school-work transition.

Institutionally, then, an important similarity between Japan and Germany, and a feature that is lacking in the United States, is the connection, either through testing or other formal programs, between schools and businesses. Because of this connection, academic performance has more direct and visible consequences for individuals in the school to work transition. Tests lead to very clear winnowing in both systems. In Japan, besides the exams that determine access to further education, grades are routinely forwarded to potential employers, and references to jobs are often made on the basis of achievement. Similarly, in Germany, formal ties between schools and businesses are part of a system for providing extensive training and apprenticeship experience. In both systems students have rather clear incentives for performing, and there are clear institutional paths to be followed in the school-work transition. There is considerable coordination and communication between schools and businesses within a system that rewards performance.[44]

None of this is to say that the United States should create exam hell or a dual system. Rather it is to say that although rhetorically one might have one's cake and eat it too, in policy one seldom does. On the one hand, other nations seem to have made clearer, although different, choices about what to emphasize in relating schools and the economy. On the other hand, the United States seems to have kept things rather vague and "messy," in part because of its commitment to equal opportunity. Again, Americans tend to interpret equal opportunity as meaning that one's life prospects should be expanded, or at least not overly limited, by the educational system. Even though they know that winnowing occurs, they cannot bring themselves to fully institutionalize it. Creating an open system in the name of equal opportunity may undercut incentives to perform and make the school-to-work transition more difficult. The question is what kinds of trade-offs or institutional gaps are created by the American configuration and how they might be coped with (or changed) through policy.

The current rhetoric about education and the economy implicitly or explicitly suggests that schools can contribute to the economy and provide expansive opportunity within a loose institutional configuration. An emphasis on critical thinking for all students will hold these elements together. Even a cursory glance at others' institutional configurations, not to mention American educational history, casts doubts on this rather rosy picture. These doubts are reinforced by the rather tenuous linking of schools to (generic, transferable) skills. The perennial dilemmas of equity versus excellence, common education versus tracking, education for citizenship versus education for likely economic role cannot be swept away by appeals to vague notions of critical thinking. These dilemmas pose some tough policy questions that have not been fully addressed by the current rhetoric on education and the economy.

Continuing Dilemmas: Human Capital and Equal Opportunity

To summarize the above discussion, first, it is doubtful that the America's education system has played much of an immediate role in its current economic woes. It is not clear it could play a direct role in any economic turnaround. Whatever the future of school reform, the schools should not be scapegoats for collective economic failures. Second, there does not seem to be a very refined understanding of the relationship(s) of education and skills, in part at least because of the theoretical apparatus and mode of economic analysis through which these issues have been approached. The largely theoretically established link of education and productivity in economic models has distracted attention away from the knotty empirical issues of just how schools prepare (or fail to prepare) students to become workers. Similarly, the current enthusiasm for "critical thinking" implies answers to a number of pedagogical questions about relevant skills, training versus education, and transfer of skills. It is not clear that these answers are empirically supported. Third, pedagogical issues aside, there is, as illustrated by Japan and Germany, a difference between an institutional scheme that directly aims at producing trained, productive workers, and one that emphasizes common, general education. The compromise the United States has produced in response to these different aims seems unsatisfactory, producing neither outstanding results for basic education nor smooth school-to-work transitions. Institutional questions of this sort are generally absent from current discussions of educational reform and the economy or they are implicitly answered by expecting the schools to be both educator and trainer through promoting "critical thinking."

America's rather muddled approach to issues of education and the economy is not just a function of a lack of knowledge about productivity, critical thinking, and the like. It also reflects some continuing dilemmas with regard to the human capital theme. There is the conflict between the two major variations on this theme, general education versus technical training. As noted above, the United States has never fully resolved whether the schools can best serve the economy simply by setting high academic and personal standards as opposed to taking on some more specific training mission(s). In doing some of both, comprehensive American schools seem to be doing neither particularly well.

There is also the dilemma of excess and deficit. To the degree that either strategy involves sorting students into groups, a contemporary version of "head" and "hand" students, it may be open to the charge of going too far and compromising equal opportunity. This would be especially true if the schools were to take on some more direct tracking and training akin to the German dual system. It might also arise if the United States were to adopt the strict, examination-based winnowing of the Japanese system. On the deficit side of the ledger, the now familiar rhetoric of the reform movement suggests schools are doing too little, on either variation, to serve the economy. Schools, it is argued, are producing neither sufficient basic skills nor high academic achievement, let alone any reservoir of technical talent.

At least some of these difficulties derive from conflicts between the human capital theme and the ideal of equal education expressed in the common school. There is and always has been a conflict between, on the one hand, the notion that all students should have the same curriculum that recognizes their common status as citizens and, on the other hand, the idea that differences between and among students should be recognized for meritocratic and economic reasons. The moral and political equality at the core of the common school approach is not easily squared with the equality of opportunity to achieve and advance (principally economically) that is central to the human capital theme. The former emphasizes a common political and moral equality and the latter posits a shared initial state of equality of opportunity, which is then transformed into a more individualized (economic) inequality. The former emphasis on what is shared by individuals is different from the latter emphasis on what, perhaps legitimately, separates them. These dilemmas are additional examples of the problem in liberal democratic ideology of finding what is shared and what is legitimately different among individuals.

Perhaps the clearest practical manifestation of this conflict is the ongoing debate about ability grouping. The argument in favor of grouping students by ability is, of course, that it provides a learning environment that appropriately matches individual students' needs. Students who can handle more advanced work in a subject are appropriately challenged. Those who either cannot or have not reached a certain level are given materials suitable for them. Critics charge that this common practice has little educational value for the more advanced students and is harmful for students who are not on the "fast" track in a subject matter. One interesting experiment in this regard is Henry Levin's "accelerated learning" program in which supposedly less-able students have had greater demands placed upon them and have shown some remarkable gains in achievement. More broadly, while the clear, if not complete, weight of scholarly opinion is against ability grouping, it remains the predominant practice in most schools, even in elementary grades. Those critical of these practices clearly seek some more common approach, and those in favor of it claim that recognizing differences in individual achievement is pedagogically and morally sound.[45]

This conflict between commonality and difference goes deeper than a debate about pedagogical practices. It extends to questions about what equal opportunity means and its relationship to educational institutions and credentials. Specifically, there is a tremendous ambivalence about the concept of equal opportunity and the schools' role in providing it. As noted previously, the development of secondary education in the United States suggested that the schools would play a more active role in directing students toward their future roles by sorting students by ability. Instead of being prior to the starting line in life's "race," schools are now an important part of the race itself. Public education, the "great balance wheel of the social machinery," supposedly provides all students an equal opportunity for developing and displaying skills that in turn open up further opportunities. There is a general sense that schools should play a key role in making up for social inequalities and past discrimination, giving all groups, and especially minorities, a genuinely equal chance. Schools then are seen as an essential component in providing equal opportunity. Equal opportunity in turn serves collective economic needs by ensuring that individual talents are properly developed.[46]

Leaving aside any difficulties with how and even whether schools serve economic needs, it has been seldom clear whether the schools can provide truly equal opportunities for all individuals. There are still many indications that the schools simply reinforce the effects of class differences. The studies of James Coleman and Christopher Jencks, among others, seem to cast a shadow over the possibility of obtaining equality through public education.[47] The specific policies designed to lessen educational inequalities--aid to poor districts, desegregation plans, preschool education and other special programs, including affirmative action programs at the postsecondary level--have had mixed results at best. Special programs in poor districts and preschool programs such as Head Start have had some clear successes. Academic achievement gaps between blacks and whites have closed somewhat, but the economic premium for advanced educational credentials seems to have grown, widening some racial and class gaps in income. Affirmative action remains controversial and its effects are unclear. Overall, school achievement and adult economic prospects remain stubbornly correlated with class and race. The differences that Adam Smith referred to as an "effect . . . of the division of labor" may now be seen, in part, as an effect of divisions of race and class within schools.

Part of the difficulty here is that it is not clear what schools can be reasonably expected to do to provide equal opportunity. There is an analogy between the demands made upon the school in the name of economic competitiveness and those made on behalf of equal economic opportunity. Specifically, the expectations concerning the schools and economic opportunity place a large, vague burden on the schools that might best be dealt with by other institutions in other ways. For example, it would seem that the distribution of economic opportunities and income are as much or more a function of government policies and changes in labor markets than school practices. To expect the schools to be the primary force in affecting a redistribution of income without dramatic changes in other institutions or policies is a rather unreasonable demand. As David Tyack and Elizabeth Hansot put it, "Whoever claimed--before the 1960's at any rate--that school could create equality of adult income? It is odd to criticize educators for not accomplishing what they never tried to do and could not do under the most favorable circumstances."[48] This large and vague burden is not lessened by the rather loose ties between the schools and the economy. In the absence of some clearer definition of the schools' proper role in creating equal opportunity, it is hard to say what the schools can, let alone should, do to equalize *economic* opportunity.

Although there is no "solution" to these dilemmas and conflicts, there are some ways in which the schools can appropriately respond to them. Clearly the schools can do more to equalize *educational* opportunity. One area in which there is some consensus about what might be done concerns preschool education, for example programs like Head Start. The educational goal that all children start school "ready to learn" is uncontroversial. We all understand that the so-called race, with its consequences for both individuals and society as a whole, is well under way before a child reaches school. Many children, particularly the poor and minorities, start behind and stay behind. The most obvious educational response to differences in family and cultural background has been to provide preschool programs such as Head Start that would bring children to school better prepared. After they begin school these children would also be eligible for other support to help ensure that schools could provide needed services for them. The controversies, if any, about these programs have mainly concerned how to maximize their effectiveness rather than with the legitimacy of their aims.

There is also considerable consensus that equal educational opportunity in school means that all students must reach some level of basic literacy and numeracy. If the schools cannot become the primary guarantor of economic opportunity, they can at least ensure that all students reach some minimal level of basic skills. If schools cannot fully redress the inequalities of family background, the vagaries of labor markets, and shortsighted corporate and government policies, they can provide at least the assurance of the development of basic skills essential for employability. The assurance that every student is ready for further schooling or training is crucial for all students but especially so for the large minority that is at risk of dropping out of the system altogether.

Thinking of equal opportunity in this way parallels the previous discussion of skills. Instead of somehow thinking of an expansive economic role for schools in terms of the development of (higher order) skills, we should focus more on basic skills that are more clearly within both the charge and the competence of schools. Likewise, instead of thinking that the schools should somehow be the prime guarantor of equal economic opportunity, we might narrow our focus to the question of guaranteeing equal educational opportunity. Schools might therefore be given the more narrow charge of bringing *all* students to a level of literacy and numeracy, as well as instilling good habits and attitudes toward work, that makes employment or further training possible. Instead of pursuing vague and ambitious goals like "knows how social, organizational, and technological systems work and operates effectively with them," we should narrow our expectations for schools and hold them strictly accountable for achieving basic aims. These tasks are what the schools are most likely to be able to do, what can be most clearly observed and measured, and what is widely agreed they ought to do better.

There have been a number of recent proposals for testing and certification that attempt to address the issue of ensuring some level of basic skill. For example, Oregon is in the process of implementing a proposal for a test in tenth grade that leads to a "Certificate of Initial Mastery," a guarantee that a student has passed some basic educational threshold. Again, it also provides for special assistance to students who do not meet standards, as well as direction toward college or training and apprenticeships for those that do. As with proposals in a number of other states that are currently considering various kinds of certificates, the apparent virtues of the Oregon proposal lie in the specific charge it gives to schools, the accountability implied by certification, and institutional support for students who would otherwise be at risk of dropping out. It focuses on basic education, and therefore equal educational opportunity, for all students; it also specifies at least one clear institutional link between schools and businesses through the signal sent by certification.[49]

This kind of proposal does not settle the more general issue of equal opportunity, again, because there is little agreement about the concept generally, or the schools' role in sorting people in particular. Critics of the Oregon proposal charged it with tracking and sorting students in ways that would inevitably be unfair, especially to minorities. Supporters of the proposal replied that comparable "tracks" already existed and that the proposed certification and remediation would actually provide greater equity, especially with regard to basic skills. This debate reflects the continuing tensions between the common school and human capital themes. Again, the apparent choices in response to this conflict seem to merely create further dilemmas. On the one hand, American notions of equal opportunity make it very unlikely that the United States will embark on the reconfiguration required to create something akin to Japanese system, even though proposals for certification clearly tend in that direction. The U.S. is further still from contemplating anything like the German dual system. On the other hand, we must wonder whether genuinely equal opportunity is provided by the American emphasis on prolonged general education and loose institutional ties of schools to businesses. Low achievement scores, the dropout problem, and the lack of clear institutional alternatives for those without educational credentials suggest that the American system is not providing the opportunity it emphasizes so strongly. For a significant minority of students, the educational system, as currently structured, is simply a dead end.

If the United States wishes to have a system that emphasizes prolonged and widely available general education, then it must recognize and respond to the gaps in "institutional design" this produces. Beyond the guarantee of basic skills for all students, there should be more systematic school-business ties as well as institutional alternatives for students at risk. At the very least there is more room for communication between schools and businesses, for example, the forwarding of transcripts and the establishment of partnerships. There are other possibilities for exchanging information or for cooperative ventures using and going beyond the Job Training Partnership Act.[50] There could also be the use of business settings for pedagogical purposes in which students might come to see the real world implications of academic work. There are many institutional and policy options in this area that bear exploration. Indeed, the United States may need new and different institutions to deal with the gaps in the current system, especially for dropouts. In any case the linkage of schools and businesses should be a genuine partnership rather than a matter of "what work requires of schools." Creating new relationships or institutions is preferable to expecting schools to be both educator and trainer or believing they can do both by promoting critical thinking.

One benefit of such linkages might be that it would lead us to reconsider how we think about skills and how to help students develop them. The appealing notion at the core of the human capital theme is the idea of recognizing individual differences in both needs and talents. However, it seems that we have more or less settled on one kind of measure of merit--academic achievement--that seems both too blunt and too sharp an instrument. It is too blunt in that it does not take into account the variety of skills that might be relevant to the workplace. It is too sharp in that it tends to create a large class of losers in the academic marketplace, including the forgotten half, who see little point in schooling. As Howard Gardner suggests, if schools would recognize skills or intelligences beyond the analytical intelligence emphasized in school work, it might be easier to develop individual talents and smooth the school-to-work transition.[51] If we are going to have a "deliciously messy" system of connecting schools and jobs, we might at least have one that does more to look at the needs and talents of individuals as they actually are rather than reducing them to narrow academic credentials. Obviously this requires much more exploration of and research on the nature and transfer of skills. For all the testing that we do as a society, we have really only started to examine the varieties of human abilities and talents.

Again, developing linkages between schools and the economy will inevitably raise serious questions about the aims of schools and the role of educational or other credentials in our society. Certification or any formal ties of schools and businesses, whether as part of restructuring or for explicit referral and training, will raise issues of tracking and equal opportunity. As a society, we have simply not settled on the schools' legitimate role, if any, in steering people toward certain kinds of jobs and opportunities. We are similarly unsure of the precise role of testing and credentials in the process of competition for jobs. These are issues that go well beyond the context of educational reform. For example, the arguments about the potential effect of the civil rights laws on educational requirements as job screens and arguments about the practice of race or gender norming are both instances in which the value of educational credentials are hotly contested.[52] These debates obviously are rooted in conflicting interpretations of basic values such as equal opportunity, competing conceptions of the priorities of public education, and differing views of how to best arrange institutions to fulfill these values and aims. Certainly there will be institutional settlements of one sort or another--through the current system, or a more formalized system of certification or training, or even a return to some common curriculum as discussed in Chapter 3. But these do not and perhaps cannot answer the fundamental normative and conceptual questions of equal opportunity at issue here.

If we look at the various controversies and policies surrounding the relationship of the schools to equal opportunity, something of a pattern emerges. Those areas that are least controversial are those in which there is an overlap with the common school theme. Guaranteeing basic skills and ensuring that all students have a real chance at acquiring them through programs such as Head Start are not likely to be controversial because they are congruent with the egalitarianism of the common school. Equalizing educational opportunity, although not easy, is more within the reach of schools than equalizing economic opportunity. Also, there are potentially appropriate, consensual policies and programs that give due recognition to individual differences in background, need, or talent. Compensatory preschool programs, institutional alternatives for students who are not academically inclined, and recognition and development of different talents all seem to take into account individual differences in ways that go beyond narrow academic criteria. These take seriously the individualistic thrust of the productivity-achievement theme and provide a fairer chance for individuals. Still, as schools do more by way of differentiating among students, through ability grouping or certification or other programs, the more it seems that controversies about equal treatment and fairness arise.

Fairness to individuals and responsiveness to their separate needs may also require schools to do more and different things. It is commonly recognized that the increasing number of problems outside the school makes equal educational opportunity, or any of the other aims of the school, difficult to achieve. It has often been suggested that these problems are more important than academic issues. The schools have sporadically attempted to respond to the many nonacademic problems affecting students' academic prospects. These have mainly continued the individualistic thrust of the human capital theme but have tried to refine the response of the schools in ways that go beyond differences in academic abilities. The attempt to further tailor education to the needs of the individual suggests another, often implicit, theme in public education, "clientelism."

Notes

1. On the difference between conferring and confirming status see Joel Spring, *The American School, 1642-1990.* New York: Longman, 1991, pp. 10-11.

2. For a succinct history of this movement see David Tyack and Elizabeth Hansot, *Managers of Virtue: Public School Leadership in America, 1820-1920.* New York: Basic Books, 1982, Part Two.

3. On the economic thrust of the reform movement, see Mark Yudof, "Education Policy and the New Consensus of the 1980s," *Phi Delta Kappan.* 65 (1984), "Children are in public schools to learn skills . . . and, ultimately, to achieve a secure and productive job . . . The emphasis is on turning out engineers, scientists, computer programmers, health specialists, and other occupational groups that serve collective interests," p. 456. For a critique see Ira Shor, *Culture Wars: Schools and Society in the Conservative Restoration, 1969-1984.* Boston: Routledge, 1986.

4. *Report of the Committee of Ten.* New York: Arno Press, 1969, reprint of the 1893 report of the National Education Association.

5. On this shift and its relationship to pedagogical theory, see R. Freeman Butts, *Public Education in the United States.* New York: Holt, Rinehart, and Winston, 1978, Chs. 7, 8.

6. As John Dewey put it, "A division of the public school system into one part which pursues traditional methods, with incidental improvements, and another which deals with those who are to go into manual labor means a plan of social predestination totally foreign to the spirit of democracy." Cited in Butts, *Public Education in the United States*, p. 222.

7. National Education Association, Commission on the Reorganization of Secondary Education, *Cardinal Principles of Secondary Education*. Washington: U.S. Bureau of Education, 1918.

8. Tyack and Hansot, *Managers of Virtue*, p. 111.

9. For an interesting analysis of these results see "Origins," in Arthur Powell, Eleanor Farrar, and David Cohen, *The Shopping Mall High School: Winners and Losers in the Academic Marketplace*. Boston: Houghton Mifflin, 1985, Ch. 5.

10. William T. Grant Foundation, *The Forgotten Half: Pathways to Success for America's Youth and Young Families*. Washington, D.C.: Commission on Work, Family, and the Future, 1988. See also Powell, Farrar, and Cohen, *The Shopping Mall High School*. Ch. 4 on "The Unspecial."

11. For a discussion of Conant's views, see Robert Hampel, *The Last Little Citadel: American High Schools Since 1940*. Boston: Houghton Mifflin, 1986, pp. 59-73.

12. Respectively, National Commission on Excellence in Education, *A Nation at Risk*. Washington: Department of Education, 1983, p. 7; *America 2000: An Education Strategy*. Washington: Department of Education, 1991, p. 14.

13. The major reports include *Workforce 2000: Work and Workers for the Twenty-first Century*. Indianapolis, Ind.: Hudson Institute, 1987; *Making America Work: Productive People, Productive Policies*. Washington, D.C.: National Governor's Association, 1988; Anthony Carnevale, Leila Gainer, and Ann Meltzer, *Workplace Basics: The Skills Employers Want*. Washington, D.C.: American Society for Training and Development/ U.S. Department of Labor, 1988; Anthony Carnevale and Leila Gainer, *The Learning Enterprise*. Washington, D.C.: American Society for Training and Development/ U.S. Department of Labor, 1989; Commission on Workforce Quality and Market Efficiency, *Investing in People: A Strategy to Address America's Workforce Crisis*. Washington, D.C.: U.S. Department of Labor, 1989; Ira Magaziner, *America's Choice: High Skills or Low Wages*. Rochester, N.Y.: National Center on Education and the Economy, 1990; The Secretary's Commission on Achieving Necessary Skills (SCANS), *What Work Requires of Schools*. Washington, D.C.: U.S. Department of Labor, 1991. The *Investing in People* report is certainly the most comprehensive of these, including two volumes of over 2400 pages of background papers.

14. For example, one report suggests that these matters of habit and discipline are as important as academic training. Committee on Economic Development, *Investing in Our Children*. New York: Committee on Economic Development, 1985, pp. 17 ff.

15. For an argument that we should imitate the German system, see William Nothdurft, *Schoolworks: Reinventing Public Schools to Create the Workforce of the Future*. Washington, D.C.: Brookings, 1989.

16. For a general critique of tracking, see Jeannie Oakes, *Keeping Track: How Schools Structure Inequality*. New Haven: Yale University Press, 1985; for some of the institutional incentives for tracking see Sarah Glazer, "Why Schools Still Have Tracking," *Congressional Quarterly Editorial Research Reports*. 28 (December, 1990).

17. Robert Reich, "Must New Economic Vigor Mean Making Do with Less?" *NEA Today*. (January, 1989), p. 17.

18. Robert Reich, *The Work of Nations*. New York: Knopf, 1990; Ray Marshall and Marc Tucker, *Thinking for a Living*. New York: Basic, 1992.

19. For one of the few explicit examples of this argument, see John Bishop, "Is the Test Score Decline Responsible for the Productivity Decline?" *American Economic Review.* 79 (March 1989), pp. 178-197.

20. William Baumol, Sue Blackman, and Edward Wolff. *Productivity and American Leadership: The Long View.* Cambridge: MIT Press, 1989, especially Ch. 9.

21. Andrew Hacker, "The Schools Flunk Out," *New York Review of Books.* XXXI (April 12, 1984), pp. 35-39. On the contribution of education to growth, see Edward Denison, *Trends in American Economic Growth.* Washington, D.C.: Brookings Institution, 1982, pp. 36-39. On alternative hypotheses concerning falling real wages and wage gaps in the labor force, see Gary Burtless, ed., *A Future of Lousy Jobs?* Washington, D.C.: Brookings, 1990, especially Ch. 1.

22. For example, one former corporate executive, now an educational consultant, suggests that schools are like a supplier for a business that is producing 75 percent or more defective "parts," dropouts and poorly prepared students. Jack Bowsher, *Educating America: Lessons Learned in American Corporations.* New York: Wiley, 1986. The "upscale" quote is from *Workforce Crisis,* p. 96.

23. Charles Murray and Richard Herrnstein, 'What's Really Behind the SAT Score Decline?" *The Public Interest.* 106 (Winter 1992), pp. 32-56.

24. SCANS, *What Work Requires,* p. 15

25 For evidence that there is not a skills gap, particularly at the high end of the scale, see Magaziner, *America's Choice,* pp. 3ff; also, Lawrence Mishel and Ruy A. Teixeira, "The Myth of the Coming Labor Shortage," *The American Prospect.* 7 (Fall 1991), pp. 98-103. On shortages in specific fields, see W. Norton Grubb, "Responding to the Constancy of Change: New Technologies and Future Demands on U.S. Education," in Gerald Burke and Russell Rumberger, eds. *The Future Impact of Technology on Work and Education.* New York: Falmer, 1987, Ch. 7.

26. *Workforce Crisis,* p. 99

27. On the deployment of new technology and its consequences, see Patricia Flynn, "Introducing New Technologies into the Workplace: The Dynamics of Technological and Organizational Change," and Gary Kearsley, "Introducing New Technologies into the Workplace: Retraining Issues and Strategies," both in *Investing in People,* pp. 411-457, 458-493. On the current excess of educational credentials, see *Making America Work,* pp. vi, 3, which notes that 55 percent of youths go on to college even though less than a quarter of all occupations require a college degree. Similarly, *America's Choice: High Skills or Low Wages,* predicts that in the year 2000 "more than 70 percent of the jobs in America will not require a college education," p. 5.

28. On the contribution of training to productivity, the distribution of training, and arguments that we underinvest, see Carnevale and Gainer, *The Learning Enterprise;* Stephen Magnum, "Evidence on Private Sector Training," in *Investing in People,* pp. 381-387; U.S. General Accounting Office, *Training Strategies: Preparing Noncollege Youth for Employment in the U.S. and Other Countries.* Washington, D.C.: General Accounting Office, 1990.

29. See Magaziner, *America's Choice: High Skills or Low Wages,* p. 3; SCANS, *What Work Requires,* "Nine of ten employers are operating on yesterday's workplace assumptions," p. viii.

30. On this general finding and its implications for minorities, see Gordon Berlin and Andrew Sum, *Toward a More Perfect Union: Basic Skills, Poor Families, and Our Economic Future*. New York: Ford Foundation, 1988.

31. For an overview of the human capital approach, see George Psacharopoulos, ed., *Economics of Education: Research and Studies*. New York: Pergamon, 1987, Introduction; Henry Levin, "Mapping the Economics of Education," *Educational Researcher*. 18 (1989), pp. 13-16; Alan DeYoung, *Economics and American Education*. New York: Longman, 1989, Ch. 6. For a review of some other ways of applying economic analysis to other areas of education, see Eric Hanushek, "The Economics of Schooling: Production and Efficiency in Public Schools," *Journal of Economic Literature*. 24 (1986), pp. 1141-1177.

32. Arne Kallerberg and Ivar Berg, *Work and Industry: Structures, Markets and Processes*. New York: Plenum, 1987, p. 170.

33. For a general review of criticisms of human capital theory, see DeYoung, *Economics and American Education*, Chs. 8, 9. For a brief statement of the signaling hypothesis, see L. C. Solmon, "The Quality of Education," in Psacharopoulos, ed., *Economics of Education: Research and Studies*, pp. 56ff; the more radical view is expressed in Samuel Bowles and Herbert Gintis, *Schooling in Capitalist America*. New York: Basic, 1976. The "null hypothesis" is best expressed in Ivar Berg, *Education and Jobs: The Great Training Robbery*. New York: Praeger, 1970, and Randall Collins, *The Credential Society*. New York: Academic Press, 1979.

34. SCANS. *What Work Requires*, xvi.

35. Susan Berryman, "Education and the Economy: A Diagnostic Review and Implications for the Federal Role," Seminar on the Federal Role in Education. Aspen, Colorado: Aspen Institute, 1988, p. 2.

36. On the several categories of skills, see Russell Rumberger and Henry Levin, "Schooling for the Modern Workplace, in *Investing in People*, pp..85-144; Russell Rumberger, "The Potential Impact of Technology on the Skill Requirements of Future Jobs," in Burke and Rumberger, *The Future Impact of Technology on Work and Education*, pp. 79ff. On the several forms of intelligence, see Howard Gardner, *Frames of Mind*. New York: Basic Books, 1983.

37. Gary Kearsley, "Introducing New Technologies in the Workplace: Retraining Issues and Strategies," and Rumberger and Levin, "Schooling for the Modern Workplace," in *Investing in People*, pp. 460, 101, respectively.

38. Berg, *The Great Training Robbery*; Linda Gottfredson, "Education as a Valid but Fallible Sign of Worker Quality," *Research in the Sociology of Education and Socialization*. 5 (1985), p. 128. "For example, differences in the educational level of workers are not consistently related to differences in their performance within different occupations; the rise over time in the educational requirements of jobs cannot be accounted for by increases in skill demands."

39. Thomas Sticht, "Functional Context Education: Policy and Training Methods from the Military Experience," in *Investing in People*, pp. 2267-2308. On the problem of transfer of skills across contexts, see Lauren Resnick, *Education and Learning to Think*. Washington: National Academy Press, 1987. One might even speculate that "generic" skills are a by-product of specific ones rather than vice versa.

40. Lauren Resnick, "Learning In School and Out," *Educational Researcher*. 16 (1987), pp. 13-19.

41. SCANS, *What Work Requires*, xv.

42. On the differences of the American institutional configuration from others, see U.S. General Accounting Office, *Training Strategies: Preparing Noncollege Youth for Employment in the U.S. and Other Countries*, Ch. 3; William Nothdurft, *Schoolworks: Reinventing Public Schools*. On the need for a longer school year, see Michael Barrett, "The Case for More School Days," *Atlantic Monthly*. (November 1990), pp. 78-106.

43. "The Big Test: How to Translate Talk of School Reform into Action?," *New York Times*. Sunday, March 24, 1991, sect. 4, p. 4. "There are few more cherished national beliefs than that of America as a land of opportunity, where most people can make it, at most any time in their lives."

44. On incentives to perform in school and school-business ties, see John Bishop, "Incentives for Learning: Why American High School Students Compare so Poorly to Their Counterparts Overseas," in *Investing in People*, pp. 1-84.

45. See Henry Levin and W.S. Hopfenberg, "Accelerated Schools for At-risk Students," *Education Digest*. 56 (May 1991), pp. 47-50. Such grouping is not the same as the larger difference between academic and vocational curricula, rather it is an issue of how the same subjects will be provided to different students.

46. For some of the knotty problems of what it means for the schools to provide equal opportunity, even equal educational opportunity, see Christopher Jencks, "What Must be Equal for Opportunity to Be Equal?" and Jennifer Hochschild, "Race, Class, Power, and Equal Opportunity," in Norman Bowie, ed., *Equal Opportunity*. Boulder: Westview Press, 1988, pp. 47-74, 75-113.

47. James Coleman, *Equality of Educational Opportunity*. Washington: U.S. Department of Health, Education, and Welfare, 1966; Christopher Jencks, *Inequality*. New York: Basic Books, 1972; *Who Gets Ahead*. New York: Basic Books, 1979.

48. Tyack and Hansot, *Managers of Virtue*, p. 216.

49. "Katz Unveils Revolutionary Education Plan," *The Oregonian*. Portland, March 29, 1991, p. C1. The proposal's most visible feature was the tenth grade certificate, but it also included provisions for school-based social services and pre-school programs. Although the Oregon plan won legislative approval, many issues of implementation, including financing, are still being addressed.

50. On school-business cooperation, see Jorie Phillippi, "Facilitating the Flow of Information Between the Business and Education Communities," in *Investing in People*, pp. 701-756; on parallel government efforts, see Bert Barnow and Laudan Aron, Survey of Government-Provided Training Programs," in *Investing in People*, pp. 493-564.

51. See Gardner, *Frames of Mind*. Robert Jacobson, "Research on Different Ways of Being Smart Leads to 6-Year Project on Teaching and Learning Practical Intelligence in Schools," *Chronicle of Higher Education*, October 21, 1992, pp. A9, 15.

52. On "race norming" test scores in screening for government job referrals, see Jan Blits and Linda Gottfredson, "Equality or Lasting Inequality?" and the response by Alexandra Wigdor and John Hartigan, "The Case for Fairness," *Society*. 3 (1990), pp. 4-11, 12-16.

5

"Clientelism" and the Odd Couple: Choice and Welfare in Education

That the whole or any large part of the education of the people should be in the State's hands, I go as far as anyone in deprecating. . . . A general state education is a mere contrivance for molding people to be exactly like one another. . . . as it is efficient and successful, it establishes a despotism over the mind, leading by natural tendency to one over the body. An education established by the State should only exist, if it exist at all, as one of many competing experiments, carried on for the purpose of example and stimulus to keep the others up to a certain standard of excellence.

--John Stuart Mill

What the best and wisest parent wants for his own child, that must the community want for all its children. Any other ideal for our schools is narrow and unlovely; acted upon it destroys our democracy. All that society has accomplished for itself is put, through the agency of the school, at the disposal of its future members. All its better thoughts of itself it hopes to realize through the new possibilities thus opened to its future self. Here individualism and socialism are at one. Only by being true to the full growth of all the individuals who make it up, can society by any chance be true to itself . . . Whenever we have in mind the discussion of a new movement in education, it is especially necessary to take the broader, or social view.

--John Dewey

Chapter 4 looked at the development of the human capital theme in public education. For both economic and pedagogical reasons, that theme takes a more individualistic approach to public education than the common school orientation. The development of differentiated curricula and programs for students, particularly in the secondary schools, was originally justified as meeting both individual and social needs. Instead of imposing one curriculum on all students, there would be a matching of programs with individual talents. Different curricula would better prepare students for their different lives after school, thereby serving collective, particularly economic, needs. In its crudest and perhaps most pernicious terms, "head" and "hand" students would find different curricula better suited to their abilities. Despite ongoing controversies about ability grouping and tracking, most schools offer differentiated curricula and programs based on students' current or likely achievement.[1] These practices are seen as best meeting individual student needs and thereby serving the larger community.

Even in its more benign forms, a focus on individual needs opens a potential Pandora's box for schools. The comprehensive high school's commitment to student-centeredness and realistic individual preparation is, if carried to its logical conclusion, potentially so complex as to be impractical. It suggests the possibility that the schools can and should respond to all kinds of individual differences. Conceivably each student might have a different set of needs, requiring a distinct program or specific services. This problem is exacerbated by the schools' role as referee in the equal opportunity "race." Schools, it may be argued, should respond to various physical, familial, cultural, and social problems as a way of creating fair opportunities for access to jobs or further educational credentials. The overlapping mandates of responding to individual differences and compensating for factors beyond the school suggest that schools might need to do more than simply set up different academic groupings. It can also imply that schools should find some means for addressing the great variety of individual characteristics, circumstances, and backgrounds.

This potential for overwhelming complexity has been reduced in two ways. First, academic records and test scores have been used to group students and place them in specific programs. Instead of trying to develop a curriculum for each student, there are overlapping curricula that provide a range of options. With the help of guidance professionals and testing programs, each student receives one of a small set of curricular options that is supposed to best fit his or her talents or needs. Second, schools have provided ancillary services and programs that respond to nonacademic problems that might impede the educational process. School nurses and social workers, meal and day care programs, and, as will be discussed below, a recently growing array of other programs address needs that go well beyond academic testing and classification. In either case, the point is to reduce complexity but still respond to individual needs through some combination of academic and support services.

Described in this way, these practices and programs might seem to be merely an adjunct to the human capital view of education. Academic classification is the primary means of designating an individual's talents and likely type of role in the economy. Support services merely guarantee that students are able to participate in the academic race on a more or less equal footing. For example, poor students can be provided a free or reduced-price meal so that they can simply be physically able to learn. Other services such as school nurses or social workers play a similar role, usually for some or all groups in the school.

However, the notion of meeting individual needs can go beyond the limited issue of academic classification or support services. There is no obvious reason why these categories should not continually expand, as indeed they have, or that new services to meet needs should not be provided through the schools. In Dewey's terms, the schools, like the "wisest parent," ideally might attempt to support children in as complete a way as possible. The schools might strive to meet the individual needs of each student defined as broadly as possible ("full growth") in both academic and nonacademic terms ("social view"). In a common way of phrasing it, schools would seek to educate the whole child.

If the notion of meeting a range of needs is taken far enough, it is then possible to see an entirely separate theme or strand of educational ideology. Providing a common educational experience or preparing students for their economic roles would be only a part of a broader mission of addressing the needs of each individual student. On this view the school is a social service agency with a broad mandate to assist young people not only in their academic pursuits, but in personal development and adjustment in the broadest terms. Since family problems obviously affect student development, this mandate might extend to students' families as well. The school then might become a professional agency that responds to the needs of its clientele, students and their families. "Clientelism" becomes a distinctive theme that develops the basic notion that schools should be responsive to the needs of their clients.

Of course, there are difficult questions as to how those needs are defined and, for that matter, by whom. The prospect that the school might try to act as the wisest parent to its clients raises questions whether the state can or should play that role. Mill's suggestion at the beginning of this chapter that education should be a private matter, lest it become a "contrivance for molding people," implies a very different response to meeting the needs of clients, school choice. School choice would shift the burden of defining students' needs from the state to the family by allowing families to choose where and how their children will be educated. Instead of the state trying to act as the wisest parent, families would be free to choose their own schools to meet their children's needs as they see them. Families would, through market mechanisms, define what educational programs and services would be provided and in what ways.

In its most extreme form, school choice suggests replacing state-provided education with a market approach. The state would provide vouchers to families to cover the cost of education and set some broad regulations about what schools must do to provide a basic education. But otherwise schools would be free to provide education and services much as a firm in the market provides a product to its customers. Even in more limited versions of choice plans among public schools, there still would be considerable latitude for schools to compete by offering different and better "products." Through competition, schools would be pressured to meet the needs of their clients or go out of business.

At first glance, these variations on the theme of clientelism, "welfare" and "choice," make a very odd couple. Proposals for providing welfare services through the schools seem utterly contradictory to the idea of school choice. In one sense, these variations are contradictory in that they envision very different educational roles for the state. One anticipates an expansion of the school into welfare services and the other reduces the state's role to merely setting the most basic regulations for (public or private) schools. At the same time, both variations do reflect the central idea of clientelism, that schools should adapt to the needs of students and families. Both suggest that the diversity and variety of those needs cannot be met by one common school or even through the standard academic vehicles of testing and curricular grouping. Therefore the schools, on either variation, must be more flexible and adaptable in what they do. Welfare and choice are very different means to a similar end, making the schools responsive to the great variety of needs. The key difference is whether the state or the family will be the primary mechanism for doing so.

If recognized at all, clientelism has always been a kind of subordinate theme in educational ideology. Schools have always been involved to a greater or lesser degree in providing social services, but this involvement has typically been ad hoc and unsystematic. Programs have expanded by accretion rather than as part of some systematic view of the schools' role. For example, some of the schools that have been most effective in difficult settings are those that have reached out to the community, especially to immigrant groups or the poor, in various ways.[2] However, these "welfare" tasks have typically been seen as secondary, driven more by the necessity to make academic endeavors possible than by some larger theme or aim. Similarly, the idea of choice has, until very recently, been mainly a matter of theoretical interest. When Milton Friedman suggested a voucher plan over thirty years ago, it was seen more as novelty than as a genuine policy alternative.[3] It is only recently that states and localities have seriously considered or experimented with choice as a possible strategy for educational reform, and these initiatives have thus far been very limited.

The vast majority of choice programs have involved only modest departures from current practices in the public sector.

Both welfare and choice proposals for the schools represent a fuller extension of the logic of individualism in defining educational aims. That such disparate kind of proposals could be simultaneously considered, as they currently are, is testimony to the rhetorical strength of arguments based on individual need. This reinforces the idea that "clientelism" is a theme worthy of consideration in its own right. This chapter explores both kinds of arguments (welfare, choice) as different ways of making schools more responsive to the clientele. Here, as in previous themes, there is some tension, and in this case perhaps an outright contradiction, between the variations on this theme. Again, as in other themes, both variations face a dilemma of excess and deficit and the "bias toward the minimum" has been the typical and safest institutional course.[4] The suggestion here is that clientelist proposals, on either variation, are most plausible when they operate in ways consistent with each other and with aims for public education expressed in other themes. Public schools can and should be more responsive through "welfare" programs and choices, but these should be pursued within the broad parameters of a common, publicly provided education. Even so, there are many empirical and practical questions about how to make schools more responsive through either welfare or choice.

Clients and Needs: Families, Communities, "IEPs," and Choice

There has always been some ambivalence and tension in the relationship between schools and families. The natural posture of the public school in a liberal democratic society is to defer to the family in nonacademic matters. To do otherwise is to have a state institution intruding into the private sphere. Even in many academic matters, such as the question of moral education discussed in Chapter 3, there is similar deference. At the same time, in its custodial function and the authority it must exercise over children, the school is always acting to some degree *in loco parentis.* It becomes a kind of second family. Moreover, the school is more than simply an educational institution. Its educational task inevitably involves building broader social relationships with students and families. Few can doubt that the family has an important educational role or that the school's social role unavoidably goes beyond its primary educational tasks. Ideally, the roles that the family and school play are complementary and mutually supportive. A loving family and an effective school provide the child with the means for healthy emotional and intellectual development. In performing their overlapping tasks, the family and school should strengthen one another.

Obviously, this ideal has never been perfectly attained. Periodically it has been suggested that the school must change its practices and programs because of changes in the families it serves. The school, it is argued, must do what the family, for whatever reasons, cannot do. Even the original common school was understood as providing a civic identity that transcended family and group ties, especially for the first wave of immigrants. At the turn of the twentieth century, the conditions in the larger cities created by further immigration and industrialization led many to recommend new services and programs for the schools. The development of kindergarten programs, school lunches, health services, playgrounds, and recreational facilities on school sites, as well as other community programs, were part of an expanding view of the social role of the school. As Joel Spring puts it, "The changes in the late nineteenth century made the school more than a center of instruction by turning it into a major social agency."[5] This role was perceived as a necessary response to an environment that was no longer adequately supportive of children generally and education in particular.

It is important to note that there is considerable variation in the above package of proposed and actual services. Some are more directly aimed at the child as student-client. These include kindergartens, physical education and playground facilities, health courses, and school nurses. Other proposals have a broader sweep and take in the family or the broader community--literacy instruction, "Americanization" programs, and family assistance of various kinds. The broadest proposals, endorsed by Dewey and embodied in the settlement house movement associated with Jane Addams, envisioned the school as a social center for the entire community. It would offer a variety of social services going well beyond education, including providing a forum for community meetings and political discussion.[6] In this range of options both the concept of the client and the range of educational needs can be defined narrowly or broadly. The concept of client ranges from the individual student to the entire community. Educational needs might be narrowly defined as academic or more broadly in terms of the "whole child." They might even extend to family outreach or community organizing. Although these categories may overlap, they reflect the underlying idea that a more social view of education was both necessary and desirable.

Not surprisingly, the schools have tended to display a bias toward the minimum, toward narrower notions of clients and needs, and therefore of programs and services.[7] Programs that sought to directly "educate" the child through kindergartens, physical and health education, for example, were specific responses by schools to the condition of children. They seemed a natural, logical development. Ideologically they also fit better with the individualistic focus of the emerging human capital theme. Moreover, as a practical and political matter those options that could demonstrate a direct benefit to children were more readily justified and easily institutionalized as part of the school's mission. Progressive pedagogical notions about educating for the "full growth of individuals" could be more easily accommodated through these options than more speculative and politically risky ventures in community building. Politically, community building was regarded with some suspicion since it was important to "take the schools out of politics."[8]

To be sure there is no sharp line between programs and services directed at children and those that serve families and communities. For example, it was often hoped that the kindergarten experience would have a salutary effect on the home by educating parents (especially immigrant parents) about proper habits and virtues. Language instruction or other forms of "Americanization" could likewise be extended to adults. Health and recreation programs developed for children could also serve communities, as could school facilities in general. Nonetheless, any broader ambitions for the school as a community center typically did not come to fruition. As the various elements of social programs were folded into the school, the idea of community building was subordinated to the narrower role of the school as an academic institution. Those tasks that most clearly affected and fit with the schools' emerging academic organization, as an education "factory," were most readily accepted and institutionalized. For example, kindergartens and school nurses could be readily justified as making education possible, and even recreational facilities could be seen in this light. The larger enterprises of social work with families and community building more generally were less clearly within the schools' perceived ability or legitimate sphere. Welfare became a separate enterprise from education as the secondary school developed.

To the degree that schools have played a role in broader community building, it has often been through less institutional or programmatic efforts. One of the commonly cited characteristics of effective schools has been their ability to reach out into the community, especially in encouraging family involvement. For example, some kind of personal and informal interaction between the school, on the one hand, and families and communities, on the other, has been rather common in may good suburban districts. However, in these settings it often involves academic liaison, recreation, and boosterism rather than welfare.[9] In poorer districts some of these less programmatic efforts at community building have been effective or even inspiring. There are numerous stories of teachers and administrators who took a broader view of their relationship with students and the larger community and succeeded in difficult circumstances. One commonly cited example is Leonard Covello, a principal in East Harlem in the 1940s. Covello made it a point to know the students and their families personally; he respected (and shared) the Italian-American culture of the area. He "celebrated multiculturalism long before it became fashionable" and created a number of specific institutional arrangements that made the school a kind of community center.[10] The key to this reaching out, however, was Covello himself. His personality and even his authoritarian view of his relationship with his "clients" defined the issues. His leadership was more charismatic than bureaucratic.

The personalistic relationship of someone like this to the community is not a program. Periodically, the idea that educational services needed to be understood in a larger social context and provided in a more systematic way has gained temporary legitimacy, although not in any consistent form or with any lasting effect. For a short period after World War II the idea of "life adjustment" exerted a powerful influence on educators. It suggested that for noncollege youth, particularly those not in vocational tracks, the school should aim at developing a broad range of social skills as part of educating the "whole child." It explicitly involved many nonacademic subjects such as interpersonal relationships, practical skills, and even hobbies. Here the notion of education was broadened to include social skills as a way of serving a category of clients whose needs were allegedly not being met by existing academic or vocational curricula.[11] Another example of an attempt to expand educational institutions to meet the needs of specific clientele arose in the 1960s as part of the War on Poverty. As part of the package of poverty programs the schools would be involved in a range of social services. Head Start programs would extend the reach of the school to the preschool years, often including families in the process of getting children ready for school. Title I money would provide schools with the opportunity to add educational and other services for poor and minority students. More comprehensive programs through Model Cities suggested that the schools might become community centers for a range of activities. The school would begin to approximate a community center akin to the settlement house.[12]

In these cases, as in the progressive era, the attempted expansion of the schools' role was rather short-lived. As with several other movements toward student-centered instruction, the idea of life adjustment was condemned as antagonistic to academic rigor. It was deemed too soft on students given what was expected from the schools. Specifically, the postwar threat of Communism was taken to require that the schools mobilize for the global struggle by increasing academic demands. Likewise, the War on Poverty quickly fell victim to the demands of another war. It became apparent that fighting poverty by expanding the programmatic efforts of the schools would require more knowledge and resources than we had or were willing to bring to bear, especially given the demands of the Vietnam War. In either case, the conceptually and politically safest route was to limit expansion of the schools' role to those kinds of programs and services that could be seen as directly impacting the child's academic potential. Certainly the school's role in these areas has increased incrementally over the years, for example, in preschool education through Head Start, but it has never become a systematic part of the schools' mission. For example, it is widely noted that Head Start programs are available to only a small proportion of those eligible.

Perhaps one area in which we can see what a full-blown clientelist approach might mean comes from the area of education for students with special needs, such as those with physical or learning disabilities. In these areas each student is given individual treatment depending upon his or her situation. The development of an individualized educational program (IEP) reflects tailoring the program to the specific requirements of the student. The program makes use of both academic and nonacademic services as needed.[13] Any IEP might use the services of a physical therapist, psychologist, social worker, and various other special services. What is crucial in this process is the diagnosis and classification of the problem that specifies the individual needs that must be met. Although there may be considerable dispute in any particular case between and among parents, teachers, specialists, and others, all parties are presumably interested primarily in meeting the needs of the individual student in question. The legitimacy of such programs stems from a recognition that these students do have special needs that require individualized attention. Equally important, these programs recognize that such efforts must be made in a coherent and systematic fashion. The various parties in this process are constantly and necessarily coordinating their efforts with one another. In the absence of this kind of holisitc, sustained effort, these students would have little or no chance to gain the benefits of public education. It is widely agreed that these students need and deserve a range of services that go well beyond academic programs, and that these services cannot and should not be separated from one another.

Although it is not often articulated, there is a clear analogy between these students with special needs and others. Many students live in circumstances and conditions that give them little or no chance to receive the benefits of public education. Their "disabilities," although not as overtly physical as those of a child with a handicapping condition, can be every bit as debilitating. Indeed, the first goal of the current reform movement, that all students start school ready to learn, represents public acknowledgment of these kinds of problems. It also reflects the sense that the appropriate reach of public education might go beyond the schoolhouse and the academic or vocational programs within it. The great obstacle, of course, is how to define, conceptually or programmatically, what the schools can and should do to address the range of factors that makes it difficult or impossible for students to learn.

Despite the historical difficulties of addressing these issues, most notably the definition of "client" and "need," and the patchwork and partial quality of existing programs, there is a growing sense that still more comprehensive, integrated services and programs should be developed. As I will discuss below, there are a number of examples of a more self-conscious and systematic "welfare" approach on the part of the schools to their clients. The school is increasingly seen as a welfare agency providing a range of services with education being first among equals. This variety of services aims at allowing students the chance at a quality education. There have been any number of proposals and experiments, but it is only in recent years that more formal programs have been developed that anticipate linking education and social services in a more systematic, client-centered approach.[14]

It may seem that there is quite a gap, both theoretically and practically, between a welfare approach and proposals for school choice. One way to bridge this gap is to mention some of the criticisms of the welfare approach. For example, some historians have expressed skepticism about the expanded social role of the school. They suggest that the aim was to exert a greater degree of social control over immigrants and make them "good citizens." This implied that immigrant families were somehow deficient and that their values or norms should be subordinated to those of the school and therefore the state. Ironically, this kind of critique, often made from the left of the political spectrum, suggests a version of clientelism, school choice, that is more congenial to the right. That is, implicit in the development of a wider range of programs and services for families is the notion that some families are incapable of coping with their situation, especially the education of their children, either narrowly or broadly defined.

However, it might be suggested that it is not the family that has failed but the school or perhaps even the larger society. What families truly need, it might be argued, is some means for dealing with the failures of their local schools, as well as the opportunity to define their own needs. Instead of looking to schools to define and meet students' needs, the idea of choice shifts this task to families. It suggests that families can, if given the chance, better define and pursue their needs than some paternalistic state agency. Choice becomes the vehicle for letting families determine their needs through market or quasi-market mechanisms. These mechanisms will in turn lead to the provision of improved education because of competition.

There is, as in the welfare approach, a wide variety of programs and proposals that currently fall under the rubric of choice. Friedman's original choice proposal was both simple and radical. Students should be given a voucher that could be cashed in for educational services at any appropriately certified school. Educational institutions would then compete for students just as other firms would in a market. Although vouchers are the most radical option for choice, most current options for choice occur within the public sector. These include everything from statewide choice programs to selection among "schools within schools." The central idea underlying these varied options is that by giving families greater discretion in choosing programs or schools, the needs of students, as more directly defined by families, will be better met.[15] The key here, of course, is that individual families determine what their needs are. The "client" becomes a "consumer," and consumers collectively determine what will be offered through their choices. This is preferable, it is argued, to the situation in which the public school, as a legal monopoly, determines what children need, academically or otherwise, and therefore what will be offered. Where a welfare approach expands the reach of the state, choice limits the state's role in defining clients' needs.

The development of programmatic social services in the school and proposals for extensive choice plans indicate that clientelism is becoming a distinctive theme in American public education. For either welfare or choice, a clientelist approach entails, insofar as possible, a broadening and individualizing of schools' services. Obviously, as these programs and proposals develop, their problems become more apparent. For example, there are questions about the definition of welfare needs and the coordination of services and the practicality and propriety of choice. Moreover, clientelist concerns become a potential competitor for attention and resources of the other themes discussed previously. Before exploring these problems it is useful to review these variations on the clientelist theme, especially as they pose the dilemma of excess and deficit.

"What?" and "How Far?": Variations on the Clientelist Theme

There are several things that make clientelism a distinctive theme in public education. It implies a different and broader notion of the relationships between schools and students and their families as clients or customers. On either variation clientelism takes a more individualistic approach to education, one that brings to the fore issues concerning the fundamental relationship of public schools to families. Tailoring education to the individual (family) is not confined to a few academic or curricular categories, as in the human capital view, rather it involves a greater concern for the range and variety of needs (the "whole child"). A shift in emphasis from using education for some larger social purpose such as cultural integration or economic development to meeting individual needs makes it possible to rethink many things about public education, including what education

	Choice	Welfare
Maximum	Privatization/vouchers	"One-stop shopping," schools as community centers
	Stipends, tax credits	Schools as coordinating agencies
Minimum	State, inter-district choice	Family support, services, outreach programs
	"Controlled," intra-district choice	School development programs

FIGURE 5.1 Variations on the "Clientelism" theme

means and how public it should be. Indeed, in the case of school choice the question becomes whether the state should be directly involved in education at all.

What is interesting about the variations on the clientelist theme (see Figure 1) is that they both reflect departures from the current enterprise but in very different directions. The question of "what" the schools shall do in the clientelist theme is really a question of "who." Specifically, who will be the primary source of authority in defining individual students' needs, the state or families? Obviously, meeting the child's needs has always been a shared responsibility and source of tension between schools and families. The variations on this theme suggest different ways of negotiating these responsibilities ("What?"). For each variation there will again be minimum and maximum variations ("How far?") that are likewise in tension with one another.

The welfare variation suggests that schools must move beyond a narrow academic definition to a broader, social view of the needs of students and families. Minimally, the schools are already doing some of this through various services (nurses, school lunches, social workers), but these have been mainly ad hoc, offered to students with acute and apparent problems. As the schools have gradually expanded their services, it becomes possible to more closely tailor programs to individuals, and look to an ever broader and more open-ended definition of need. Some in the current reform movement suggest this still simply isn't going far enough (deficit). A more ambitious approach would offer a broader, more integrated program to students. It would particularly reach out to families and provide a range of (welfare) services that might not be traditionally seen as academic.[16]

But in expanding these programs and services the schools may be going beyond their capacity or legitimate purview (excess). Clearly there are some formidable practical obstacles to the schools' developing a set of welfare services, especially in a time of fiscal constraints. There is also the obvious conceptual problem of defining individual needs. Conceivably each individual can, and probably does, have a set of distinctive needs. Defining, let alone meeting, them for each student would of course be impractical. Even if we had settled on a view of precisely what kinds of services were legitimate, we might not have the practical knowledge, political will, or fiscal capacity to deliver them. Equally important, the schools have often been criticized when they have ventured into this territory. It has been suggested that either they have taken on too many tasks or, worse, have let a "therapeutic" orientation compromise the academic purposes of the school.[17]

Here again there is the dilemma of excess and deficit. On the one hand, the developing welfare programs imply that the state should do more to compensate for problems outside the school. There is an understandable impulse for schools to try to respond to family situations or other external problems that make education difficult or impossible. On the other hand, the concept of clients' needs is so broad and open-ended that, at the limit, the state could become a surrogate or substitute family. The prospect of government doing so raises some questions about the legitimacy of its activities in relation to this "private" sphere. There are serious questions about how far the state can and should go in defining and serving students noneducational needs. In such a situation, it might be feared that the state is less likely to act as the "wisest parent" than a "contrivance for molding people."

The choice approach tries to meet the variety of student and family needs by contracting rather than expanding the state's role. It might be argued that, instead of relying upon the schools to define and respond to student needs, families should be given more autonomy and responsibility in choosing schools that meet their needs as they see them. Proponents of choice plans argue, as in Mill's statement at the beginning of this chapter, that school choice opens up the possibility for "competing experiments" that provide a constant "example and stimulus to keep the others up to a certain standard of excellence." It is ironic that Mill saw state schools as performing this function whereas contemporary advocates of choice see private schools playing this role. Proponents of choice also point to the organizational efficiency and academic focus (and success) of private and parochial schools and claim this is the result of choice and competition. These schools succeed where the public schools fail, they claim, because market mechanisms provide a stimulus for these schools to succeed.[18] The competition engendered by creating a market for schooling, it is argued, will serve needs better, because it leaves the definition of those needs up to families. Schools that serve their clientele's needs better will prosper and those that do not will fail.

One of the most powerful rhetorical devices used by those in favor of choice is to note that the public schools are a monopoly. Unless a family moves from the district, it must take whatever "product" the school gives it. Choice would break this link in a way that creates an ironic variation on the dilemma of excess and deficit. As a monopoly, it is argued, the schools have already gone too far in defining students' needs. The current system has thus done too little to allow families to choose children's educational programs and schools. The (unacceptable) "bias toward the minimum" in this case is the minimizing of parental autonomy and choice. To do "more" by way of choice means lessening the role of the state in making these educational decisions. The maximum version of the choice variation, then, is for the state, as in Mill's view, to minimize its role. It would take itself as far out of the educational system as far as possible, for example, through vouchers or some other form of privatization.

Needless to say, proposals for choice have been very controversial since they potentially challenge the traditional system of publicly provided education. Many of the disputes about choice revolve around practical and empirical issues, for example, how to implement choice plans or whether choice in any of its forms will produce better academic results than the current system. There are also concerns that choice may produce worse results for certain groups, particularly the poor and minorities. They might lack either enough economic leverage or consumer savvy, or both, to obtain quality educational services. Other objections are more theoretical, suggesting that privatization destroys a key aim of public education, namely that all students should develop some sense of public involvement and citizenship. Many of these objections are aimed at a radical privatization of public education through some kind of voucher system. There is greater support for controlled choice within the public system as one possible strategy for reform. However, the basic criticisms of choice in any form suggest that its educational benefits are modest if not dubious, and that education should not be primarily considered as a kind of private or consumer good.[19]

In either form, clientelism raises some of the most fundamental questions about education posed by liberal democratic theory: the role of the state in education, the boundary between public and private, the merit of "regulatory" and "market" mechanisms, the nature of the family and its relationship to the state. Although the choice variation on this theme is the more recent development and is still largely a theoretical idea, it is worth examining first. It most starkly poses the issues of what best serves the clients' needs by suggesting a major reconceptualization of how families and schools should be related. Where welfare implies broadening and institutionalizing a long-term trend in the expansion of school services, choice implies moving in a somewhat different direction. In some of its forms choice implies a radically different institutional framework altogether. Examining this alternative first makes it easier to see what is at stake in the welfare variation on this theme.

Choice: Educational Markets

Many of the dilemmas of public education described in previous chapters arise because of the suspicion of state power in a liberal democratic society. For example, as discussed in Chapter 3, on one hand if the state actively promotes certain moral precepts, it may be open to the charge of imposing its views and thereby compromising individual freedom. On the other hand, to the degree it seeks to avoid such issues, it can be charged with doing too little to provide for cultural and political integration. Proposals for school choice, in the libertarian tradition of Mill, suggest a different way of dealing with this dilemma. They would, to a greater or lesser degree, take away the power of the state to define the goals and programs of educational institutions. This power would be shifted to families who through market mechanisms ultimately decide what the schools will offer. Such a shift is desirable, not only intuitively as a matter of family autonomy and consumer sovereignty, but also as a matter of producing better educational results through market-style competition.

Some forms of school choice have always existed. Private provision of secondary education was the rule well into the nineteenth century, and the formation of separate parochial schools dates from the middle of that century. There is still a robust private sector today. Recently there has been an increase in Catholic and Christian school populations. There has always been a constitutionally recognized "exit" option from the public schools as part of the normal exercise of freedom in a liberal democratic society. (Of course, there has been a premium attached to availing oneself of the private option, even if that premium is subsidized in various ways by religious organizations or indirect forms of aid to parochial schools.) Even within the public sector, there has been some degree of choice through decisions concerning where to reside and expressions of parental preferences for placement within schools. In the 1960s, alternative schools, including magnet schools that were part of desegregation efforts, also offered to increase family options. The allure of these and other kinds of options has helped make recent choice proposals more attractive.[20]

The appeal of choice as a strategy for educational reform steadily gained momentum in the 1980s. Two studies by James Coleman suggest that private and parochial schools are more effective than their public counterparts and that this effectiveness is independent of any background characteristics of students.[21] This lends credence to the argument that public monies supporting private and parochial schools might be well spent. In 1983 the courts upheld the idea of states' granting tuition tax credits for students attending nonsectarian private schools. A number of states and localities implemented various choice plans, and some existing successful programs, such as Harlem's District 4, began to receive national attention and even acclaim.

More recently, there have been a number of experiments and proposals for privatization that take the idea of choice to its logical conclusion. Some school districts have contracted the operation of schools to private firms. Wisconsin has created the Milwaukee Parental Choice Program to provide a limited program of stipends for low income families to choose a private school. Several states are experimenting with similar programs in which state aid supports students in "charter" schools. The Edison Project, underwritten initially by Whittle Communications, began the process of planning and seeking funding for building schools as a private, for profit venture. Finally, a widely discussed book in 1990 by John Chubb and Terry Moe, *Politics, Markets, and America's Schools*, suggests that the very existence of publicly controlled schools was the source of America's educational problems. They argue that choice, in the form of a voucher or "scholarship" program, is a "panacea" for improving educational performance.[22]

It is striking how quickly the idea of choice has become a visible part of the agenda of the reform movement. This is due to a combination of factors. Given the severity of the original indictment of the schools and the lack of progress of early reform efforts, something that promised a very different approach would no longer necessarily be condemned as radical. Indeed, it might be welcomed because it held out the prospect of being a "panacea." The natural sympathies of the Republican administrations that have held power during most of the reform movement would give, if nothing else, rhetorical support to the idea that market mechanisms might be a remedy for school problems. The idea of choice also gained some unlikely political allies in educators, especially minorities, in urban settings who were willing to lobby for choice as something that could be no worse than the existing situation. Similarly, Chubb and Moe's proposal was published by the Brookings Institution, a think tank not known for promoting conservative political views. In short, the yearning for real reform, a willingness to experiment, and a broad, if unlikely, political coalition, have given increased legitimacy to the idea of choice.

One of the reasons choice plans can gather such support is that the idea has always spanned several different kinds of proposals. Choice has come to mean almost any program that gives families options beyond what they have traditionally had in their local schools. These might include programs of choosing schools within local districts or statewide, as well as voucher plans that would allow public funds to underwrite the choice of nonpublic schools. Part of the difficulty in evaluating the idea of choice is the fact that the concept has come to cover an incredible variety of different and even contradictory programmatic possibilities. One early review of the literature suggests that there are at least "36 categories and subcategories of family choice models," including magnet schools, schools within schools, public vouchers, specialty schools, specific instructional activities and programs, programs for special target populations, among others.[23] There are other typologies that are as complex and produce as many or more alternatives. The idea of choice is therefore only meaningful when it is specified what kinds of choices are available to families and under what terms.[24]

Perhaps the most proximate, and most common, departure from traditional practice is what is called "controlled" or "intradistrict" choice. Parents in a district have the option of choosing which public school their child will attend. Within certain restrictions like availability of space and racial balance, parents can select their child's school, presumably on the basis of their assessment of their child's needs. There are many wrinkles on the idea of controlled choice, including the notion that schools will consciously differentiate their programs to provide real choices. For example, one school might specialize in performing arts, another in math and science, and so on. In effect, each school tries to become a magnet school by offering an attractive program or a "theme" that will both give it a distinctive identity and convince parents to choose it. There may also be several different kinds of schools within the same building. District 4 is often cited as the prime example of how the use of such thematic offerings within a choice plan can dramatically improve a district. The logic of such controlled choice can, of course, be extended beyond a district. Some states, most notably Minnesota, have adopted "open enrollment" plans that allow students to register in any school in the state. A number of other states are currently experimenting with various choice plans.[25]

It is important to note that even where choice programs "look" the same, there can be many local nuances and differences that can affect how the programs function. For example, in "controlled" intradistrict programs decisions concerning school assignment might be made at either the school or district level. This difference in the admissions process may have important implications for how a program functions. Even where programs seem to have the same rules and procedures, there may be many other contextual factors (needs for transportation, the availability of information, or the profile of the clientele) that will affect what "choice" means. There are also many other possible differences in implementation regarding internal organization, teacher autonomy, governance, and so on that might have significant impacts.

There is something of a fault line between the above programs and proposals that would give families an expanded option to exit from publicly controlled schools. The key to such options is public financial support. The provision of tax credits for private school tuition is perhaps the first step in making a wider range of choices available to families. The development of "charter" schools and stipends for selecting a private school are yet more ambitious provisions of financial support. These programs, it should be noted, are not inconsistent with the existence of a public school system. Rather they imply that public schools will no longer have a monopoly in the educational market.[26] It is but a short step, theoretically at least, to the prospect that families would be free to choose where to spend an educational "allowance" or "scholarship" from the government. In its most radical form, as originally articulated by Friedman and recently revived by Chubb and Moe, the state would more or less get out of the education business, save as a kind of third party payer within a lightly regulated industry.

It is testimony to the growing salience of the idea of choice that such voucher plans, once considered a radical idea, are now being seriously debated and considered. One major focus of the recent debate is the argument for privatization offered by Chubb and Moe. Building upon a longitudinal data set of surveys and records of teachers, administrators, and students used by Coleman and others, Chubb and Moe suggest that private and parochial schools are simply academically more effective. What Chubb and Moe add to this finding is an explanation of what they see as the source of these differences. Specifically, they claim that the system of democratic control in the public sector produces organizational patterns that are inconsistent with educational excellence. The administrative apparatus that governs schools renders them less autonomous and less responsive to the clientele, and therefore less effective:

> Like many observers of contemporary American education, we believe that the bureaucratization of educational governance has simply gone too far. Many public school systems seem to have become so bureaucratized that their schools cannot possibly develop clear objectives and high academic expectations or attract and keep the kinds of principals and teachers that are required for effective performance.
>
> We have a different theory than other observers, however, about why all of this has happened. Our reasoning is that much of it is an inevitable and logical consequence of the direct democratic control of schools. Except under special conditions, we believe, the existing institutions of democratic control are simply inconsistent with the autonomous operation and effective organization of schools.[27]

Chubb and Moe's solution follows directly from their analysis. The state should set minimal criteria for licensing schools just as it does now in accrediting private schools, and approved schools should have the right to accept students using their own admission criteria. Most important, public monies should follow students. Chubb and Moe do suggest a number of other conditions for financing, information, governance, and racial balance. However, the key to the program is that, within very broad limits, families will have choices among highly autonomous schools underwritten by public money.

In whatever form, the underlying logic supporting various choice plans is essentially the same as that articulated by Chubb and Moe. Schools, like firms in any other industry, will compete for customers. Those that best respond to what "customers" want will succeed and those that do not will go out of business. Within some broad limits, families will not be coerced, politically or economically, into sending their children into schools that do not meet their needs. This resonates with our suspicion of state power and monopoly in any form. Moreover, freeing up the school industry will presumably have collective benefits as well. Competition of this kind will be a constant spur for school improvement and innovation (as Mill put it, "many competing experiments"). There will be natural incentives to provide better education that are lacking in the current bureaucratic system. In a sense choice, it is argued, frees teachers and principals as much as it does parents and children. It allows them to use their best knowledge and judgment to provide better education by throwing off the bureaucratic apparatus that constrains them.[28]

Proponents of choice suggest that there is already considerable evidence that choice is a promising strategy for reform. Although there are some programs that have not succeeded, there are few, if any that are outright failures. Choice, it seems, does no harm. Chubb and Moe's ambitious study attempts to give the choice movement a more general grounding in a broad database on the correlates of school achievement and a theory of what makes schools effective. What are the exceptional "effective" schools in the public sector, they argue, are more the rule in the private sector precisely because of the need to be competitive.[29] Finally, the continuing demand for educational reform provides a political environment more receptive to what would have been dismissed out of hand not so long ago.

But Does It Work?

Needless to say there has been tremendous controversy about the idea of choice, particularly as it has implied the privatization of public schools through vouchers. Much of the argument concerning choice plans in any form has revolved around logistical and empirical issues. Even when it is acknowledged, as it must be, that some choice programs have been apparently successful, there are further doubts about whether those successes can be duplicated in other districts. There are some formidable logistical difficulties in even the more modest controlled choice plans, let alone any voucher program. Transportation and information are just two of the obstacles commonly cited. It would be difficult and costly to ensure adequate transportation for many choice plans. Similarly, ensuring that parents know what their options are requires a great deal of effort. Moreover, most analysts agree that dealing with these practical issues, particularly in the public sector, will inevitably cost more money. This presents some obvious political problems for states and localities that are resistant to further educational expenditures. This is not to say that these problems are insurmountable, merely that there are many practical questions to be answered in moving from small-scale demonstrations to some more systematic choice program.[30]

Perhaps more basic questions and arguments concern whether in fact choice programs produce the benefits attributed to them, whether choice programs in any form, "work." There has been considerable debate about how significant an effect choice has or whether the apparent positive effects of choice are merely the result of other variables that lead to school improvement. For example, a Carnegie Foundation report notes that there is little or no significant difference between choice and nonchoice districts in achievement. Similarly, even in those "model" districts widely cited as evidence for the efficacy of choice, like District 4, the benefits of choice may be overstated. For example, that district has enjoyed a relatively high level of funding and control over admissions, yet there are questions about whether its successes are as impressive as the publicity about them. There are more general issues as well, particularly whether some comparisons of public and private school achievement are valid, given that the latter inevitably can be selective.[31] Finally, almost all parties to the debate admit that there is still much we do not know about the conditions under which choice plans might work well. This lack of knowledge is compounded by the fact that we suspect that many contextual variables and matters of detail in implementation can have important effects on any choice plan.

Many, if not most, of the practical objections imply that the small-scale successes of choice programs, if they are successes at all, are not readily extended to the entire system. The logistics of transportation, information for all parents, and deciding priorities are all likely to undermine any attempts to make choice the guiding principle for education. It is very difficult to create a "market" for education. Moreover, behind these practical objections lie some deeper fears that choice programs will merely accentuate some of the undesirable features of current arrangements. The well-off will make sure that their educational needs are met and at the same time the poor will be even more isolated in less desirable schools. Finally, it is unclear how broad-based choice plans might deal with populations that have very specialized needs, such as students with physical disabilities.[32]

These fears suggest that perhaps the real issues concerning choice may not be mainly empirical, at least not in some straightforward way. Rather they are conceptual, theoretical, and ultimately normative. They involve some very basic issues of the relationship of schools and families, and the questions become more serious the further one moves toward privatization. First, there is a conceptual equivocation about the very idea of choice. Lumping together a number of very different public and private programs and proposals under the heading of choice may lead to attributing too much to choice and too little to other kinds of factors that we also know can improve performance. For example, the development of high schools that have different themes is usually accompanied by grants of greater discretion to faculty, clarification of goals and standards, improved morale, and so on. But the question then is whether any resulting improvement is a function of choice or a result of the flexibility and self-scrutiny occasioned by the development of a choice plan. That is, there are many good "effective" schools in suburban and urban districts that have created these organizational characteristics and improved performance without choice. To attribute to choice or to market forces any improvement that goes along with what might otherwise be called restructuring or an effective schools program is conceptually, and therefore perhaps empirically, misleading.[33]

This conceptual issue suggests another problem relating to consumer sovereignty. The arguments for the limiting of state control over education appeals not only to consequences but rights as well. The notion that parents have rights with respect to what kind of education their children should receive is rhetorically powerful. This is especially true given the natural suspicion of state power over what choice proponents call "the last monopoly." It is fairly easy to translate that argument into the language of consumer sovereignty. Parents should be able to choose what educational services they will "consume." It is not surprising, therefore, that polls show strong support for the idea of choice.

Granting the appeal of arguments from the perspective of parents' rights and even the assumption that parents know their child's needs best, there is something of a conceptual paradox in the argument for consumer sovereignty. The movement for choice has not been the product of some upsurge of consumer demand. It has primarily been the brainchild of academics and educational officials. Moreover, in many instances when choice has been made available, only a very small percentage of families has availed themselves of the option. Although opinion polls do show support for the *idea* of choice, they also register parental satisfaction with their own schools, even as they have serious doubts about others' schools. Thus, if we take seriously the notions of consumer sovereignty and parents knowing best, choice programs are not, no pun intended, the widespread choice of families.[34] To be fair, this kind of parental inertia is not something that only confronts choice as a reform strategy. As will be discussed in Chapter 6, even after more than a decade of discussion about the failures of the schools and initiatives to reform them, parental evaluations of their own schools remain generally high and certainly higher than assessments of reformers. Nevertheless, this is particularly problematic for choice programs given their rhetorical reliance on the idea of consumer sovereignty.

A similar problem with the choice approach, especially in its maximum variation as represented by Chubb and Moe, is that it can simply be oversold. To see choice as panacea requires believing that organizational features of American schools are so rigid that a completely different institutional design is the only effective path to reform. This sweeping assertion flies in the face of the fact that other countries' school systems are as bureaucratic, or even more so, than those in the United States yet seem to be able to create school environments conducive to learning. There may be something unique about American federalism or culture that makes bureaucratic constraints more of a drag on educational performance, but Chubb and Moe do not address this possibility. In any case, the example of other countries suggests the possibility that state control and educational achievement are not mutually exclusive. Putting choice at odds with other reforms and creating a rigid dichotomy of market versus state is simply too reductive. It does not allow for the subtleties of various mixes of incentives and programs. As Nicholas Lemann puts it, "There's something facile about totally dismissing all education reform schemes that have ever really been tried, while presenting as flawless one that exists only in the theoretical realm."[35]

These conceptual issues point to larger and more fundamental theoretical questions. Ultimately, perhaps, the most serious objection to choice is normative and concerns how far the state should go in privatizing education. Choice programs, especially in their more radical form, imply that education can and should be treated as a kind of market good, an item for individual (family) consumption. But to conceive of education in this way is to more or less abandon the idea of education as a public good. As the Carnegie Foundation report puts it:

> Arguments for choice are stated in the language of individual self-interest, while downgrading the ways in which our vision of public education, including the neighborhood school arrangement, has served larger social ends. Adopting the language of the marketplace, education is portrayed as a solitary act of consumerism. . . . To frame the issue in these terms is to distort the vision of public education beyond recognition. From the very first it was

understood that the nation's schools should serve both private benefit and the public good. And this was to be accomplished, at least in part, by the way we organized our schools.[36]

The most radical choice plans discount anything but the most minimal notion of common education for moral or civic purposes. They likewise leave to the market the use of the schools for any social purposes other than those that evolve from the choices of families. In short, it subordinates educational aims expressed in other themes to the wants of families and the market results of their choices.

On Chubb and Moe's part, this subordination is justified because it will produce academic achievement of the kind seen in the private educational sector. Indeed, any legitimate collective educational aims, it is argued, are best served by schools that, through market pressure, are academically sound. Moreover, and perhaps more important, advocates of choice point out that many of these theoretical objections to the idea of choice are based on a romantic notion of common schools that simply do not exist. Schools do not treat all their students equitably, as the endless debate about tracking and grouping illustrates. The differences between and among schools, for example between suburban and urban schools, are even more pronounced and less defensible. Many inner city schools are a far cry from the "great equalizer" envisioned by Horace Mann. Proponents of choice are also quick to point out that the absence of choices in the name of a common school creates a dual kind of inequity. Poor schools are less able to provide educational opportunities than their better-off counterparts. Moreover, wealthier parents typically have the option to choose a market alternative that is unavailable to poorer parents. To consign the latter to schools that all admit are failures is more inequitable than almost anything that might be envisioned under a choice plan.[37]

There is some merit to these replies, especially as they remind us of the inequities in a public, supposedly common system of education. However, they are not fully compelling. First, the evidence for the academic effects of any kind of choice plan, let alone speculation about some radical market solution, are ambiguous or mixed. Much of the strongest evidence in favor of choice is actually derived not from the private sector but from more controlled public-sector experiments. To assign the label choice to these and very different proposals is misleading. Second, as a general proposition, we have no compelling reason to believe that educational markets automatically produce quality any more than we believe that economic markets always work. There still may be inequities--in parental attentiveness, student needs, available options--that academic markets cannot readily handle. As many thoughtful supporters of public choice programs point out, markets of various kinds handle some things well and not others.[38] Finally, to assert that schools do not meet the ideals of equity or common education does not mean we should jettison those ideals. It perhaps should be taken as a spur to better fulfill these ideals for all students. Perhaps the bottom line, so to speak, is that education cannot and ought not be simply reduced to a consumer good, given the variety of needs and aims schools should serve.[39]

Rendering some overall judgment on choice is difficult given the diversity of what falls under the label. Its current political prospects are dimming given a basically unsympathetic administration and the natural political opposition to it. Political prospects aside, it can be said that radical privatization should not be regarded as a panacea. To do so would require us to believe that it is a unique solution, one that is so powerful that it allows us to give up all else in the name of market forces. More positively, it can be said that choice, especially within the public sector, is a strategy that has some promise. It necessitates family involvement and tries to make schools more sensitive and responsive to their clientele. Moreover, all admit that whatever else choice does, it does force administrators to look at their practices in a way many reforms often do not. Even many of the staunchest critics of choice proposals acknowledge these benefits. Many likewise approve of local experimentation with choice as a means of diversifying and specializing programs, but this is what any good program for school reform might do anyway. It is certainly possible to imagine that public schools could, without or with only modest public options for choice, do more to reach out to families in this way. Choice may be less a unique strategy than another lesson in how to approach school reform. Indeed, even as the choice option has been debated and tried there have been other experiments in broadening the range of services provided by the schools as a way of meeting family needs.

The Welfare State in the Neighborhood: The "Wisest Parent"?

Almost every discussion or analysis of educational reform has commented upon the increasingly difficult environments in which schools must function. There are common references to crime and drugs, poverty and deteriorating neighborhoods, disintegrating, neglectful, and even abusive families that make education, especially in many inner city schools, all but impossible. Perhaps the most important change of all has been the decline in the ability of the family to play a socializing and stabilizing role for children. The statistics are daunting. Owing mainly to economic pressures, two-thirds of the mothers of school-aged children work outside the home. One-fourth of children are being raised in single-parent homes, the vast majority of which are headed by women. Out-of-wedlock births have increased. Children born in marriages face at least even odds that their parents will divorce, with uncertain and probably negative consequences for the children. Not surprisingly many of these statistics, and there are many more negative statistics, are worse for poor families, as are the prospects for other sources of support like quality health and child care.[40] Leaving aside any other problems that might be suggested by these statistics, they do indicate that there is less available support for the schools from families.

Schools have seldom responded to family problems in an integrated or coordinated fashion, and they have generally been slow to address the issue of how to respond to the recent deterioration of the family. Certainly, there have always been some on-site social services most notably social workers, school psychologists, and professional counselors for specific, acute problems. And, as mentioned above, more recent programs have specifically targeted poor families for special preschool and in-school support; health and child-care services are becoming increasingly common as well. Nevertheless, this patchwork of programs and services has tended to be fragmented, discontinuous, and uncoordinated with other social services.[41] This is partly due to an institutional history in which specialized social services developed apart from schools and produced a division of labor that has been difficult to overcome. There are therefore bureaucratic problems in coordinating the activities of schools and other social service agencies.

Although choice plans and experiments have received a great deal of public attention, there have been quieter but no less significant developments in the area of coordinating or directly delivering social services through the schools. These programs suggest that the boundary between academic and other programs is somewhat artificial, both conceptually and practically. It is not merely that academic progress might be difficult or impossible without these services, it is rather that the school is trying to serve the student as a client in a more holistic fashion. Instead of defining students' needs narrowly or academically, the schools provide an expanded array of services that aims to support education. With each instance of these kinds of programs and services the schools are developing a welfare variation of the clientelist theme.

Moving in this direction requires that schools develop new relationships with social service agencies and families, as well as viewing a child's education in a broad way. As Harold Hodgkinson puts it, schools and welfare agencies are beginning to realize and act as if they serve "the same client," which they do. Their combined services become part and parcel of what it means to educate students. Since supporting students means responding to family problems that affect the prospects for learning, the school must treat the family as a "client" as well. It must either enlist families in the educational process or provide services to them so that education can proceed, or both. In any case, the schools must take into account and deal with the nonacademic situations and needs through these expanded relationships. Thus the school becomes a social service agency in its own right in which education is inextricably bound up with other services.[42]

As in choice programs there is considerable variation in what might fall under the heading of a welfare approach to education. There are any number of strategies for providing such services in a more integrated fashion. One way of sorting through this variety is to note the degree to which schools and community agencies must collaborate in a program, and the degree of outreach implied by any effort. Just as at the turn of the twentieth century, the current range of possibilities includes programs that are more focused on school-related and school-based services and those that involve broader family or community efforts. A survey of some examples illustrates that, like choice programs, there is some uncertainty about what precisely works, let alone how what works well in one setting might be applied in others. Still, there is an increasing awareness and self-consciousness about how schools might engage these problems.

The most ambitious proposals and programs envision taking previously separate social services and moving them into, or at least near, the school building. Some districts have developed on-site child or health care, both for students and families. There are more ambitious attempts to make the school become the hub of social services--integrating health and child care, counseling and psychological services, family education, and any other social services that students and their families might need. This "one-stop-shopping" approach offers the possibility of coordinated effort by schools and social service agencies in or near the school. A good example of this is the Dunbar project in Baltimore that makes "the school building the pivotal institution in the neighborhood. It is an anchor, a place where children not only learn but receive health care, socializing skills, good food in many cases, and recreation. . . . a place for parents to meet, to receive job training, or to earn . . . their GED . . . a place for community leaders to set goals based on the needs of their individual schools and for businesses and non-profit organizations to channel resources into the community."[43]

Instead of attempting to bring together existing social services, many schools have sought to offer their own programs. One common means of extending social services through schools falls under the rubric of "family" or "parent education." The schools develop or coordinate educational programs that directly target families. Whether on a case or group basis or through an organized class, the point of this kind of program is to support families so that children might be ready for and able to learn better in school. This support can start with prenatal advising, go through classes in infant care and development, and continue into classes for adults for basic literacy. For example, Arkansas has developed HIPPY (Home Instruction Plan for Preschool Youngsters), a program linking hospitals and health agencies with schools to provide education and other services to families with young children. For a number of years several states have sponsored family education programs that provide a range of courses for parents with young children as well as other specific social services.[44] In these and a variety of similar programs, the assumption is really quite simple: education for the parent(s) is a key factor in educating the child. The school's clientele expands to include families, and it becomes the focal point for education in a very broad sense. Ideally, this approach has the practical advantage of avoiding or minimizing difficult issues of coordination or turf battles with other social services. These programs often function within the school or through very specific cooperation with existing agencies.[45]

Educating the whole child may not require new outreach programs like those described above. A somewhat narrower, but no less ambitious, model for a more integrated, social education is the School Development Program associated with the work of James Comer. Begun in New Haven in 1968, the program works primarily within the school rather than through existing social services or established agencies. It seeks, on-site, to reconfigure the actual and potential resources of the school, family, and community to integrate academic and social skills. In each school, the program has three main components: a governance and management group, a parents program, and a mental health team. The school governance team has teachers, administrators, parents, and mental health professionals. It sets out the general goals for the school, trains others to carry them out, and evaluates and assesses results. Parents, besides being represented on this body, have a separate program involving school activities and volunteer work, including one parent per professional staff member in the classroom itself. There is a constant working relationship between these two groups and the mental health team of classroom and special education teachers, a social worker and a school psychologist. The latter's general responsibility is "getting teachers and parents to think developmentally, to think relationships" as well as dealing with individual referrals from classroom teachers for "cases" of students who need assistance.[46]

What might be lost in this description of these organizational elements is the relatively simplicity of the program's aims. Instead of narrowly focusing on the academic side of schooling, the program seeks to create positive interactions between children and adults. It engages in self-conscious, systematic socialization. The school, in cooperation with the families of its students (or other significant adults), seeks to provide what "children from better-educated families . . . gain . . . *simply by growing up with their parents.*" As Comer puts it:

[Giving] children the kinds of experiences that allow them to go to school and interact with adults and other school children in such a way that they are able to sit still, invest in tasks, and engage in and be spontaneous and curious about learning when it is appropriate to do so. All of these responses and behaviors impress school people and enable adults to feel good about children and children to feel good about adults. They make possible the kinds of attachment and bonding that then allow adults to become meaningful persons in the lives of children and that aid children's performance and growth in school. From that point, children can begin to imitate, identify with, and internalize the attitudes, values, and ways of school people. The program of the school becomes meaningful through children's relationships with teachers and other school people.[47]

The school and the family become part of a "conspiracy of adults" that not only educates in the academic sense but socializes students into interacting with the larger world in healthy ways, "so that children did not have to choose between their parents and their social networks and their school people." The child's family and the school "family" become coextensive. "In the same way that children attempt to gain the approval of their parents, they also attempt to gain the approval of school people. This then is what enables academic learning to take place as children begin to move forward."[48]

That the intent of the program is more than academic achievement is indicated by the way in which it assesses its results. Measurement of basic skills on standardized tests are used, but schools following the plan also look at rates of absenteeism, punishments, and suspensions. Not surprisingly, as schools have improved their performance on these measures, their academic performance has also improved.[49] This alone would make the program attractive, but it also does not seem to require fundamental organizational changes or large amounts of new funding (beyond start-up costs) as other programs might. The Comer program has generally been successful, so much so that it has received a number of foundation grants and government support. It may be in as many as a hundred cities within a few years.

But Does It Work?

As with choice plans, there are many tactical and strategic questions involved in deciding what kinds of social services the schools might offer and how to offer them in effective ways. The very comprehensiveness of the approach offered by one-stop-shopping creates some severe practical obstacles. The current professional separation of service providers makes it difficult to imagine that services could be readily coordinated, let alone suddenly moved into one setting. Differences in approaches and goals as well as organizational self-protection suggest that it would be difficult to implement one-stop-shopping soon. Moreover, while such an approach might be more efficient in the long run, there is little doubt that moving to a new system of social service coordination and delivery requires money. For example, a California proposal ("New Beginnings") in San Diego envisioned locating more comprehensive social services in the schools. But the most recent debate concerning school services was whether in fact the state could afford kindergarten. In short the total overhaul of the social services through the schools might be an ideal proposal, but seems a dim possibility.

Another practical issue concerns whether schools that embark on such programs are simply overreaching. Namely, it might be objected that school involvement in these areas is, at best, simply a distraction from its more important academic purposes. It is impractical, it might be argued, to dump all of society's woes onto the education system that can barely do its educational job adequately. One observer suggests that if the schools become involved in nonacademic activities of any sort (including sports and other cocurricular programs), these should be placed in a "parallel" school, leaving the academic work to the regular schools. Moreover, many of the field studies of the schools have suggested that therapeutic approaches and attitudes have helped erode demands for academic excellence.[50] At worst, these programs may make demands that schools cannot or will not meet. For example, a highly touted Rochester, New York, teachers' contract envisioned teachers working as advisors to students and families outside the classroom. The program floundered on the simple fact that teachers were not trained to take on this role and were unable, if not also unwilling, to do so.

These practical objections have some merit as a cautionary reminder of the obstacles that must be overcome in developing a broader view of schools' relationship with their clients. Nevertheless, there are numerous examples of programs, including the Comer model, that have successfully blended social and academic concerns. There is cause for optimism in the quiet success of these varied and increasingly numerous efforts. No one approach has a formula for success, and how well a program succeeds will depend upon many political, fiscal, and local factors. "Failures" may occur, especially if programs are hurriedly or thoughtlessly implemented, but they may also occur if nothing is done at all. The real problem is translating particular success stories into some more comprehensive program, but this is also a problem that arises with more strictly academic reform strategies or choice proposals. Finally, regarding finances, at a time that reformers bemoan the fact that greater expenditures for education have not yielded much progress, it would seem that programs like these are a wise investment.[51]

What is perhaps most surprising about the schools' steadily increasing movement into welfare services is how relatively little political or theoretical controversy it has generated. In other policy areas that have touched the family, especially concerning welfare more typically understood, there is continuous, strident debate. These disputes have been part of public dialogue at least since the Moynihan Report in the mid-1960s pointed to the deterioration of ghetto families. Recently there has been yet another eruption of these debates, this time around the phrase "family values." Conservatives rail against dependency and call for more responsibility of the part of individuals and families. They point out the growing evidence that the decline of the two-parent family has done tremendous damage to children. Both public policy and broader cultural trends are to blame, it is argued, because they have been either indifferent or hostile to the two parent family. Alternatively, liberals reject the idea that we can somehow turn back the clock to another era. Both for economic and cultural reasons, they claim, there is no going back to a form of family that was a historical anomaly--and that may not have been very healthy anyway. In any case, the changing role(s) of women in our society demands that public policy attend to and support changes in traditional family roles. Finally, liberals object to the idea of "blaming the victim," of talking about a "culture of poverty" or "the disintegration of the black family" without pointing to the social and economic discrimination and declining government support that is primarily responsible for these problems.[52]

These familiar battle lines have have not been very visible with respect to school-based services. There are at least two explanations for this. First, schools have generally not promoted programs that touch upon contested values. It is hard to condemn prenatal care, preschool education and other support for families, or the promotion of health or basic literacy. As in the case of moral education embedded in school curricula and practices described in Chapter 3, the values embodied in these programs are often simply so basic that they do not generate controversy. More generally, there is a kind of "halo" effect in the association of these programs with the more consensual area of education. Moving them from the category of "welfare" to "education" somehow makes them less contentious. Second, and similarly, these programs are further shielded from criticism because their primary beneficiaries do not seem to be responsible, nor could they be responsible, for their situation. Most of the questions of individual responsibility and dependency that arise in the discussions of welfare seem inapplicable to children. Indeed, the prospect of avoiding these problems and issues later on is a key attraction of these efforts.

If the schools continue to expand their welfare programs, there will probably objections from both the right and left that echo the welfare debate. These objections will pose the dilemma of excess and deficit, although how this argument will be framed depends upon the political perspective from which it arises. From the right of the political spectrum, the complaint might be that school-based family services are likely to encourage or even endorse alternative family patterns and habits. The state is simply going too far in using schools (and other policies) to (re)define the family. The analogy to welfare dependency is pretty clear. "Families" will find that government will provide what they cannot or will not, with unfortunate consequences. Government should support, to the extent it can, two-parent families, especially in light of the growing evidence of the social consequences of family breakdown.[53] From a more liberal perspective, many of those who are critical of the literature on the "underclass" and the "culture of poverty" would suggest that these programs have not gone far enough to support the changing nature of the family. Without more comprehensive and integrated programs that intervene to support families and children, school-based programs, although welcome, are likely to be limited in their effectiveness. The point is not to try to create a family that perhaps never truly was, but to respond to the needs of families as they are and are likely to be.[54]

Even where there is no standard ideological stance, there may be similar doubts about the unexamined assumptions and unintended consequences of welfare or therapeutic approaches to the family through schools. These programs, it might be argued, invade the family "haven" in ways that are ultimately destructive of values and attitudes that underlie a healthy culture. The boundary between public and private concerns will always be crossed by therapeutic professionals, even where there is no overt sign of conflict. The very engagement of the state in defining healthy development and behaviors, it might be argued, automatically compromises the private sphere.[55] The threat is that in acting as the "wisest parent" in these programs the state will, perhaps inevitably, compromise the autonomy of the family. The therapeutic intentions of professionals who might help the family can lead to its subordination to larger political agendas or even to its destruction. Thus it is not merely that involvement with the social dimension of education may distract from the academic priorities of schools, it is that the state has no business doing these things.

Evolving school-family relationships raise many issues about the reach of the state, the boundary between public and private matters, and the proper scope and understanding of education. Similarly, there can be little doubt that the entry of the state into family matters is fraught with practical risks. Not the least of these is that families might cede to the schools roles they are unable or unwilling to play. But these issues cannot be profitably addressed in the same sterile way as the current welfare debate. If we think in more modest terms about what the schools might aim to do in this area and look at what some programs and other nations already do, these more theoretical or ideological objections are more cautionary reminders than severe obstacles.

The existence of some successful models and programs suggests that there is some modest consensus, and perhaps something reasonable about, broadening the welfare efforts of schools. For example, family support programs do try to encourage family responsibility and independence, and can serve the cause of maintaining a two-parent family. That they are done under the aegis of the state does not, at least not obviously, make them intrusive or create unacceptable dependency. Similarly, the kinds of social skills that are encouraged in the Comer program are hardly intrusive or destructive of family autonomy. It is also hard to see them as some kind of cultural imposition, as if the notion of cooperating with adults in the school setting were a form of cultural denial. Equally important, things like day care and other forms of family support are quite common in other industrialized countries, and these hardly seem repressive. They and the programs cited above stand as a clear counterargument to the claim that governments are incapable of legitimately or competently providing such services. Indeed, what seems unfair and even truly destructive of families is the lack of support in the United States of the kind found in other countries.[56]

Public Choice and Public Welfare

It is odd that as educators and other observers have commented upon the effect of the decline of the family on the educational process that more attention has not been given to emerging school-based responses to these problems. It is not quite so odd when we consider that schools and families have typically been considered as relatively isolated, autonomous realms. Despite the constant tension and interaction between them (and between them and the larger society) both the family and the school have been treated as if they were somehow separate from larger social and political processes. This represents both a misplaced idealism and liberal democratic society's natural suspicion of the state.[57] We would like to believe that all families, whether two- or single-parent, nuclear or extended, were functional and competent, and were surrounded by a supportive culture and institutions. We would like to approximate a previous time when there was a positive adult presence in children's lives (a "conspiracy of adults") wherever they went. Whether or not this idealized picture ever fully existed, most would agree that the gap between such ideals and reality has grown greater recently. We still do not commonly think that government should develop more programmatic ties to the family through the schools. Perhaps there is a vague fear of the state becoming involved in what is the paradigmatic private sphere. There may also be more specific doubts about state competence and the unintended consequences of state involvement. Nevertheless, the gap between idealized and actual families widens, as the steady drumbeat of statistics on broken families and childhood poverty remind us.

In the past the schools' response to these kinds of problems was generally limited to the most acute or egregious problems affecting the possibility of education. It is only recently that it has been recognized that some more comprehensive and programmatic approach might be necessary. Ultimately, then, arguments about whether the schools should provide social services of one kind or another may simply be moot. If schools are going to deal with children as they currently are, the kinds of initiatives described above or something comparable are almost inevitable. Unless we are prepared to continue to act as if the process of education is separate from the dramatic pressures on the family that all acknowledge, some programmatic responses of this sort are probably unavoidable. The main issues are practical and empirical. We need to ascertain what kinds of programs best support families and how these can be delivered in efficient, effective ways.

How well these clientelist efforts will work depends in no small measure on the larger economic and policy environment. The schools cannot do everything, and it would be naive to think that somehow the schools can more or less singlehandedly transform the social service landscape. Broader policies concerning welfare, health, and child care will have a profound effect on how successful any school-based programs are. It is not easy to be optimistic about the development of new policies in these areas that will make the tasks of education easier. Neither generous fiscal nor political support seems forthcoming. Moreover, we no longer seem to have a consistently growing economy with a stable base of well-paying jobs. It is ironic that our faltering economy is often portrayed as a victim of the educational system. It is perhaps more accurate to say that the problems of the educational system have been made worse by an economy that has not created conditions for families to properly support children.

Still, there is some modest cause for optimism in school-based initiatives like the Comer approach, family support programs, and other efforts. They do not, at least on a small scale, require huge commitments of resources, and they do not seem to overstep the bounds of state authority. They seem to have had some success, even where the odds were highest against them. They suggest that there are effective interventions that, if properly done, show "that the cycle of disadvantage can be broken through systematic social action."[58]

Attempts to build on these successes will naturally face questions of transferability and cost. First, it is seldom clear how to move from these smaller-scale projects to any more comprehensive approach, let alone one that coordinates and integrates education and other social services. This is no small obstacle given a current system that is a minefield of jurisdictional conflict that puts professionals at odds with one another and needed services out of reach of clients. Second, any more systematic efforts will almost certainly require new investment of resources. The cliche that money will not solve the problems should really be taken to mean that money that is poorly spent will not solve problems. In any case, our expenditures for social and educational support of children and families are less comparatively than many countries. Again, although it is difficult to do some precise cost-benefit analysis, it stands to reason that money spent on these programs may save resources devoted to less desirable expenditures such as imprisonment or welfare.

The above examples of successful school-based programs provide the most compelling critique of radical choice programs. It is unclear that a privatized school system would generate such programs or that the families in such programs could be brought into the educational process in the same way. This is not to say that *public* choice programs are unwise or unworkable. Rather it is to say that more extreme versions of choice are less likely to address directly the obvious needs of families. To leave such needs to the "market" is not only less likely to work, it is, in Dewey's phrase, a "narrow and unlovely" ideal. It is narrow in that it reduces education to a limited view of education as academic achievement. It is unlovely in that it cedes our collective responsibilities to the next generation to a melange of competing, impersonal forces. Even from a merely practical viewpoint, there is little reason to suspect that more radical choice plans would be successful in responding to these problems. If there is legitimate skepticism about a systematic welfare approach, even in light of some successful examples, there should be far greater skepticism about privatization as a means of addressing these issues.

At the same time, to the degree that public choice programs reach out and involve families, they overlap considerably with the welfare programs described above. (As I will discuss in Chapter 6, there is also overlap with the other major themes in public education.) Choice then is merely another version of the same process of serving clients by working with families. At their best such programs build a somewhat different bridge between school and family, but it is one that assembles the conspiracy of adults to serve the needs of children. There is no a priori reason that the two approaches cannot be used simultaneously with (public) schools of choice offering different kinds of services appropriate to their clientele. The key, again, is that the focus is on the clients' needs, broadly understood, and how the education and other services can be mobilized to meet them.

In the emergence of clientelist programs, then, there is both cause for modest optimism as well as a rather perplexing puzzle. These programs suggest that we do know what works, or at least some things that work, with regard to coping with the changes that families have undergone. Practical responses to these changes are within our reach. Here, as in other areas and with respect to the other themes discussed in the previous chapters, there are programs and districts that provide models for what might be accomplished in the schools. And yet these seem exceptional and not, at least not yet, clearly applicable across the board. Although we may know many things that work, we do not seem to know how, or be able, to make them work comprehensively. Clearly, this problem is important for the prospects of the educational reform movement. We can now address this puzzle in light of the previous analysis of themes in public education.

Notes

1. Even where schools have professed to have abolished tracking in principle, they often end up tracking in fact. See Philip Cusick, *The Egalitarian Ideal and the American High School*. New York: Longman, 1983.

2. See David Tyack and Elizabeth Hansot, *Managers of Virtue: Public School Leadership in America, 1820-1980*. New York: Basic Books, 1982, pp. 194-211.

3. Milton Friedman, *Capitalism and Freedom*. Chicago: University of Chicago Press, 1962. For another early statement, see John Coons and Stephen Sugarman, *Education by Choice: The Case for Family Control*. Berkeley: University of Chicago Press, 1978. A more recent and more refined view of private options is offered by Myron Lieberman, *Privatization and Educational Choice*. New York: St. Martin's Press, 1989.

4. It is interesting that choice proposals literally invert the logic of that dilemma. The "maximum" version of choice actually has the state doing too little to promote the public's interest in education. The "minimum" version says the state is going too far in defining individual and family needs.

5. Joel Spring, *The American School: 1642-1990*. New York: Longman, 1990, 2nd. ed., p. 163.

6. For a concise summary of this movement, see Robert L. Church and Michael Sedlak, *Education in the United States*. New York: Free Press, 1976, Ch. 9.

7. It is probably also true that schools have never been willing participants in the expansion of services, and "the 'progressive' influence was a good deal less pervasive than we have become accustomed to believe . . . with regard to the addition of social services and nonacademic course work. Most of the 'progressive' agenda died aborning, was most imperfectly realized, or has only recently shown signs of coming to fruition." Michael Sedlak and Steven Schlossman, "The Public School and Social Services: Reassessing the Progressive Legacy," *Educational Theory*. 35 (1985), p. 371.

8. Besides the vagueness of any mandate to build community, urban schools became increasingly centralized as part of the movement for organizational efficiency and against local favoritism and corruption. Local control and close ties to the community were less likely in this organizational environment. The increasing professionalization and division of labor within the school and among social service personnel more generally worked against centering services, let alone efforts at community building, in the schools. "The conservative progressives wished to impose a centralized control over the public schools in order to make them serve the interests of the whole city more effectively. They thought that local control of schools caused corruption that was expensive and that impeded high quality instruction." Church, *Education in the United States*, p. 281.

9. As pressure on families in these middle- or upper-class areas has increased, these schools too have broadened their programs to provide family counseling, drug education, and similar programs.

10. Robert Hampel, *The Last Little Citadel: American High Schools Since 1940*. Boston: Houghton Mifflin, 1986 pp. 7 ff.; Tyack and Hansot, *Managers of Virtue*, pp. 207-211.

11. See Hampel, *The Last Little Citadel*, pp. 43-51.

12. See Hugh David Graham, *The Uncertain Triumph: Federal Education Policy in the Kennedy and Johnson Years*. Chapel Hill: University of North Carolina Press, 1984, especially, Chs. 3-6.

13. For a mixed review of IEPs and special education generally, see Jeannie Oakes and Martin Lipton, *Making the Best of Schools*. New Haven: Yale University Press, 1990, Ch. 8, especially, pp. 188-189.

14. On the case for a more integrated and comprehensive approach, see Lisbeth Schorr, "What Works: Applying What We Already Know About Social Policy," *The American Prospect*. (Spring 1993), pp. 43-54. For a more general view, see her *Within Our Reach: Breaking the Cycle of Disadvantage*. New York: Anchor Doubleday, 1988, especially Chs. 8-9. For some specific models and programs, *Joining Forces*. Washington, D.C.: National Association of School Boards, 1989.

15. For a brief history and survey of the issues surrounding school choice, see Richard Wornsop, "School Choice: Would it Strengthen or Weaken Public Education in America?" *CQ Researcher*. 1 (May 10, 1991), pp. 255-275.

16. See Michael Kirst, "Improving Children's Services: Overcoming Barriers, Creating New Opportunities," *Phi Delta Kappan*. 72 (April 1991), pp. 615-618. "What's needed is a complete overhaul of children's services, bringing together public and private organizations to meet the comprehensive needs of children, adolescents, and parents. Schools should constitute one of the centers of a coordinated network of total children's services," p. 616.

17. "The schools have been victimized long enough, the critics charge, by the ambitious and fuzzy-headedness of educators who envision an endless stream of services justified in the name of 'child welfare' or 'community uplift.' Since the Great Society era, they allege, the schools' intellectual mission has been diluted by the incorporation of numerous ill-conceived social services and curricular innovations that sap limited economic resources and do little to enhance students' academic achievement." Sedlak and Schlossman, "The Public School and Social Services," p. 371.

18. "The resulting competition for students, say proponents of choice, would bring to the education system the diversity and quality that free economic markets have recently brought to computers, communications equipment, and cable television." Kevin Hopkins, "A Question of Choice," *Business Week*. December 7, 1992, p. 4.

19. For this mix of grudging support for public choice and criticism of privatization, see Ernest Boyer, *School Choice*. Princeton: Carnegie Foundation for the Advancement of Teaching, 1992; Albert Shanker and Bella Rosenberg, *Politics, Markets, and America's Schools: The Fallacies of Private School Choice*. Washington, D.C.: American Federation of Teachers, 1991.

20. For a brief history, see Wornsop, "School Choice," pp. 258-266.

21. James Coleman, Thomas Hoffer, and Sally Kilgore, *High School Achievement*. New York: Basic Books, 1982; James Coleman and Thomas Hoffer, *Public and Private High Schools*. New York: Basic Books, 1987.

22. For a survey, see Wornsop, "School Choice," and Lieberman, *Privatization and Educational Choice*. For a description and assessment of the Milwaukee experiment, see John Witte, "Private School Choice: The Low Income Voucher Experiment," paper presented at the annual meeting of the American Political Science Association, Chicago, September, 1992. John E. Chubb and Terry M. Moe, *Politics, Markets, and America's Schools*. Washington, D.C.: The Brookings Institution, 1990.

23. Mary Anne Raywid, "Family Choice Arrangements in Public Schools: A Review of the Literature," *Review of Educational Research*. 55 (Winter 1985), pp. 435-467.

24. For an even more complex typology of choice plans as well as an excellent discussion of the issues at stake, see John Witte, "Choice and Control: An Analytical Overview," in William F. Clune and John Witte, eds., *Choice and Control in American Education Volume 1: The Theory of Choice and Control in Education*. New York: Falmer Press, 1990, pp. 11-47.

25. For a useful survey of the variety of public choice plans, see Timothy W. Young and Evans Clinchy, *Choice in Public Education*. New York: Teachers College Press, 1992. On state efforts, Joe Nathan, *Public Schools by Choice*. Bloomington, Ind.: Meyer Stone, 1989; "Results and Future Prospects of State Efforts to Increase Choice Among Schools," *Phi Delta Kappan*. 68 (June 1987), pp. 746-752; Boyer, *School Choice*, pp. 99-111.

26. See Lieberman, *Privatization and Educational Choice*, for a discussion of the monopoly issue and public-private differences.

27. Chubb and Moe, *Politics, Markets*, p. 183.

28. For a good example of current arguments for choice, see James R. Rinehart and Jackson F. Lee, *American Education and the Dynamics of Choice*. New York: Praeger, 1991. It includes a very sympathetic analysis of Chubb and Moe's work.

29. "Private schools are organized more effectively than public schools are and this is a reflection of their far greater autonomy from external (bureaucratic) control . . . the crucial feature of private schools is that they emerge and operate under very different institutional conditions than public schools do." Chubb and Moe, *Politics, Markets*, p. 24.

30. For a review of many of these practical issues, see Joe Nathan, *Public Schools by Choice*.

31. Boyer, *School Choice*, Ch. 2; Shanker and Rosenberg, *Politics, Markets*. Also see John Witte, *Public Subsidies for Private Schools*. Madison: Wisconsin Center for Education Policy, 1991, for a review of some of the the the difficulties of assessing the causes of achievement and its relationship to choice.

32. Amy Stuart Wells, "Choice in Education: Examining the Evidence on Equity," *Teachers College Record*. 93 (1, Fall 1991), pp. 139-153: "The myriad school-choice policies that have been implemented or are under consideration around the country vary radically in the degree to which they address equity issues," p. 139.

33. See Abigail Thernstrom, "Is Choice a Necessity?" *The Public Interest*. 101 (1990), pp. 124-132. "The choice rhetoric, with its emphasis on schools' 'missions,' confuses distinctive schools with good ones, and it is the latter we should want." p. 128.

34. Boyer, *School Choice*, Ch. 2.

35. Nicholas Lemann, "A False Panacea," *The Atlantic Monthly*. 267 (January, 1991), p. 104. See also Frances Fowler, "The Shocking Ideological Integrity of Chubb and Moe," *Journal of Education*. 173 (3, 1991), pp. 119-129: "A close examination of public education in those countries [France, Germany] would reveal organizational structures which combine centralized bureaucracy with participatory democracy at the building level," p. 123. See also Richard Elmore's review of Chubb and Moe's book in *Journal of Policy Analysis and Management*. 10 (1991), pp. 687-695: "Variations in the politics and governance of public education are of no particular interest to the authors because they are driven by a need to simplify. . . . Getting beyond the details, unfortunately, is not a virtue in a system in which details matter," p. 690.

36. Boyer, *School Choice*, p. 90. See also Thernstrom, "Is Choice a Necessity?"

37. For these arguments see Hopkins, "A Question of Choice," and Rinehart and Lee, *American Education and the Dynamics of Choice*, Ch. 11.

38. See Elmore, "Politics, Markets," on Chubb and Moe's treatment of markets, "markets, like systems of democratic control, vary enormously in their structures and operating characteristics . . . some markets . . . are characterized by highly collusive and coercive behavior . . . professional services markets are, after all, based on an asymmetry of information. The authors aren't, however, any more interested in the complexities of markets than they are in the 'details' of the educational system," p. 690.

39. See Thernstrom, "Is Choice a Necessity?": "Education has purposes other than meeting individual needs. . . . Society too has a stake in what's taught. Schools must educate children in our civic culture," p. 129, and "Choice advocates want the impossible: educational policy removed from the normative context in which it is inextricably embedded," p. 131.

40. See *SOS America! A Children's Defense Budget*. Washington, D.C.: Children's Defense Fund, 1990; Harold Hodgkinson, "Reform vs. Reality," *Phi Delta Kappan*. 72 (September 1991), pp. 9-16.

41. See Schorr, "What Works," These problems begin before a child reaches school age: "In most cities, a woman with a newborn who wants to climb out of poverty faces a dizzying array of obstacles. . . . If she is seeking medical and child care for the baby, drug treatment, family planning, and job training for herself, and housing for the two of them, she will have to go to six different locations, each with different--and often conflicting--rules for establishing and documenting eligibility, each with a time consuming and cumbersome acceptance process. . . . The process

is now so onerous that only a Mother Theresa who is also a Machiavelli *and* a CPA can succeed," p. 48. See also Kirst, "Improving Children's Services."

42. Harold Hodgkinson, *The Same Client: The Demographics of Education and Service Delivery Systems.* Washington, D.C.: Institute for Educational Leadership, 1989; for a survey of some state efforts, see Janet Levy and Carol Copple, *Joining Forces: A Report From the First Year.* Alexandria: National Association of State Boards of Education,1989.

43. Testimony of Baltimore's Mayor Kurt Schmoke before United States Senate Committee on Labor and Human Resources Hearing, "Meeting the Goals: Collaborating for Youth," May 8, 1991, p. 15.

44. Levy and Copple, *Joining Forces.*; see also *Family Support: Education and Involvement: A Guide for State Action.* Washington, D.C.: Council of Chief State School Officers, 1989; Bonnie S. Hausman and Heather B. Weiss, "State-Sponsored Family Services: The Case for School-Based Services," *Community Education Journal.* 15 (January 1988), pp. 12-15; Jean Heifetz and Patricia Sepparman, "'The Most Important Thing We Do'," *Community Education Journal.* 3 (Spring 1989), pp. 6-11.

45. Similarly, although the most obvious target for these programs has been "at risk" families, they are often universal-access programs. Indeed, these kinds of programs are now taking root in areas, such as middle-class suburban districts, that previously would not have been seen as having needed them.

46. James P. Comer, "Child Development and Education," *Journal of Negro Education.* 58 (2, 1989), p. 137; *School Power.* New York: Free Press, 1980.

47. Comer, "Child Development," pp. 128-129.

48. Comer, "Child Development," p. 129.

49. For an example of an assessment, see Norris Haynes, James Comer, and Muriel Hamilton-Lee, "The School Development Program: A Model for Improvement," *Journal of Negro Education.* 57 (1, 1988), pp. 11-21.

50. James Banner, "The Parallel School," *Phi Delta Kappan.* 73 (February 1992), pp. 486-488: "We have placed on schools the responsibility to take up where the family, the community, the political party, and the business system have long ago abdicated. The school has become an institution . . . that shatters under the weight of its promiscuous obligations. No institution can be expected to accommodate--without disintegrating--the burden of expectations under which the school now labors." p. 487. See also Hampel, *The Last Little Citadel,* Chs. 4, 5.

51. See Schorr, "What Works," especially pp. 53-54 on costs and benefits; for a more general perspective see her *Within Our Reach: Breaking the Cycle of Disadvantage.* New York: Anchor Doubleday, 1988, Chs. 1, 10.

52. For a general survey of these issues see E. J. Dionne, *Why Americans Hate Politics.* New York: Simon and Schuster, 1991, Chs. 3, 4.

53. For recent conservative views, see Barbara Dafoe Whitehead, "Dan Quayle Was Right," *Atlantic Monthly.* 271 (April 1993), pp. 47-84; James Q. Wilson, "The Family-Values Debate," *Commentary.* 95 (April 1993), pp. 24-31.

54. See Stephanie Coontz, *The Way We Never Were: American Families and the Nostalgia Trap.* New York: Basic Books, 1992; David Hamburg, *Today's Children.* New York: Random House, 1992, especially Section II.

55. Christopher Lasch, *Haven in a Heartless World: The Family Besieged.* New York: Basic Books, 1977: "The history of modern society, from one point of view, is the assertion of social control over activities once left to individuals or their families.

... capitalists took production out of the household and collectivized it, under their own supervision. . . . Finally, they extended their control over workers' private life as well . . . as teachers, child guidance experts . . . and other specialists began to supervise child-rearing, formerly the business of the family. The socialization of production, followed by the socialization of reproduction . . . have made people more dependent on the managerial and professional classes . . . and have thus eroded the capacity for self-help and social invention." pp. xx-xxi. See also, Eugene Lewis, *American Politics in a Bureaucratic Age.* Cambridge, Mass.: Winthrop, 1977: "A clientele is represented in the policy process by the agency responsible for for it. The professionalization of social service personnel, educators, and medical people explains much about the idea of a clientele. . . . Clients have their lives influenced in important ways by professionals who act with the authority of expertise and the legitimacy of the state," pp. 18-19.

56. Hodgkinson, "Reform vs. Reality," "American young people are at far greater risk for social, economic, and health problems than are children in the world's other developed nations," p. 13.

57. Wilson, "The Family Values Debate," "The dominant tendency in legal and philosophical thought has been to emancipate the individual from all forms of tutelage. . . . This emancipation has proceeded episodically and unevenly, but relentlessly. Liberal political theory has celebrated the individual and constrained the state, but it has been silent about the family," p. 28.

58. Schorr, "What Works," p. 43.

6

The Future of Educational Reform: Political Choices and School Culture

It is now the conventional wisdom that schools have to change. We are at a point where we are more willing than ever to confront the annoyingly provocative queries of the man from Mars about alternatives. I fear that as people confront these queries, they sense they are going in a direction that will be so radical in its consequences, so strewn with obstacles and turmoil, so necessarily uncertain in its outcomes, that they retreat from confrontation. Paradoxically, that fear represents optimism on my part. My pessimism is reflected in a second fear, realistically grounded, that although the reformers speak the language of change, they are still unable to consider the kinds of questions our visitors from outer space raised. Let us not gloss over the attitude implied by his questions: that alternatives are not of a piece, that their virtues (if any) do not reside in novelty but in the salience for achieving educational aims, that aims should inform means and not be transformed by them, that the more you narrow the universe of alternatives--worse yet, if you are not even aware that there is a universe of alternatives--the more you ensure that the existing regularities are in no danger of change.

--Seymour Sarason

Were we to evaluate people, not only according to their intelligence and their education, their occupation, and their power, but according to their kindliness and their courage, their imagination and their sensitivity, their sympathy and generosity, there could be no classes. Who would be able to say that the scientist was superior to the porter with admirable qualities as a father, the civil servant with unusual skill at gaining prizes superior to the lorry-driver with unusual skill at growing roses? The classless society would also be a tolerant society, in which individual differences were actively encouraged as well as passively tolerated, in which full meaning was at last given to the dignity of man. Every human being would then have equal opportunity, not to rise up in the world in the light of any mathematical measure, but to develop his own special capacities for leading a rich life.

--"The Chelsea Manifesto"
(Michael Young)

185

The previous chapters began with a quote from a past philosopher or theorist juxtaposed with one from a more contemporary commentary on philosophy or education. It is perhaps appropriate that the final chapter should start with the present and look to the future. The first quote comes from a recent work evaluating the prospects for, actually what it calls "the predictable failure of," educational reform. Sarason's comment suggests that our failure to connect fully the political choices of educational aims with the culture of schools will likely leave things unchanged. He suggests that we need to ask very basic questions about schools and evaluate our practices accordingly. These questions are ones that might be posed from the very broadest perspective we can imagine (the "visitors from outer space").

Written over thirty years ago, Young's imaginary "manifesto" from insurgents in the year 2009 suggests a way of viewing such choices. It challenges a rigid meritocracy based on educational achievement and proposes a view of education that is committed to the development of each individual. That manifesto goes on to urge "that the hierarchy of schools should be abolished and common schools at last established." While the first quote suggests an understandable pessimism about the likelihood of dramatic reform, the second invites us to envision a new commitment to equal, common education.[1]

It has been more than ten years since the publication of *A Nation at Risk* began the current educational reform movement. The tenth anniversary of that report was not the opportunity for celebrating the dramatic improvement of schools. It was mainly the occasion for noting how little had changed, despite all the talk of reform and infusion of more money into public education. Certainly, there have been some qualified successes and modest indications of improvement. The gap between white and black achievement scores and dropout rates has closed somewhat, although the gap is still striking. Achievement scores have inched up, though the gains of the last decade are modest and the SAT scores of the top students have actually moved down slightly. At the same time, indicators of other problems, including school violence, drug use, and teen pregnancy have worsened. In supposedly better schools that have fewer of these problems, there have not been dramatic changes in the everyday business of schooling. A "man from Mars" dropping in at the beginning of the reform movement and ten years later might be forgiven if he concluded that there had been no reform. Viewed in the broadest terms, there seems to be relatively little change in the public schools, despite a decade of "reform."

It is too soon, however, to write off the reform movement as a failure. At a minimum, there has been a continuing, wide-ranging discussion of the "universe of alternatives" both in terms of educational aims and specific practices. These discussions have been more than theoretical or academic. There is a large number of interesting experiments going on under the broad and vague rubric of "restructuring." These encompass a range of possibilities for school governance, organization, and pedagogical approach. A number of books have tried to glean the lessons from successful schools. These examples of "schools that work" or "smart schools" seem to indicate that genuine reform is possible.[2] In 1992 the New American Schools Development Corporation, as part of the *America 2000* program, announced grants to eleven projects that offer promising alternatives to current practices. These vary considerably and include building schools "from scratch," reintroducing classical curricula, experiments in choice in the form of "theme" schools, and new pedagogical strategies emphasizing real-world problems and the creative use of technology.[3] Both the "smart schools" and these "New American Schools" suggest that genuine reform is possible. Though the overall picture of the public schools remains fairly static, there are identifiable instances of real change and dramatic reform.

This combination of small-scale success and systemic inertia presents at least two puzzles that any assessment of the future of educational reform must address. First, there is the obvious question of why we cannot translate what we know "works" into across-the-board reform. The obvious answers, lack of political will, institutional inertia, simple human and organizational failure take us some way toward answering this puzzle, but there is more to it than that. At least part of the problem concerns our failure to deal with the competing themes discussed in the previous chapters. In terms of the man from Mars (perhaps a political theorist) we have not taken sufficient note that "alternatives are not of a piece, that their virtues (if any) do not reside in novelty but in the salience for achieving educational aims." There is, as critics of the reform movement have repeatedly pointed out, a need to discuss broader questions about the aims of reform ("that aims should inform means and not be transformed by them"). These questions go beyond the buzzwords of "excellence" and "competitiveness."

Second, and similarly, any casual glance at what works indicates that a number of things can and do work, even though they seem very different from one another. It is unclear whether these may represent contradictory ideas or merely different means to the same ends. This puzzle is another indication of the importance of the question of aims and its relationship(s) to the universe of alternatives. Equally important, the apparent variability in these successful cases indicates the significance of school culture for educational reform. What succeeds depends heavily on local factors that are very difficult to program from the top down. Thus although our political choices can encourage some common direction or tendency through policy, ultimately changing schools is a matter of transforming school culture by enlisting all those directly involved in the cause of reform.

The purpose of this chapter is to gather together the conclusions of the previous chapters and discuss the prospects for reform, particularly in light of the two puzzles just mentioned. Revisiting the "first triangle" of ideas, interests, and institutions in light of the discussion of the major themes in education suggests a direction for the reform movement and some of the formidable obstacles in its path. Again, such an analysis will not yield theoretically determined conclusions. Rather, it will suggest a sensibility, a way of looking at reform efforts from a more theoretical or thematic standpoint, as well as suggesting particular conclusions about what reform possibilities are more or less desirable and reasonable. Specifically, it suggests the priority of creating a new common school, one that emphasizes the moral and civic aims of education. The practical means for fulfilling this general aim cannot be theoretically determined or specified, especially given the problems posed for reform by current interests and institutions. Moving in this direction, as in the "schools that work," will necessarily and appropriately emerge, if at all, from changes in school culture. These include "how principals, teachers, and students think about their work" as well how parents and citizens think about the aims of reform.[4] This conclusion is neither as pessimistic as Sarason's analysis nor as optimistic as a vision of the schools as the vanguard of a moral transformation by the year 2009, let alone the year 2000. Finally, this result is also consistent with a view of "the task of political theory" that overlaps with the task of education in a liberal democratic society.

Ideas: "Overlapping Consensus" and Themes

The previous chapters have arrayed a formidable set of theoretical and practical problems confronting efforts at educational reform. First, there are the natural obstacles to reform discussed in Chapter 1, the conflicts in the "first triangle" of ideas, interests, and institutions. These obstacles loom larger in a massive, diffuse, and potentially contested policy area like education. In trying to address these problems we might seek principled guidance from more general theories of liberal democracy. But, as discussed in Chapter 2, the search for neutral principles of various kinds, the "theoretical mystique," is likely to be futile. It is difficult to find some central theoretical principles that can guide policy yet be consistent with the pluralistic nature of liberal democracies. Certainly there are some general, broadly shared values such as individual rights, rule of law, equality. There are also shared views of certain virtues such as tolerance, sympathy, respect for others, critical self-awareness.[5] However, this does not provide a well-defined (consensual) theoretical vantage point from which we can derive clear guidance concerning policy. This very loose "overlapping consensus" allows different, competing, and changing interpretations of these commitments. These differences define the various groups--liberals and conservatives, egalitarians and libertarians--within a shared liberal democratic culture. The varied interpretations of these commitments occasionally or even often conflict, and the resolution of these conflicts must be negotiated in and through policies and institutions. What these commitments mean in practice is often dependent upon contextual considerations and political judgments and processes.

When we move from the overlapping principles in liberal democratic theory to the different themes in public education there seems to be a similar pattern and analogous problems. Taken together, the three themes discussed in Chapters 3, 4, and 5 provide a simultaneously ambitious and consensual list of expectations for schools. We want the schools to build a common culture, strengthen the economy, help each individual realize his or her potential, and so on. Much of the "merged rhetoric" surrounding the reform movement suggests that these aims are consistent with one another. There is a kind of overlapping consensus about the aims of reform, as well as an assumption that these can all be achieved through the (reformed) public schools. As is commonly noted, we want it all and try to obtain it in practice through a mixed program of common and differentiated curricula and support services.

A more specific and practical version of an overlapping consensus is the strategy of setting widely agreed-upon policy goals, as represented in the *America 2000* program. This strategy suggests that a common ground can be found in listing specific outcomes such as a reduced dropout rate, universal school readiness, and so on. Similarly, as noted above, a number of recent works have looked at examples of reformed schools, trying to find the overlap among these schools--the common ingredients leading to success--as a way of offering practical guidance for future reform efforts. The search for an overlapping consensus concerning public education thus arises at both the level of general aims and specific policies.

The analysis of themes in public education presented in Chapters 3, 4, and 5 suggests a different way of understanding these overlapping thematic and policy commitments. The examination of different themes in education policy indicates that there is both overlap and conflict in both theory and practice. We cannot necessarily have it all since the different themes potentially suggest different priorities and practices. Moreover, each theme faces conceptual, empirical, and normative problems specific to it. There is also a problem common to all themes, the dilemma of excess and deficit, that is inevitable in the relationship of public policy and state action in a liberal democratic society. Even as a thematic analysis raises these problems, it also draws attention to the better and worse ways they are dealt with in practice. This in turn indicates the need for a more theoretical or thematic way of thinking about and evaluating what works.

The discussion of the three themes does indicate some overlap among them. For example, basic, common education is necessary for both civic education and preparation for the world of work. Trying to recognize and respond to the needs of individual students as clients is likewise part of meeting the needs of the larger economy. There is general agreement that improving the quality and performance of schools will serve the variety of aims suggested by the major themes. This overlap in themes is more than rhetorical. For example, the school development program associated with James Comer is an instance of clientelism, but it is also clearly a program of moral education. Helping children "imitate and identify with the adults around them and to internalize adult attitudes, value, and behavior" combines moral, developmental education with the academic mission of schools. Similarly, some programs, like the Coalition of Essential Schools, try to draw analogies between academic performances and the world of work -- "The governing metaphor of the school should be the student as worker" --bringing together the academic and economic functions of schooling.[6] If we look at both themes themselves and some of the ways in which they are worked out in practice, there is something like an overlapping consensus concerning the various aims of public education.

Though they overlap, the three themes also provide different ways of conceiving of the proper aims and priorities of public education. These differences suggest that there are political choices concerning the direction of the schools, and some choices clearly foreclose others. For example, if we gave priority to the economic aims of schooling expressed in the human capital theme, the institutional design of American schools might be radically different. We might move toward the German model of apprenticeship training within a clear tracking system. Or if we took seriously the notion that the diverse educational needs of students could be best defined by families, more ambitious choice systems or vouchers would be the answer. And of course there is much rhetoric about what we can or cannot borrow from the Japanese, but that system presents yet another institutional configuration that is more akin to our tradition of the common school. That these choices exist should not be surprising. A liberal democracy can be consistent with different kinds of educational regimes. Although we may want it all there are political choices to be made about what aims we will pursue and in what ways. "Alternatives are not of a piece" even as rhetorically and institutionally we try to knit them together.

Moreover, each theme, whether overlapping or conflicting with others, faces problems. Some problems are specific to certain themes, for example, the empirical issue of relating educational achievement and economic competitiveness. Still other problems face all three themes and involve tensions that are deeply rooted in liberal democratic theory. The ambivalent view of the state in a liberal democratic society suggests that we want the public schools to play a major role in pursuing certain aims, but are suspicious about the reach of state power. This creates the dilemma of excess and deficit in which the pursuit of any aim suggested by a theme leaves the state open to the charge of doing too much or too little. For example, the state may be open to the charge of moral imposition if it promotes a didactic program of moral instruction but will be charged with doing too little if it tries to be neutral in moral matters. The result has been a bias toward the minimum, the pursuit of more modest versions of any of these aims, even as the perennial cry of reformers has been for schools to do more. This result is not peculiar to educational policy. Americans have always had a "dread and yearning" of the state.[7]

These problems within and among themes are embedded in the very nature of liberal democratic theory and educational policy. A thematic analysis cannot solve them. However, it can provide a framework for analyzing them, especially as they are negotiated and responded to in practice. For example, an analysis of the common school theme can remind us that the academic purposes of schools have a moral basis and that moral education, for good or ill, goes on daily in the schools. It can tell us that the economic role of schools is often overestimated, and that we have not developed adequate institutions for the transition from school to work. Similarly, it can suggest that the schools' relationships to their clients, students and families, are not purely academic and that we need to find ways in which schools can broaden and build new relationships that serve the varied needs of clients. In each case, for each theme, such an analysis can suggest the more or less plausible ways that the schools can and should, as reformers have suggested, do more: more to encourage moral behavior and create common bonds in the schools, more to ensure that each student has the basic skills so that they can receive training or transitional support in an increasingly hostile job market, more to meet a broader range of clients' needs, perhaps including those of families. These results do not come from applying some theoretical principles to practices but by looking at the kinds of evidence and arguments relevant to different themes, especially with regard to practices within the schools.

Current discussions of "smart schools" reveal similar patterns of overlap and conflict. Descriptions of these schools emphasize certain "building blocks" common to these schools. These features include: a safe and orderly environment, a clear and shared set of aims, high expectations that all students can learn, consistent monitoring and assessment of student performance, flexible leadership that allows collegiality and empowerment among teachers, parental and community involvement. The lists of characteristic features of these schools are generally consistent (overlapping) with one another, as well as being similar to lists developed in the literature on "effective schools" that predated the current reform movement.[8] These descriptions suggest a variety of more or less general policies that can work. Indeed, it is striking how much we seem to know about "what works" and how many things work. For example, programmatic initiatives like controlled choice are often cited as vehicles for successful reform, as are classroom level strategies that use technology creatively or bring real-world problems into the classroom in productive ways, as are several other approaches to reform. Although it is repeatedly emphasized that "nothing. . . . is offered as a blueprint or a recipe," these schools "are models, examples of what is possible, visions that help us think in new ways about the organization and mission of the public schools."[9]

There is something both obvious and puzzling about schools that work. It seems plain to most observers that they do work and that they are similar to one another in specifiable ways. Rather than making threats or minimal "treaties," they create order through "the values of unanxious expectation ('I won't threaten you but I expect much of you'), of trust (unless it is abused), of decency (the values of fairness, generosity and tolerance)."[10] They thereby create a common set of purposes and a feeling of community. Similarly, teachers are given considerable discretion to exercise professional judgment. They help shape the school, and they respond to their tasks with commitment and enthusiasm. There is often considerable parental and community support and involvement. Further, these schools typically set clear goals and have high expectations for all students. Both objective measures of academic achievement and subjective satisfaction of all involved indicate a high degree of success. Moreover, these schools seem to succeed not only by conventional test-based measures of achievement but also in terms of higher order skills. They often do more both academically and in other ways without raising questions about the legitimate reach of school authority. Overall, then, these schools reflect some (overlapping) consensus about what is a good school; they apparently develop satisfactory solutions for theoretical problems in practice.

That these are obviously good schools creates the two puzzles mentioned earlier. First, although these examples all work in some sense, there seems to be no ready way to translate their experience into a programmatic effort for reform. We know what works but we have difficulty systematically applying this knowledge in practice. A further, related problem is that although there is considerable overlap among these schools, there are also some apparent differences in what they do. That is, in the lists of things that work there are some ideas and practices that, if not contradictory, are different from, and likely to exclude, others. For example, if we look at the group of schools that have been selected as "New American Schools," we find some schools that consciously pursue a classical curriculum and others that emphasize real-life problems. One of the grants explicitly takes "Total Quality Management" in corporations as its model, and another emphasizes "Expeditionary Learning" that reaches out to, and takes it cues from, other segments of the community. Many different, and perhaps mutually exclusive, things seem to work.

These problems are not specific or unique to these schools. We can also find successful examples, schools that work, that reflect the themes discussed previously. But these examples have not been broadly applied, nor is it clear they all could be consistently. For example, there are examples of community-based services that seem to have produced positive results, but these may not be consistent with apparently successful choice plans that move students across district lines. Similarly, the development of schools with distinctive curricula, or programs tailored to individual student needs, is actually or potentially inconsistent with the notion of a common curriculum. And yet these instances of varied approaches and practices also all seem to work. It may seem odd to say, but we perhaps know too many things that (might) work, even as we seem chronically unable to apply what we know systematically.

These puzzles suggest that there are questions about political choices that have yet to be fully addressed by the reform movement. Namely, as some critics of the reform movement have noted, the issue of different aims and priorities has been buried by a combination of merged rhetoric and consensus on specific policy goals. Perhaps the closest thing to theoretical debate has been the argument over school choice. Because it is so different and poses such a direct challenge to the most basic understandings of *public* education, it requires us to think seriously about our aims and choices. The general lack of theoretical discussion also helps partly explain how so many different kinds of educational experiments could be going on simultaneously without developing any general program of reform. If there is no guiding thematic sensibility, then we can simultaneously have programs for choice alongside "restructuring" of public schools alongside attempts to restore classical curricula and create "cultural literacy." All of these can rightly claim to be success stories, yet apparently point us in different directions. Optimistically viewed, this variety (and the oft-noted faddishness) that marks cycles of educational reform reflects an ongoing desire to experiment and improve. Viewed in a more pessimistic light, it suggests a lack of theoretical clarity about the kinds of things we want schools to achieve and a failure to have some relatively clear view of the aims of public education. This produces a relatively narrow focus on what works either through setting specific policy goals or through looking at instances of successful schools.

In sum, we can find instances of overlapping consensus among the several themes in public education and the practices of schools that work. At the same time this overlap is partial and incomplete. The different themes suggest different directions for schools and potentially very different institutional configurations. Even within a particular theme, there will be differing interpretations and conflicts, for example, about what more can legitimately be done to fulfill certain aims. Similarly, although there are many common features in schools that work, there are also differences. In the absence of some more principled or theoretical understanding about the aims of schooling, it is not only difficult to analyze the consensus about what works, but also to evaluate the merit of different and perhaps competing things that seem to work.[11]

The question then becomes whether the analysis of the different themes can be drawn together in any coherent way for evaluating the aims of, and current efforts at, educational reform. Or to put the matter another way, the issue is not primarily what works, for we know that a number of things work or can be made to work on a small scale. We can point to a variety of success stories that have arisen out of the educational reform movement. The question then is what more or less reasonable aims can be drawn from the various themes and how they can (or cannot) be combined in sensible ways in policies and practices.

Toward a (New) Common School

If we look over the analysis of themes in Chapters 3, 4, and 5 we can draw several conclusions about the general direction reform should follow and suggest a way of evaluating schools that work. Perhaps the major conclusion is that the aims of the common school should have some presumptive priority over alternatives. In simplest terms, this means two things. First, insofar as possible each student should be given an equal education, one involving high intellectual standards for substantive knowledge and critical thought. There should be a common set of expectations for all students. This is the only approach that is fully consistent with the idea of a *public* school. Second, this common education should be seen as part moral and civic education, broadly understood. The primary aim of the schools should be the encouragement of responsible citizenship; "the democratic faith is rooted in the belief that all humans beings are capable of excellence and have not just the right but the capacity to become citizens."[12] The point of a common, *public* system of education should not be merely academic achievement or the creation a trained workforce or the creation of markets for educational services. It should be to give all children the intellectual and social skills that will permit them to be responsible citizens. These skills will also assist them in discharging their responsibilities in their social and economic lives as well.[13]

This priority can be initially established by default as much as anything else. As noted in Chapter 4, the rhetoric concerning the economic importance of schools is at least overstated if not simply wrong. It would be difficult to make economic aims primary without a dramatic reordering of both our thinking about schools and our institutional arrangements. Unless we were confident of great economic benefits in something like the German model, and willing to accept its notion of equal opportunity, any economic functions of schooling are clearly secondary to other aims. They are best served by basic, common education. Similarly, clientelist concerns such as the provision of welfare services through the schools are not an end in themselves. They make sense, for example in family education and the Comer model, mainly as supporting the aim of equal education. Finally, the case for radical choice is largely speculative. That alone should be enough to discount its claims, but it also offers a narrow vision of academic improvement that disregards the cultural and integrative functions of schools. What might be obtainable through choice can almost certainly be had by more modest public versions of it or by other means. As will be noted below, while each of the other themes must still be taken into account, the primary direction for change should be the creation of a new, reformed common school.

There is little need to rehearse and repeat the many theoretical or philosophical arguments in favor of the common school, but at least two considerations are worth mentioning here.[14] First, a genuinely common, public school best reflects our belief in the moral worth of each individual. It embodies a commitment to equality, in the sense of "civic equality,"[15] the respect of individuals for each other and themselves as citizens. It seeks to give "full meaning . . . to the dignity" of all individuals. If we truly believe that all individuals deserve equal respect and consideration, we should show that in our public institutions, and we must certainly communicate it to our children and act accordingly with regard to them. The very nature of citizenship in a liberal democracy implies equality in the public sphere, and the public schools are clearly part of that sphere. This equality cannot be only the formal guarantees of legal rights and basic freedoms, or merely some "basic" education. It should extend to the commitment that each person potentially has "special capacities for leading a rich life" and deserves, through the schools, the opportunity to develop these capacities. Indeed, it is hard to make sense of the other aims of the schools, even the simple goals of basic literacy and understanding, without putting them in this moral and civic context.[16]

A second, and similar, point can be made by reminding ourselves of the role of public schools as one of the bridges between theory and practice in a liberal democratic society. The analytical and moral individualism of liberal democratic theory leaves largely unspecified any agent(s) or practical means for integrating separate individuals. In the absence of some shared basis of mutuality and respect, the pursuit of separate interests and ways of life threatens to degenerate into anarchy. While this mediating task has largely fallen to the private sphere, for example to families and churches, the public schools have also played an important role. This role is even more crucial as other agents seem less able, for whatever reason, to take on the task.

As *public* institutions the schools have the responsibility to help all students develop the skills, knowledge, and traits of character necessary for life in a liberal democratic society. They must prepare individuals to participate in, and even change, the varied ways of life in a liberal democratic society. The public schools must also help provide some common basis of culture and morality that is the precondition for, as the "Chelsea Manifesto" put it, "a tolerant society, in which individual differences were actively encouraged as well as passively tolerated." This common base is not provided if the schools are seen as primarily an arena for economic competition among nations or individuals. Similarly, the liberal democratic state's commitment to treating its citizens equally is compromised if the state is primarily in the business of using the schools to sort students or treat them as consumers. Although divisible, education remains primarily a public good that should be provided in a common fashion. The liberal democratic state has, in the educational realm, an interest in social unity that overrides the excessive individualism all too characteristic of our economic and social relationships.[17]

Pointing in this general direction or creating this sensibility may be reasonable, but it provides little programmatic advice concerning school organization and practices. Of course, it really cannot do so. To analyze themes is, again, merely to suggest what is at stake in our political choices, some of the problems we face in making them, and some of the more or less reasonable responses to these problems in light of that analysis. At the same time, there are clearly some general policy implications that follow from the presumptive priority of a new common school. First, and perhaps most obviously, there is a fundamental need for some basic level of order and discipline in the schools. This would be necessary for any of the legitimate aims of schools, but it is particularly important once we see the schools as conveying moral lessons and preparing young people for their role as citizens. As noted in Chapter 3, this goes beyond merely maintaining an orderly environment, as many schools do, to the more positive task of encouraging a set of moral and intellectual virtues appropriate for citizens in a liberal democratic society. Almost every account of effective schools, or dramatic transformations of bad schools, or schools that work notes the establishment of not only a safe environment but also the development of shared expectations about behavior and cooperation. The best schools go even further and encourage "traits such as a commitment to community and a desire to participate, values such as a sense of justice, equality, or liberty, skills of interpretation, debate, and compromise, habits of reflection, study, examining multiple perspectives, [that] form the basis of democratic citizenship."[18]

A second change in school practices that is implied by the vision of a new common school is the limiting or abolition of academic segregation. The current presumption in most schools, even those that deny that they track, is in favor of various forms of grouping. By itself this may not be problematic. Unfortunately, it is usually accompanied by the assumption that all students cannot be asked to meet high expectations. We should presume instead that each student, in whatever "group," should be given the same curriculum and standards and asked for the same efforts to meet them.

It is testimony to the inherent inertia of schools as institutions that these practices continue even as there has been mounting evidence against them and some demonstration that suitable alternatives are available. Most scholars agree that tracking does little for the advanced students and is positively harmful for students who, for whatever reason, are not in the top group.[19] Moreover, one of the most interesting current experiments in this regard are programs for accelerated learning for less accomplished, and often disadvantaged, students. Instead of setting more modest expectations for those who are behind their peers, these programs demand more and do so successfully.[20] Finally, if we look at the narratives about smart schools, they almost all have dispensed with the idea of rigid grouping. They convey the expectation that all students can learn, "each student should master a number of essential skills and be competent in certain areas of knowledge . . . the school's goals should apply to all students."[21] There is a growing consensus among scholars and practitioners on the need to change in the direction of a common set of expectations and standards.

These are some of policy areas that might be addressed if reform moved in the direction of a genuinely common school, but again moving in a certain direction does not guarantee clear answers. For example, there are issues about the content of a common curriculum, as debates about multiculturalism and national standards illustrate. On the one hand, it would seem possible to have national standards and even tests, as other nations do, as a means of expressing common educational ideals and setting high expectations. These would ideally act as a spur for states and localities to work, in their own ways, at meeting standards for all students.

On the other hand, there would be difficulties in setting standards that give due weight to concerns for diversity and local discretion. The same tension between commonality and diversity arises in a number of areas of curriculum and practice--for example, between accountability and professional discretion for teachers. Even if these tensions could be successfully resolved, there may be other difficulties. For example, national standards might face what Toch calls "the paradox of standardized testing," that the setting of specific test-bound standards has actually discouraged teaching higher-order skills.[22]

Another policy area where a thematic direction does not yield a clear solution to a problem concerns equity in school finance. Few would endorse the "savage inequalities" in financial support for some schools, especially in poorer urban areas.[23] Fewer still have solutions to the patchwork of ways of financing schools. This patchwork has made school finance issues a zero-sum game. Instead of seeing educational expenditures as an investment in a common enterprise, the current system pits groups and districts against one another. Moreover, although greater equity in expenditures is certainly desirable, more money, if poorly spent, does not produce improvements and exacerbates conflicts concerning school finance. In these and in many other areas, the ideal of common education can provide some presumptive priorities, for national standards and more equitable financing, but not necessarily provide strong guidance for policy. How we determine, among other things, what ought to be common in the curriculum or how to give truly equitable financial support requires ongoing interpretation and debate about the meaning of a common public education.

Similarly, to give presumptive priority to the aims of a common school will leave some of the legitimate concerns raised by other themes partly or totally unanswered. We cannot have it all, and certainly not all of it through the schools. For example, while there are legitimate concerns about the relationship of schools to the economy, it is clear that schools have been asked to take on a transitional function for which they are ill-suited. Moreover, they have been asked to do so without much help from the larger community. As noted in Chapter 4, one of the great gaps in America's institutional pattern is the transition from school to work. There are a number of proposals currently being discussed including specific certification by schools of certain job-related academic skills, formal apprenticeship programs, or other opportunities for training to smooth this transition. Without gainsaying the validity of any of these proposals, such initiatives are likely to make most sense after the schools discharge their basic academic/ moral mission. And this assumes that the schools do their basic job adequately, something that reformers have been quick to point out has not always been the case. At the very least there need to be more transitional alternatives, especially for those students who drop out or are otherwise not ready for further education or perhaps even training.[24] In any case, government and industry policies on training and employment might ultimately be a better and more direct answer to the issue of the school-work transition. Moreover, regardless of the locus and nature of such policies and programs, there are still vexing, unanswered questions of equal opportunity and its relationship to educational credentials. Any proposed program or policies will surely need to address these issues.

There are also legitimate questions about how a common school approach might be related to the clientelist proposals discussed in Chapter 5. Many of these are still at a stage where it is difficult to see how they might be related to the aims of a new common school. For example, *public* choice programs would ideally provide a variety of means to common ends. Within some common set of curricular expectations there should be room for parental input and choice within the public system. But the current enthusiasm for choice among schools with distinctive themes, taken to an extreme, may actually undercut the aims of common education. At a more individual level, it is also clear that pedagogically we are still at an early stage, conceptually let alone practically, in discovering how to respond appropriately to differences in student learning styles or how to deal with "multiple intelligences."[25] Still, there is something to be said for tailoring curriculum and pedagogy to student needs and giving some play to students' interests within a common setting. These were after all the original reasons for a more comprehensive high school.

Responding to individual needs is not merely a matter of developing an appropriate curricular or pedagogical response to student differences. It also means dealing with the differences in background and out-of-school factors that can impinge upon the academic enterprise. This means viewing education as going beyond academics to the needs of the whole child. The current division of labor and lack of coordination between welfare and education undermines policy in both areas. However, there are examples of programs, such as family education and Comer's school development program, that show how the two can be successfully combined. But the key to this combination is, at least initially, to see these issues as a legitimate concern of the schools. Unfortunately, much of the rhetoric in the reform movement has condemned in (over)broad terms nonacademic endeavors as distractions from the main academic enterprise. This is unfortunate because it is becoming increasingly clear that concern with the social side of education may be a necessary precondition for academic success. The two can and perhaps must be made mutually supportive, as in the successful programs described in Chapter 5.[26]

To note that the schools cannot shoulder completely the burden of the economy or the welfare system is a useful reminder that how well schools function depends upon the larger social and political environment. Without economic and social support of various kinds, the schools' task becomes that much more difficult. A healthy economy, sensible policies on health care, welfare, and housing, and equitable financial support all make the prospects for a new common school brighter. Likewise, there are simply many questions that cannot be answered in or through the schools, for example, the difficult issues of equal opportunity and its relationship to schools, or the ways in which government policies can or should assist families of various kinds. Some of the concerns expressed in other themes simply should not be seen as the sole or primary responsibility of the schools. Many of the policy problems confronting the schools reflect issues that confront society more generally, and the schools can be only part of the solution to these problems.

More positively, the idea of a new common school can incorporate many of the aims expressed in other themes as well as many of the legitimate concerns of the reform movement. Increasingly there seems to be something of an overlapping consensus, in both theory and practice, in favor of a new common school. Reformers of different political persuasions might disagree on the content of the curriculum, but they tend to agree that whatever is provided should be provided to all equally. Both "right" and "left" agree on the desirability of setting similar, high expectations for all students within basically the same curriculum. Even those who emphasize the economic importance of the schools are increasingly advocating common standards and high expectations. Moreover, they also suggest that these academic skills must be complemented by explicit or implicit moral lessons about responsibility. As the Committee for Economic Development puts it, "For most students, employers would prefer a curriculum that stresses literacy, mathematical skills, and problem-solving skills. . . . The schools should also teach and reward self-discipline, self-reliance, teamwork, acceptance of responsibility, and respect for the rights of others."[27] Similarly, the school readiness goal, consensus about the desirability of expanding Head Start, and the support and acclaim for other programs such as the Comer model indicate the public's willingness to see a broader "welfare" mandate for schools. It is increasingly recognized that in order to guarantee equal education, schools must respond to external factors. As noted in Chapter 5, welfare in these forms seems far less controversial, and potentially far more effective, than more conventional welfare programs.

Further support for this vision of a new common school can be found in the recent descriptions of schools that work. These schools are models for what a new common school might look like. Although their pedagogical approaches might vary, these schools typically set the same (high) expectations for all students and expect all students to be able to learn. Perhaps more important, the academic expectations set in these schools are not independent from the moral and civic aims of education, properly understood. What is commonly noted about them is that they have established, for students and faculty, for parents and administrators not merely a moral legitimacy, but a genuine "ethos" and sense of pride concerning the moral relationships within the school community. In the ordinary course of doing their work these schools engage in moral and civic education, becoming "sites where we prepare active participatory, democratic citizens."[28] At the core of it, Theodore Sizer suggests, is the concept of respect--of various groups within the school for one another, of all groups for the common undertaking in which they are engaged. "There is nothing radical about such propositions. . . . They are indeed *values*; they reflect fundamental moral--democratic--convictions, ones long embraced by Americans."[29]

Some might balk at the notion that these schools are engaged in moral and civic education. The phrase "moral education" conjures up didactic preaching and "civic education" creates images of civics texts, pledges to the flag, visits to the courthouse and voting booth. But these are not necessarily the most important moral and civic lessons. As noted in Chapter 3, the schools' engaging in civic and moral education is simply unavoidable. In how it organizes itself, deals with students, in the content and style of the curriculum, and in many other ways the school will convey a moral message. That message should be one that encourages the characteristics we value in citizens in a liberal democratic society. In schools that work that message is both explicitly and implicitly conveyed throughout the school.

Unfortunately, the message that is currently being sent in too many other schools is a far cry from one that encourages responsible citizenship. The most common observation emerging from field studies is that most schools lack a sense of purpose or mission. Students fail to see any meaning in their activity, and they often treat academic endeavors with irony or barely concealed contempt. Teachers learn to live with the compromises they make in the name of maintaining some minimal requirements of order and opening up the possibility for academic achievement for motivated students. Too often then school seems little more than a set of bargains or treaties between and among different groups of students, teachers, and administrators, for peaceful coexistence. This is a far cry from what a common school in a democracy should be, namely a school for encouraging responsible citizenship. Again, the other aims of the school, as well as the expenditure of large sums of public money, only make sense as part of some broader moral enterprise of education for citizenship.

We are now in a position to provide some further, albeit still incomplete, responses to the two puzzles of the current reform movement. Regarding the first, why some schools work, but we are unable to generalize what works, the simple fact is that the public schools have simply not fully embraced the ideal of a genuinely common school, let alone the idea of its moral and civic function. This is most obvious in the continuation of differentiated curricula, with the more or less explicit message that not all students can, or even should, be expected to achieve. This message is especially troublesome as these academic divisions reflect or reinforce differences of class, race, and culture. Even where schools have set high and perhaps even common academic standards, these are often interpreted narrowly so that they do not communicate some broader ethos of individual responsibility or collective purpose. The bias toward the minimum inclines schools away from any larger vision of schools as moral, public agents. Study after study has criticized and commented upon the "factory model" of schools that treats students as products to be moved along rather than as future citizens. In the absence of a larger vision of schooling it should be little surprise that schools create treaties that ensure minimal, mutual expectations. Likewise it should be no surprise that "apathy and alienation are at the heart of contemporary school culture," especially for those students who are implicitly or even explicitly told that they are "unspecial" or simply incapable of academic and personal achievement.[30]

Similarly, the second puzzle, that there are very different and seemingly conflicting ways of creating an effective school, is somewhat less troubling in light of the priority of the common school ideal. Clearly there can be several or even many paths to developing a school that has high common expectations and a sense of purpose. To set the priority of the common school theme provides ways of assessing these differences, not in the sense of applying a principle deductively to practice, but more as rules of thumb for evaluating schools. For any school it might be asked whether it maintains a safe and orderly environment that communicates not mere compliance but moral community, whether it extends opportunities for achievement to all students, whether it sets high expectations for both behavior and academic achievement, again for all students, whether it also includes teachers in the moral community of the school, not as mere workers, but as individuals concerned for the well-being and direction of future citizens.[31] Not surprisingly most of the schools that work seem to meet these kinds of tests. There may and should be many debates about what in a range of alternative organizational mechanisms, curricular approaches, and pedagogical strategies is most effective and practical in meeting these aims. The critical point is that these schools in various ways embody the possibilities for a new common school.

Again, these theoretical conclusions about educational ideals, about themes, do not spell out specific solutions, although they are clearly more congenial to some than others. To assert the priority of the aims of the common school is to express a sensibility or a direction, not provide a blueprint or recipe. The lack of some guiding direction, as noted above, provides part of the answer to our initial puzzles, but a fuller response must address the other elements of the "first triangle" described in Chapter 1. A fuller account of why this direction is not being systematically pursued, and how we can account for the variability in schools that work, requires a brief look at the other two elements of our initial triangle. The play of interests and institutions, which taken together determine school culture, will ultimately determine whether and in what ways our educational ideals will be realized in practice.

Interests and Institutions: Who Really Wants Reform?

If thematic analysis can point out a preferred direction for educational reform, it does not provide specific practical advice about making reform a reality. Ideas about reform may be widely agreed upon, but these will have little practical effect if they are not supported by interests and embodied in institutions. And if we look at these areas there is some cause for pessimism about the pace of reform, as well as its direction and content. The major interests involved have yet to be mobilized on behalf of reform, and institutions have often undergone "reform" without genuine change. There is little chance for reform unless those most directly involved are willing to question and change the understandings and practices, the culture, of the school. School culture is ultimately where the meaning of our political choices about reform will be determined. Whatever optimism there might be about the possibilities for creating a new common school depends on addressing questions of school culture.

First, one of the persistent facts of the reform movement is that, after more than a decade, all the alarms about education and calls for reform have still not penetrated public consciousness. Intellectually, parents and ordinary citizens acknowledge that there are problems in public education but by and large approve of their own schools. This reflects a kind of reverse NIMBY ("not in my backyard") syndrome. There is a need to reform other people's schools, not ours. Poll respondents have consistently rated the schools in their community higher than those in the nation as a whole. The percentage of those giving "A" and "B" grades for local schools has held at over 40 percent while the percentage for the nation's schools as a whole has been less than half that. Parents of school-age children rate their local schools even higher, giving them from 60 to 75 percent above average grades; those grades have increased in the last ten years.[32] This suggests that the potentially most powerful interest in promoting educational reform is not mobilized because it has not been fully persuaded that there is a problem. In the absence of some broad public pressure on behalf of reform, especially from parents, there is little reason to expect schools to change in any significant ways.

These ratings and parental satisfaction may reflect an inability or unwillingness to see both the problems of schools and the dangers in not responding to them. At the same time, these polls also indicate that the public sees the key problems confronting schools as drugs and discipline. This is quite different from the focus on "excellence" and "competitiveness" that have been prominent in the rhetoric of reform. It suggests that there is considerable latent support for greater emphasis in the schools on moral and civic education. This support may not be being tapped because the parents' perspective that schools are moral authorities and socializing agents is not consistently a focus for reform efforts. And yet, again, many of the stories of the reform of specific schools describe the creation of an orderly environment as part of the development of an ethos or a moral community within the school. They also typically involve parents in this endeavor. Parental interests and effort might be more readily mobilized for reform that supports the creation of this kind of school rather than one narrowly focused on improving standardized test scores.

The other powerful interest yet to be mobilized on behalf of reform are educators, especially teachers. The dispersed and shared nature of educational power in the United States would make it difficult to enlist educators in the cause of reform, but the way in which reform has proceeded has made it even more difficult. The initial rhetoric of reform was, implicitly or explicitly, critical of the teaching profession. Teachers had failed to produce the desired academic results. Rightly or wrongly, teachers rejected these criticisms as blaming them for many problems that were beyond their control. They were also, perhaps justly, skeptical of what seemed to be yet another cycle of reform efforts that imposed, from above, another shift in educational styles and strategies.

Perhaps most important, it was not clear initially, and perhaps not even recently, how teachers should respond to the reform movement. On the one hand, many of the proposals concerning teachers, especially those that arose in the first phase of the reform movement, involve increased regulation and accountability (for example, competency testing, merit pay). These reflect a kind of "factory model" of schooling with teachers pursuing goals and following rules set elsewhere. On the other hand, there has also been, more recently, discussion of increasing teacher discretion, autonomy, and empowerment in the school. These proposals for the "professionalization" of teaching suggest a very different view of the role of teachers in school reform. These mixed signals have been received against a background and history of bureaucratic school governance and adversarial union-administration relations. It should therefore not be surprising that teachers might resist, or try to fit into existing patterns, the rather vague, often shifting, and implicitly critical demands for "more." It is also not surprising that the initial opposition of the teacher's unions to the reform movement has only recently given way, at least in the case of one of the major unions, to some active support for the professionalization of teaching. It remains the case that with teachers, as with parents, the reform movement has not really been taken to heart.[33]

The reluctant reaction of educators to reform may be dismissed as self-interested or shortsighted (or both). Teachers and their unions are not totally innocent of these charges. But here, as with parents, the reform movement has largely missed the opportunity to mobilize a powerful interest by addressing its concerns in a way that could promote the cause of a new common school. That cause requires the presumption that teachers must have a significant say in both the process of reform and the schools that result therefrom. Almost all the stories of schools that work have teachers playing a significant role in the process of deciding how to restructure the "existing regularities." They also redefine their own role in the new structure. Involving teachers in decisionmaking concerning curricula, governance, and the use of time, among other things, is not merely an issue of professionalism in some academic sense. It is rather a critical ingredient in making teachers full participants in a school community that has an important moral and civic purpose.[34]

These changes in organizational structure, the rearrangement of lines of authority, and the like make most sense and are most likely to succeed when they are aimed at the creation of a community within the school. This community in turn is typically committed to equal, quality education. To be sure, moving in this direction does not resolve the many issues associated with accountability and public control, the role of administrators, the application of state or national standards, and questions of unionism and professionalism. Nevertheless, these problems are most properly addressed by assuming that teachers must be "citizens" in their schools if they are to create schools for future citizens. Moving in this direction is the choice most consistent with the ideals of moral and civic education, and the one that is most likely to mobilize teachers on behalf of genuine reform.[35]

The problems posed by the interests of teachers become inevitably intertwined with the issue of institutional structure. For all the talk about restructuring schools or breaking the mold it is extremely difficult to break with past practices and organizational routines and move into some brave new future. To suggest that time might be used differently or authority relationships changed is easier than figuring out on a day-to-day basis how to do so. Not only is it difficult in that it requires raising fundamental questions about aims and practices, but it is doubly so in that the schools must continue their task even as they consider making changes. To use an old cliche, it is something like rebuilding a boat in the middle of the ocean. There is a tremendous temptation to simply rename rather than change existing patterns and practices in order to satisfy the widespread demands for reform. Thus too often "instead of changing to fit the reforms, schools made the reforms conform to the way schools had always been."[36]

This institutional inertia helps explain why although we know what works we cannot routinely apply what we know. For example, during the first phase of the reform movement, schools simply adjusted their existing efforts toward producing test results rather than dramatically rethinking aims and practices. In more recent years the second phase of the reform movement has focused on the internal routines and culture of schools as the target, and stumbling block, for reform. But here too in the absence of some genuine movement for change from within schools, reform is often more ritual ("staff development") than substance.[37] Finally, the fact that there are so many possibilities (and no blueprint) under the heading of "restructuring," for example in the different strategies of the "New American Schools," has made it still more difficult for schools to begin the process of transforming themselves. Thus there are both obstacles and opportunities implicit in the many different specific options that might be the focus of reform efforts.

These observations about the role of interests and institutions suggest that the key to school reform is in creating a shared school culture consistent with the ideal of a new common school. The idea of a school culture is as hard to define precisely as it is to change. It encompasses many things, including an array of explicit or implicit assumptions about aims and practices within a school, the formal and informal "regularities" in the use of time, the structure of authority, the mutual expectations of various groups, and ultimately overall goals and self-understanding.[38] As noted previously, in schools that work there are certain cultural continuities, general regularities in terms of aims, expectations, and practices that are consistent with a vision of equal common education. At the same time, these schools often display very different modes of organization, curricular formats, and pedagogical approaches, for example, the different strategies embodied in the "New American Schools."

That these different strategies all work is testimony to the power of school culture, since what works depends heavily upon the commitment of those involved. That is, beyond these similarities and differences there is perhaps a more fundamental continuity, namely, that the new culture of the school, both in its general and specific features, is widely shared. All groups involved--teachers, parents, and students--share a sense of common purpose in the school and a commitment to its distinctive ways of achieving its aims. These new treaties have typically been the conscious creation of these groups.[39] The particular strategies that might be adopted to reach the general aim of equal common education is perhaps less important than the fact that the means were produced by those involved. These schools are thus both a product and an embodiment of a more democratic culture in the schools.

Much of the literature on schools that work focuses on certain organizational factors, for example the use of time, the autonomy of teachers, the size of schools, and many other practices. These are the "fixed ways of conducting schools . . .'regularities' . . . so ingrained in schooling that we hardly notice and rarely question them."[40] Without denying the validity or importance of these factors, these issues in turn raise questions about basic aims that are equally or more significant. Namely, to delve into the issues of "fixed ways" inevitably raises questions of basic aims ("that aims should inform means"). It also typically reflects a collective willingness both to participate in the process of change and to move the schools in the direction of better serving all students. When the question of aims, and specifically the goal of equal quality education, is truly engaged by those involved there is some latitude in what can be created; there are different kinds of regularities consistent with equal quality education.

Without quibbling over the semantics of what constitutes radical change, the changes needed for real reform may in some sense not be radical at all. Many of the reformed schools, for example those associated with the Comer model, work within many of the existing regularities of time and subject matter. What is radically changed is the self-understanding of the school's mission as being committed to academic and social development of all children. This in turn necessitates the participation of all groups involved in making that happen. Changing schools' views of themselves in this fashion may be as much or more the key to reform as commonly cited organizational or curricular factors.[41]

It should now be clearer why we seem to know what works but cannot apply it systematically and why so many things seem to work. Even though we know in some sense what works, the key interests involved, especially parents and teachers, have yet to be convinced that reform is necessary, and the institutional structure of American schools makes genuine change very difficult. Moreover, what works is consistent with many different strategies for change, and there is no one institutional strategy that guarantees success. The success of any given strategy, again, depends significantly upon its adoption by all those involved, by its becoming a mission and vision that penetrates and changes the existing culture of the school. That many different things work then is also less of a mystery, for it confirms that a variety of schools can work by enlisting those involved in creating a new school culture. Classical curricula and thematic schools within schools, choice programs and local restructuring of various kinds, as well as a variety of other approaches, can all apparently work once there is widespread commitment to providing equal quality education to all. That is, the odds for success dramatically increase when those involved have genuine ownership of and commitment to reform. (This result should not be especially surprising, given the common pedagogical observation about the importance of expectations for outcomes.) Thus although school culture may not be infinitely malleable, there is enough variability there to suggest that reform can occur in a variety of ways, once those involved are genuinely committed to creating a better school for all students.

Sarason's observations about reform suggest both pessimism and optimism. Although there is widespread discussion of the need for change, few schools are engaged in the kind of cultural self-scrutiny required. Many questions about basic aims and practices are not being widely asked let alone seriously addressed at the school level, despite the widespread public discussion of reform. At the same time, there is cause for optimism in the fact that there are schools that work and that there is a pattern in these transformed schools that is consistent with the common school ideal. These schools indicate that it is possible to create high expectations and real opportunities for all students. It is possible to create a school environment that both implicitly and explicitly encourages the development of responsible citizens. Finally, there is cause for optimism in the variety of paths that can be followed to this common end, once all those involved take school reform seriously. The prospect of a more participatory, democratic process that changes the culture of schooling is consistent with the ideals of civic and moral education that should be the focus of a new common school. It is also consistent with the liberal democratic vision that the people will ultimately decide upon and shape their political institutions.

The Task(s) of Political Theory Revisited

That educational reform is ultimately the responsibility of all those involved with the public schools--that is just about everyone--suggests another, somewhat different "task of political theory." Political theory's task has been primarily seen as analytical and philosophical. It typically follows philosophy's telos toward more general, coherent, objective (metaphysical) accounts, free from the particularities and contingencies of history and culture. Even where it takes a more practical, political turn and addresses itself to a specific kind of society or policy problem, its style is philosophical and rationalistic.

To the degree that the task of theory takes a practical turn, as in Rawls' political approach, this style implies a very strong view of what theoretical inquiry can accomplish. It also takes a somewhat narrow view of how it should proceed. But, as noted in Chapter 2, this approach may not fit very well with the ways in which liberal democratic societies understand themselves or approach policy questions. The overlapping consensus in a liberal democracy is not reducible to a few well-structured principles (the theoretical mystique). Rather, it is a "thicker" set of commitments that overlap and conflict with one another, often including agreements on specific policies and institutions as ways of interpreting values and resolving conflict. This looser overlapping consensus structures political debate by suggesting what principles can be invoked to justify (changes in) policies and institutions. Nonetheless this overlap is open-textured and incomplete. The implications of these consensual principles for any given political issue are often underdetermined.[42] They will, depending upon the issue and context involved, be open to interpretation and debate by different groups. The resulting political conflicts must be dealt with through institutional mechanisms and specific policies.

Given the limits on the theoretical mystique, it would seem desirable to integrate theoretical inquiries with empirical information of various kinds. This might include descriptions of how principles are reflected in actual practices (moral education embedded in schools), research on relevant hypotheses (the relationship of education to the economy), and specific experiments or attempts at improving policy (welfare and choice programs, "schools that work"). That is, political theory would overlap with more empirical studies of the process, causes, and consequences of public policy that fall under the rubric of "policy analysis" or "policy studies." A more "thematic" approach to a policy area, such as the analysis of educational policy offered in Chapters 3, 4, and 5, tries to develop a hybrid or combination of political theory and policy analysis.[43]

A thematic approach begins by taking seriously, but not uncritically, the overlapping and competing values expressed in different policy themes. It examines them particularly as they reflect the deeper problems, for example the dilemmas of state activity in a liberal democratic society. At the same time, it uses empirical inquiries as material for assessing these broad themes as they are interpreted and embodied in practices. These too are subject to critical scrutiny, as in the analysis of the relationship of education and the economy. A thematic approach is thus not wholly philosophical or directly empirical, but rather tries to blend both kinds of considerations in discussing policy. Again, it seeks to make clear what is at stake in our policy choices and discover more or less reasonable ways of approaching them. Finally, none of this denies the validity or value of philosophical inquiry as a task of political theory. Rather it is to suggest that there are other ways of relating theory and policy that might broaden our conception of the task(s) of political theory.

We have now come full circle, from theory to policy and back again. Our discussion began with a search for intellectual resources that might be brought to bear in discussing educational reform. Considering what political theory might offer policy debate suggested that the general commitments of the liberal democratic tradition could not be defined in any tightly structured way. The overlapping commitments of that tradition are, and perhaps must be, understood in a pluralistic fashion. A liberal democratic community then is self-defining, within the broad and evolving commitments of its tradition. What these commitments mean depends upon their interpretation in specific contexts, expressed in and through policies and institutions, for example, in the area of education. Theoretical inquiry can inform these interpretations and create a dialogue between philosophy and democracy, but ultimately the community must decide what its commitments are.

The discussion of the major themes in public education followed a similar path. Examining the varied aims for the schools did not produce some clear resolution of the problems confronting public education generally or the reform movement in particular. Rather, it raised some specific conflicts and problems within and among themes that must continually be resolved or negotiated in practice. This produced a view of the general direction and policy guidelines that educational reform might follow toward a new common school. However, it also indicated that reform depends upon changes in the culture of schools, the self-understandings within schools about their purpose and practices. The success of schools that work suggests the possibility of reforming schools in ways consistent with ideals of moral and civic education broadly understood. But whether such changes can occur and what form they will take must be determined district by district, school by school, by all those involved. Here again, theory can inform but not determine policy. In both liberal democratic theory and educational reform then, the concerns of philosophy and theory must be combined with those of democracy and practice.

And that is as it should be. The task of political theory is not merely the work of theorists but the task of citizens. The progress and even the survival of a liberal democratic society depends upon the ability of its citizens to understand and deliberate upon shared principles and to value, and act within, common institutions. In education policy, the intellectual resources that can be brought to bear in assisting the process of reform must include those involved directly in the schools in creating and maintaining a democratic school culture. Therefore the tasks of theory and the tasks of education overlap. Public education is a critical means by which the task(s) of theory in a liberal democratic society can be accomplished. Only by committing ourselves to the development of responsible citizens can we expect to maintain and improve all of our political, social, and economic institutions. This requires all of us to value our schools enough to do the work needed for reform. But this task in turn requires us to have an expansive vision of education that transcends narrower academic or economic concerns, one that goes beyond "any mathematical measure" to each person's "special capacities for leading a rich life." We need to regard all of our young people, whatever their future status or occupation, as citizens deserving equal respect. We need publicly to value and promote "their kindliness and their courage, their imagination and their sensitivity, their sympathy and generosity" as well. To imagine and to theorize about a truly democratic society "in which full meaning was at last given to the dignity of man" is a worthy enterprise. The actual fulfillment of that vision depends in no small measure upon the reform of our system of public education.

Notes

1.   Michael Young, *The Rise of the Meritocracy, 1870-2033.* London: Penguin, 1961, pp. 169-170. Seymour Sarason, *The Predictable Failure of Educational Reform.* San Francisco: Jossey Bass, 1990, p. 175.

2.   William Wayson, *Up From Excellence.* Bloomington: Phi Delta Kappa, 1988; Jeannie and Martin Lipton, *Making the Best of Schools.* New Haven: Yale University Press, 1990; Edward Fiske, *Smart Schools, Smart Kids.* New York: Simon and Schuster, 1991; Thomas Toch, *In the Name of Excellence.* New York: Oxford University Press, 1991, especially Part III; George Wood, *Schools that Work.* New York: Dutton, 1992; Theodore Sizer, *Horace's School.* Boston: Houghton Mifflin, 1992.

3.   "'Breaking the Mold' of Education: Eleven Design Teams Gear up to Reinvent U.S. Schools for the Next Generation of Children," *Christian Science Monitor.* July 20, 1992, p. 12.

4.   Oakes and Lipton, *Making the Best of Schools,* "This immediate culture includes the *opportunities* to learn that schools provide, their *expectations* for how well children will learn, and the *professional conditions for teaching.*" p. 10.

5.   See Stephen Macedo, *Liberal Virtues.* New York: Oxford University Press, especially Chs. 5-7; William Galston, *Liberal Purposes.* New York: Cambridge University Press, 1991, especially Parts III and IV.

6.   James P. Comer, "Child Development and Education," *Journal of Negro Education.* 58 (2, 1989), pp. 128-129; Sizer, *Horace's School,* p. 208, from the Coalition of Essential Schools' nine common principles.

7.   The bias toward the minimum has both theoretical and political advantages. It lessens the potential for conflict between and among aims or themes. For example, ensuring that all students meet minimal standards of literacy is obviously common to all themes. It is also a safe political posture in that it does not open schools to criticism for going beyond the legitimate scope of state authority. On the

"dread and yearning" toward the state, see James Morone, *The Democratic Wish*. New York: Basic Books, 1990, introduction.

8. See Wayson, *Up From Excellence*, Chapter 8 on the relationship(s) of research on effective schools to the current reform movement.

9. Wood, *Schools that Work*, p. 231. See also Wayson, *Up From Excellence*, Chs. 9, 10, for varied descriptions and guidelines concerning excellent schools.

10. Sizer, *Horace's School*, p. 208.

11. Again, as Amy Gutmann succinctly puts it, "Having invoked a concept of 'better' education, we must ask 'better' with respect to what purposes?" *Democratic Education*. Princeton: Princeton University Press, 1988, p. 4.

12. Benjamin Barber, *An Aristocracy of Everyone*. New York: Ballantine Books, 1992, "Democratic education mediates the ancient quarrel between the rule of opinion and the rule of excellence by informing opinion and, through universal education in excellence, creating an aristocracy of everyone." p. 5.

13. See James P. Comer, "Our National Dilemma," Proceedings of the conference "Making Schools Work for Underachieving Minority Students," November 1987, "So the challenge is to find a way . . . [that] allows the children to develop in a way in which they can achieve academically and develop the skills and motivation to become responsible citizens, responsible family members, responsible and competent childrearers. Unless we do that we really have not achieved the mission of the school, because the mission of the school is not simply to teach basic academic skills, it is not simply to provide employers with future competent workers, but it is to prepare children to be responsible citizens of a democratic society." p. 18.

14. For some of the arguments in favor of the ideal of equal education see Gutmann, *Democratic Education*; Wood, *Schools that Work*, introduction, Ch. 6; Ann Bastian et al., *Choosing Equality: The Case For Democratic Schooling*. Philadelphia: Temple University Press, 1985. A particularly succinct statement is offered by Barber, *An Aristocracy of Everyone*, pp. 144-150.

15. On the notion of "civic equality," see Mickey Kaus, *The End of Equality*. New York: Basic Books, 1992. It is "something beyond formal legal equality, even beyond the basic freedoms. . . . We can have all those things and still not live in a society in which everyone *feels* he is, at bottom, an equal member." p. 16.

16. Barber cites a comment of Dewey's on the relationship of academic and moral aims, "Moral education in school is practically hopeless when we set up the development of character as a supreme end, and at the same time treat the acquiring of knowledge and the development of understanding, which of necessity occupy the chief part of school time, as having nothing to do with character." *An Aristocracy of Everyone*, p. 227.

17. For a powerful argument on the public's interest in "conscious social reproduction" through the schools, see Gutmann, *Democratic Education*, Ch. 1, especially pp. 38-47.

18. Wood, *Schools That Work*, p. xxiii. To be sure, the exercise of authority for its own sake is contrary to the aim of producing responsible citizens. Effective schools enlist students in the common enterprise rather than simply commanding compliance. For all the concern with order that studies of schools have noted, and even the appearance of discipline in orderly schools, the problem is, as discussed in Chapter 3, more a lack of sensible discipline than an excess of it. This is certainly the case in schools plagued by disorder and violence, and in more peaceful schools

where there is simply more or less contempt for the enterprise. Clearly, the moral lessons drawn from such environments are hardly conducive to the fundamental aims of public education, let alone the development of academic skills.

19. For some of the arguments against tracking see John Goodlad and Jeannie Oakes, "We Must Offer Equal Access to Knowledge," *Educational Leadership*. (1988), pp. 16-22; Jeannie Oakes.*Keeping Track: How Schools Structure Inequality*. New Haven: Yale University Press, 1985.

20. Henry Levin and Wendy Hopfenberg, "Don't Remediate, Accelerate!," *Educational Digest*. 70 (January 1991), pp. 47-50; Ron Brandt, "On Building Learning Communities: A Conversation with Hank Levin," *Educational Leadership*. 50 (September 1992), pp. 19-23; Fiske, *Smart Schools*, pp. 108-114.

21. Sizer, *Horace's School*, p. 208.

22. Toch, *In the Name of Excellence*, Ch. 6.

23. Jonathan Kozol, *Savage Inequalities*. New York: Crown Publishers, 1991.

24. Albert Shanker, "Making Transitions," *New York Times*. April 18, 1993, "The U.S. has the worst school-to-work transition in the industrialized world. It would be more accurate, in fact, to say that we have no system at all."

25. On "multiple intelligences" and school reform, see Howard Gardner, *The Unschooled Mind*. New York: Basic Books, 1991

26. Bastian puts it very nicely, "Unfortunately, school people too often resent the added demands, blame underparenting or social problems for school failure, and ultimately disclaim the responsibility for making the school culture more supportive of the child. New demands on schools to meet social needs are not the enemy of school achievement; in fact, meeting these needs is a condition for effective instruction and a key to raising levels of achievement. The issue is not the demands that are placed on schools, but the resources that are provided to meet these demands." *Choosing Equality*, p. 62.

27. Committee for Economic Development, *Investing in Our Children*. New York: Committee on Economic Development, 1985, p. 15, "One thing is clear from our inquiries: Business in general is not interested in narrow vocationalism. In many respects, business believes that the schools in recent years have strayed too far in that direction."

28. Wood, *Schools That Work*, p. xxiii.

29. Sizer, *Horace's School*. pp. 123-124; for a fuller discussion of this understanding of respect, see Ch. 9 on "Thoughtful Places."

30. See Toch, *In the Name of Excellence*, Ch. 7 on "apathy and alienation," "the climate in many of the nation's public schools has alienated vast numbers of students and teachers," pp. 239-240. On the "unspecial," see Arthur Powell, Eleanor Farrar, and David Cohen, *The Shopping Mall High School*. Boston: Houghton Mifflin, 1985, Ch. 4.

31. See Oakes and Lipton, *Making the Best of Schools*, Ch. 1 on expectations and conditions as ways of evaluating schools; see Sizer, *Horace's School*, Chs. 9-11 on the roles of teachers and students in a good school.

32. Stanley Elan, Lowell C. Rose, and Alec Gallup, "The 24th Annual Gallup/ Phi Delta Kappa Poll of the Public's Attitudes Toward the Public Schools," *Phi Delta Kappan*. 73 (September 1992), pp. 41-53.

33. See Toch, *In the Name of Excellence*, Ch. 5, for a fairly critical view of the role of unions, particularly the National Education Association, in impeding reform: "Yet despite the avalanche of new initiatives in teaching, many of them reforms rarely discussed even a decade ago, the union-backed impediments to reform . . . remain in place . . . it's clear that public school teaching cannot achieve white collar status as long as traditional union policies remain pervasive within it. There is an inherent conflict between traditional industrial-style teacher unionism--with its predisposition to confrontation, its commitment to limiting the responsibilities of teachers in schools, and its opposition to meaningful standards--and the high standards and accountability inherent in the professionalism that the reformers seek for teaching." p. 204.

34. "Control of the structure, size, time, and governance may not seem like the most exciting concept in a school. But it . . . is the key that unlocks the doors, making it possible for teachers to achieve the democratic visions they have for their classrooms." Wood, *Schools That Work*, p. 246.

35. For a good description and discussion of cases of decentralized decisionmaking, see Fiske, *Smart Schools*, Ch. 2: "The premise of shared decision making is simple: Those closest to the action should have the authority and responsibility to make most of the decisions. The principle applies to both the relationship between central districts and individual schools and to the relationships within schools among principals, teachers, parents and others . . . management of the school is transferred . . . [it] includes the principal but is dominated by teachers and frequently includes parents, clerical and custodial workers, and, in some high schools, students." p. 30.

36. Oakes and Lipton, *Making the Best of Schools*, p. 9.

37. On fitting test-driven reform to current practices see Larry Cuban, "Transforming the Frog into a Prince: Effective Schools Research, Policy, and Practice at the District Level," *Harvard Educational Review.* (1984), pp. 129-151; Toch, *In the Name of Excellence*, Ch. 6: "Far from reinforcing the push for educational excellence, the new tests are driving down the level of instruction." p. 221. On the ways in which schools absorb or co-opt reform efforts, see Thomas Timar and David Kirp, *Managing Educational Excellence*. New York: Falmer Press, 1988.

38. Oakes and Lipton define school culture as the opportunities and expectations for learning and professional conditions for teaching, *Making the Best of Schools*, Ch. 1.

39. Fiske, *Smart Schools*, Ch. 2.

40. Oakes and Lipton, *Making the Best of Schools*, p. 9, borrowing Sarason's use of the term "regularities."

41. "We can, for a start, see that all our schools are genuine communities, with a shared vision of the kind of human being a young person will be when he/she leaves the school doors. These communities should engender the habits of heart and mind that are required of democratic citizens." Wood, *Schools That Work*, p. 254.

42. On the "underdetermination" of policy by ideological or theoretical principles, see David Paris and James Reynolds, *The Logic of Policy Inquiry*. New York: Longman, 1983, Ch. 8, especially pp. 260-261.

43. For a discussion of this combination see David Paris, "Policy Inquiry and Rational Ideologies," in Edward Portis and Michael Levy, *Handbook of Political Theory and Policy Science*. New York: Greenwood Press, 1988, pp. 75-90.

About the Book and Author

Ten years of educational reform have not brought dramatic improvements. In *Ideology and Educational Reform*, David Paris traces the underlying ideological problems that make genuine reform difficult. These include different and often conflicting beliefs concerning the proper role of public education as well as the public's natural ambivalence about schools as government agencies.

Paris describes three major themes in public education—common school, human capital, and clientelism. He critically evaluates current policies and explores proposed reforms associated with each of these topics, including moral education, the school-economy relationship, school choice, and the delivery of social services. Paris proposes better ways for dealing with ideological problems in school practice, and suggests appropriate directions for policy reform.

David C. Paris is James S. Sherman Professor of Government at Hamilton College.

Index